P9-DDC-874

# Nature Needs Us

Howdy Howard

# Nature Needs Us

Walter E. Howard

Published 2006

Copyright © 2005 by Walter E. Howard.

Library of Congress Number:     2005904505
ISBN :         Hardcover        1-4134-9629-6
               Softcover        1-4134-9628-8

All rights reserved. No part of this book may be reproduced or transmitted in any form or by any means, electronic or mechanical, including photocopying, recording, or by any information storage and retrieval system, without permission in writing from the copyright owner.

This book was printed in the United States of America.

**To order additional copies of this book, contact:**
Xlibris Corporation
1-888-795-4274
www.Xlibris.com
Orders@Xlibris.com
28977

# Contents

To my students

# Foreword

Why this book? It's unlike any other. What motivates me to write it? I'm worried. Too many people do not seem to understand nature in today's world, and we must for our children's sake. Who am I? In 2004 my autobiography was published by Global Publishing Services (ISBN 0-9746565-1-8). It tells about my truly unique life experiences, including World War II, academic struggles, field and laboratory research with animals and travels to about 70 countries.

In this book I reveal my empathy and deep compassion for nature. With realism and introspection, I depict the enormous impacts and benefits to conservation of properly understanding nature. This book explains social justification and virtues of "managing" nature in human-modified environments, rather than leaving the outcome to the whims of nature as if in natural environments.

The book will help the reader defend his or her biological emotional views about nature's death ethic. It is written in layman's language to help provide a wider scientific and philosophical understanding of nature. The provocative views that are presented, all of which come from the author's heart, are done intentionally to enhance the book. The book will have a significant impact by encouraging students as well as adults to examine more closely the functions of nature, and to do so in critical detail, rather than emotionally, so they will be able to better defend their own personal ethics about nature.

# Acknowledgements

A very large number of people have contributed to this book. This includes my colleagues, editors, reviewers of earlier drafts and related publications and my frequent talks on these subjects. I have also benefited from responses made by students in classes when I taught *Wildlife Biology*, *Principles of Animal Control*, *Population Problems—Issues in Human Ecology* and other classes. My 44 graduate students who got 54 doctorate or master degrees under my direction were especially helpful. With all my undergraduate and graduate students, I tried to stimulate them to be independent thinkers and to do their best to defend their own ethical viewpoints. Their responses often helped me. However, I accept full responsibility for my views about nature.

I am very grateful for the tolerance, patience and editing by Betty Howard, my wife since 1940. I used to be a workaholic, frequently leaving her and the three children while I did field research.

Finally, I am very grateful to John D. Stumbos, who was the principal editor. I am also grateful to William S. Leet and my wife for editing the final draft.

# Preface

The goal of this book is to share my perspective in the many issues surrounding nature in "human-modified" environments. I hope to spur a healthy self-analysis of your attitudes about nature. I'm not trying to tell you what is right or wrong, but rather that you should explore your own ethics about nature. People can't help but disrupt the natural scheme of things with agriculture, logging and providing for our livelihoods. How we handle this disruption depends upon our underlying beliefs and attitudes. This book will definitely help shape your thoughts on how best to alleviate many animal problems and promote humane wildlife management.

It is essential to understand nature's life-death ethic. Why? To make sense of a singularly human trait—the morality in deciding the importance of the life of an animal, which is a highly personal code, influenced by friends and family, colleagues and critics.

I wrote this book from my heart, because of my lifelong concern for nature. As a boy I was drawn to natural wild areas around my home in Davis, California, and in the Sierra Nevada Mountains. My dedication to preserving nature's beauty, diversity and welfare can be traced to my youth. Until my mid-teens I spent most summers in the Sierra Nevada rolling rocks in small streams, ripping bark off logs, etc., to explore nature's animal life. I am simultaneously humbled and inspired by the rich diversity in changes in color, the unique sounds heard during the daylight and darkness, the unusual odors, extremes of temperature and surprises in weather and the unsuspected hardships and pleasures one experiences while exploring nature's mysteries.

Nature accomplishes its amazing balancing act through a high rate within all species. All species, that is, except *Homo sapiens.*

This non-technical book is designed for a broad range of readers: students, avid conservationists, land-use managers and planners, wildlife biologists, sportsmen, environmentalists, outdoor enthusiasts and the general public. It is especially for people who love nature and are deeply concerned about the welfare of nature, or for students needing exposure to nature's ways. While no two people will agree on how nature should be managed in a world consisting almost entirely of human-disturbed environments, a number of significant issues are raised that must be considered to the extent possible, in forming one's own ethic about nature's life-death dance.

The goal is to help you, the reader, better understand nature, of which you are a part, and to ensure that you appreciate the fact that we are dealing with environments that have been modified by people. "Leaving it to nature" in modified environments is a viable option only when one is willing to accept the consequences of nature's survival-of-the-fittest struggle. Even in the wildest areas humans have physically altered the environment with pollutants or by other means.

We all need to rethink our ethics about nature and natural phenomena. The major objective of this book is to spark thought and dialogue to help the reader solidify or improve his or her own ethic regarding the diverse aspects of nature in a world that humans continue to influence—for good or for ill. I do not claim to understand all the fascinating mysteries in nature but have been helped by my extensive field experience during fifty-seven years as a professor. Also helpful have been my travels throughout much of the world, intelligent probing questions asked by my 44 bright Ph.D. and M.S. students (mostly in ecology and animal behavior) and my thousands of other students in classes.

I have insight into the mysteries of nature that I want to share with you. Nature functions in a way that is not understood by the lay public and is too frequently done a disservice by well-meaning, albeit anthropomorphic sympathizers.

I have made every effort to clarify nature's life-death ethic for both scientific and nonscientific readers. Even though this book is written primarily for the general public, teachers be forewarned that there are no right or wrong answers to most of the issues presented in this book. The "Questions for the Classroom" at the end of the book are meant to serve students and the public so they can strengthen their own ethical positions on these oft-times emotional issues.

This book is intentionally provocative to stimulate the reader into becoming more objective in formulating beliefs and attitudes about nature and our exploitation of animals—whether it be for food, materials, work, research, pleasure, sport, hunting, fishing or trapping. When we tamper with the environment, we have a responsibility to help find ways to manage animal populations—to ensure their welfare and long-term survival.

This book is designed to motivate people of all ages. It deals with the fields of ecology, wildlife conservation, biomedical research, humane treatment of animals, animal control, agriculture, hunting, trapping, fishing, forestry, political science and the social sciences. It is an analysis of what nature is all about in the "real world."

# Introduction

The world is no longer in a "natural" state. No person, group or government can restore nature to its presumed innocence, that is, what it was before human exploration and settlement. In varying degrees, people have modified all environments. Ecosystems no longer exist unaffected by the hand of man, even in our national parks and remote wilderness areas.

Human beings have introduced exotic species, altered environments and destroyed the original predator-prey balance throughout the world. The outcome is a shift in the resulting plant and animal communities, creating a new "natural world" that requires some form of management by people. Only where human modifications have been slight is it desirable to live with the outcome of nature's survival-of-the-fittest struggle by each species to survive. The challenge for us is to find the best way to coexist with wild and domestic animals and still preserve healthy environments.

From both animal welfare and environmental perspectives, it is paramount that we understand the laws of nature. People must understand nature because additional habitat modifications and the use of animals and land by societies are inevitable. The human population will continue to grow and the masses of people now in existence will not go away. One way or another, we persist and advocate on accommodation. The well-being of both domestic and wild creatures clearly depends upon how much we can improve the way humans use and manage the plants and animals of the environment. Our well-being depends on this as well. It is an immutable law of nature that the well-being of one species sometimes comes at the expense of another. How are we to choose what is best in those cases?

Sometimes it isn't morally wrong to intentionally distress domestic animals. For example, training animals to perform certain behaviors for their own good may cause some suffering and pain. Inflicting such distress may be ethically correct.

I am not surprised to hear people say they want to reestablish nature as it was in the United States before Europeans arrived, except for things that affect them personally. Changes made by people do not eliminate natural balances per se; rather, these changes initiate new balances, some of which we like and some we don't. For instance, pavement is a habitat that can be utilized by many small but living organisms. Whether the new balances are better or worse depends upon one's viewpoint, often with disagreements among us; very often one's viewpoint is a reflection of one's biases and life experiences.

In order to understand the laws of nature, one must view events through a different value system. A main tenet of this value system is that it is better when a population of animals produces an undesirable large number of individuals that the "surplus" be selectively culled. It is morally wrong for us to let surplus animals cause entire populations of the species to become highly stressed or even die from diseases, starvation or other factors, especially when we caused the overpopulation.

In the "real world," of which people are a part, anecdotal information and speculation simply won't do—hard scientific evidence is needed. It is difficult to remain dispassionate about people's use of animals. The issues are volatile, like politics, and difficult to consolidate. No one philosophy can be all things to all people, so let's start by listening to some divergent views in order to arrive at our own personal balanced opinion. We need to think of ourselves as philosophers who are seriously investigating the workings of nature.

Our well-being and the well-being of all animals depend upon how plants and animals are "managed" in a healthy functioning environment. The secret to managing native wild and feral animals in a sustainable manner is proper management of their population density, and this may include a reduction and even complete extirpation of local populations of a species—for instance, rats in the attic and pocket gophers or moles in our lawns and gardens. With domestic animals, which are genetically distinct from their wild counterparts, the goal should be to ensure them a quality life free of unnecessary pain and distress and a death that is as humane and nondistressful as possible—a fate unlike that which usually awaits animals in the wild. Domestic animals have lost their natural wildness due to selective breeding and having been reared for generations in a nonnatural environment.

To try to help both wild and domestic animal populations live a healthy life, while at the same time also protecting the environment, we need to consider a number of factors—animal welfare, research, animal control, the balance of nature, agriculture, hunting, trapping, fishing and forestry—all of which have emotional dimensions. Nature's role must be brought back into the deliberations of these highly polarized subjects. The common uses of animals for food, research and game, when done responsibly, have an acceptable place in society.

The welfare of vertebrate animals—mammals, birds, reptiles, fish and amphibians—and how we manage and protect the environment are among the most important sociopolitical issues that we will face in coming years. Fortunately, there is general agreement that we have a duty to treat higher animals kindly and not inflict unnecessary pain and distress, since sentient animals like dogs, horses, cows and pigs can experience fear, pleasure and boredom as well as pain and suffering.

Not too long ago people considered animals their property, to be used, or abused, as they liked. Fortunately, there has been a positive change in attitude toward animal welfare in the developed parts of the world, and animal rights organizations, in spite of their excesses, can be credited with having done much toward making people more sensitive to the ways animals are treated.

Because of the ever-growing human population, it is becoming increasingly more difficult to preserve "natural" animal populations.

And the number of conflicts between wildlife and people is bound to increase in the future.

Two terms need to be clarified: "Animal welfare" means ensuring that all animals used for food, experiments, clothing and entertainment are handled in an *acceptable* manner that does not cause *unnecessary* pain and distress, even though it may require killing the animals.

The animal rights movement takes the position that people should treat animals humanely and that people should not exploit animals, even when such action may be beneficial to people or animals. Ironically, animal rights advocates adhere to this philosophy even when the action may be beneficial to animals or people. Of course, many legitimate questions can and should be asked about the morality of using animals as food or game, as companion animals, or in research, and these will be discussed.

Animals do not need our sympathy, but they deserve our respect. They need to be properly understood and managed by recognizing the rules of nature. If people did not enjoy and use animals as pets, beasts of burden or for sport, food and products, a large percentage of the wild and domestic vertebrate animals we regularly see would not have been born and many "unwanted" species probably would now be extinct.

It is sometimes necessary to inflict pain and distress in the management and use of domestic and wild animals. This type of distress, however, is not only acceptable if done responsibly, but often is desirable if it is kept to a minimum and not done unnecessarily. In nature young animals experience pain and distress, which is necessary so they can learn how to survive. Today, many wild animal populations in disturbed or modified environments lack natural predation or adequate human-caused mortality factors to control their density. As a consequence, entire populations rather than a few individuals suffer severely from species' self-limiting factors, such as extreme starvation, cruel diseases and excessive cannibalism.

All animals, including humans, eventually die. Death begets life. Except for people, the bulk of all animals born die before they reach sexual maturity. This is in marked contrast to pets and animals in zoos, where many animals often live unusually long lives under man's care. What is right or wrong concerning the fate of all animals is partly dependent upon how you want to help manage nature's mortality factors.

People occupy a dominant position in nature and society has an ethical and moral right to use animals in research, teaching, agriculture, hunting, trapping, fishing and as pets, as long as they conform to nature's life-death cycle. Responsible use of animals is biologically sound. It fits well into the natural scheme of life and it has enriched species diversity in most altered environments.

Although nature is beautiful, it can be a tough arena with a seemingly cruel and brutal death ethic known as the "survival of the fittest." Living in the wild is an existence that is not free of suffering. The two main biological functions of all plant and animal organisms are reproduction and to become food for other organisms. Nature's death ethic links everything together in endless chemical communion and energy exchange. If in doubt, just watch an episode of *Nature* on public television.

In the natural world, all animals are continuously faced with inescapable life-threatening competition, predation, diseases, parasitism, weather extremes and starvation. These are some of the hazards of being able to run free, and this is why regulated killing by human predator can be an integral part of establishing nature's balance in human-modified ecosystems. Many of the current endangered species are not adapted to current human-modified habitats and, hence, will be eliminated if not helped by human intervention.

Due to evolution, new species survive if they can adapt to the current habitat conditions. Likewise, when exotic (alien) species are accidentally or purposefully introduced into a new environment, they will survive and become established only if the habitat is suitable. Some alterations of nature's natural schemes that enable exotics to become established may be considered undesirable. Imagine what the flora and fauna in different parts of the world would be like if all continents were connected by land bridges.

Species diversity on each continent would be enriched, even though some species might be eliminated.

To assure the continuance of a species in nature, each species is programmed to produce enough offspring both to replace its parents and to provide the fuel (food) needed by other species. This eat-and-be-eaten regime is necessary to preserve the balance of nature.

Over time, birth and death rates of each surviving species tend to approach equality. Nature's death ethic also requires that many offspring must die before they reproduce, not only to provide sustenance for the balance of nature, but also to prevent species from overpopulating and destroying themselves. High birth rates serve the twofold purpose of (a) providing prey for predators in nature's complex chain of sustenance and (b) ensuring that enough individuals within each species survive and procreate, thereby completing the life-death predator-prey cycle. When this balance is disturbed—as it has been to some degree today in every environment—it becomes the responsibility of humans to, in effect, fulfill nature's obligation by culling, or otherwise controlling, animal population densities through various means, which includes regulated sport hunting and trapping. Such management schemes can protect both the habitats and the animal species within a specific environment by keeping animal populations from exceeding the "carrying capacity" of their currently available habitats.

A question often raised is, "Do animals have rights?" Animals do have rights—not in the legal sense of the word, but each animal has the right to do what is necessary for survival, even if it means eating its offspring, siblings or parents. Animals cannot grasp moral principles or reason as people do. They don't have a golden rule. Even human rights are not absolute. They vary among cultures and over time. Social customs, mores and laws do not permit people to follow many of their basic instincts. For example, we do not behave like wild animals; we arbitrarily choose to restrict our sexual, feeding and other behaviors. From a moral point of view, animals deserve fair, humane and responsible treatment by people. That's a "right" we justifiably bestow on our fellow creatures.

Compared with the struggles found in the natural world, domestic animals live a life much freer of nature's cruelty and, significantly, almost all die more humanely than do their wild ancestors. A wild animal reaches maturity at the expense of other animals that served as food or were killed in territorial defense or sexual fighting. Because of our social customs, the human predator is unique in that it commonly exhibits compassion and pity toward its prey and is forced to operate under regulations designed to ensure that the treatment, even the killing, of the prey will be as humane as is feasible. Not so in nature.

By properly managing population densities of wild animals and doing all we can to preserve their original habitats, we are instituting constructive ways of helping minimize the suffering of animals wrought by fang, claw, beak and talon. Many prey are eaten or swallowed while still alive, as I discovered as a child when I forced a western garter snake to disgorge a small trout, which then swam away, as did the snake.

It is wishful thinking to believe we can find solutions to many health and behavior questions of people, as well as domestic animals, without using animals in both research and teaching. Current use of animals for these objectives, fortunately, is highly regulated. Abuses are now less frequent, thanks in part to the animal rights movement. Alternatives to using animals are ethically commendable, but not always satisfactory.

Because so many of the functions of bodies and biological systems are unknown and complex, it is impossible to always use computer simulations as is often recommended by animal rightists. Doctors cannot treat patients without using medical skills, knowledge, medicine and surgical arts that were gained primarily from the use of animals in research and teaching. However, those who exploit animals either as pets or for food, labor or their products, or use them in research were too slow in adjusting to needed changes in social attitudes about animal welfare—hence the explosion of the animal rights movement.

Many people today are urban folks who have little experience of nature in the raw. They have not lived on the land, nor have they experienced the joys, triumphs and misfortunes of producing crops, raising livestock or otherwise having to be responsible for managing and killing animals to feed the family and society. They usually don't have a clue as to what the odors of a dairy, poultry, or hog farm are like. Also, many have been deeply influenced by anthropomorphism and the "Bambi" syndrome that ignores nature's life-and-death roles. How can they understand that in order to improve animal welfare in human-modified environments it is usually unwise, except in some wilderness areas where habitats have not been sufficiently altered, to leave the outcome of any new balancing process exclusively to the whims of nature's survival-of-the-fittest regime?

Animals rarely live to a ripe old age unless people have protected them from harm. In modified environments, nature's death ethic can easily eliminate some species as has happened. The reason wild animals seldom reach old age is that they are unable to counteract nature's death ethic. People have conquered many of nature's death-ethic mortality factors by developing medical advances, pesticides and safe water to drink; producing safe and abundant food and increasing their ability to provide themselves with a safe indoor and outdoor environment in which to live. People actually show more compassion toward other members of their species and also to other species than do wild or domestic animals. Some might think that dogs and cats are an exception, but they too can become very intolerant of other cats and dogs.

Public attitudes are probably more influential than are laws and policies. They are deep-rooted in issues of values and goals and fall victim of activism. If this book will stimulate readers to think more objectively, their attitudes about nature can be based on biological principles and common sense rather than on emotionalism. By creating better awareness of the true role of the balance of nature in modified habitats, perhaps society can then set more environmentally desirable goals concerning the welfare of wildlife. Better answers are needed.

As you are probably beginning to sense, I am prone to disregard the current sociopolitical atmosphere and push for what I think is right. I take to heart my responsibility as a scientist and would rather be forthright than politically correct with both academic and environmental issues. Any one of my former students at the University of California-Davis will tell you this about me. I don't care whether you agree with me or not, just think . . . critically, openly, honestly. To borrow a phrase out of its usual context: question authority. Yes, I have an omnivorous intellectual appetite and a penchant for poking and prodding orthodox viewpoints.

There is disagreement among professional biologists and many lay persons about the interpretation of nature's life-death ethic. Many are trapped by their emotions. Read on and decide for yourself.

# CHAPTER 1

# Nature's Death Ethic

What do we mean by the term "balance of nature"? The harmony or "balance" found in "undisturbed" nature is the sum of the interactions among all resident organisms in their attempt to survive and reproduce. They sustain themselves through predation and reproduction. This is nature's life-death ethic. The balance is created in the web of relationships among the population densities of the diverse species of organisms that make up an ecological community. The natural balancing process among plant species usually leads to a "climax," which is a more or less steady state between inputs and outflows of nutrients, such as the Tall Grass Prairie that once dominated central North America. The original biodiversity of the Tall Grass Prairie no longer exists. For America's Tall Grass Prairie to be considered "balanced," would it require all original 400 plant, 300 bird and 80 mammal species to be present?

The balance of nature reflects ecosystem homeostasis. The intrinsic adjustments and feedback mechanisms continually create new "balances" in human-disturbed environments. Social and economic considerations need to take into account changing ecosystems. We cannot control or manage all of nature's processes.

From a practical point of view, the balance of nature should really be called "balancing" of nature. It is a dynamic and fluctuating survival-of-the-fittest struggle for existence. Larger, stronger and better adapted individuals feed upon or displace the weaker and less environmentally fit, even those of the same species.

It is a misconception to think that a true harmony (balance) prevails in nature, which is anything but peaceful and harmonious.

Natural balances are always in a state of flux. Herein lies the secret to survival—nature's capacity to adapt to a continually changing environment. Regardless of our level of sophistication, a sound environmental ethic should be based on accurately interpreted ecological principles which, according to Bicak (1997), is rare today.

In some cases, humans may be able to override laws of nature, but we are still part of nature and, for the most part, subject to its laws. Even though human life has become quite artificial, many aspects of nature are deeply ingrained in our culture. Only by understanding nature's role can one grasp the challenges and opportunities in dealing with disturbed ecosystems.

Since ethical values to some extent regulate the behavior of societies, education about the welfare of animals and a thorough understanding of the laws of nature are tremendously important. We should value nature in its own right, as well as for the benefit of people.

Life in the wild is not free of suffering. The average life span of wild animals is usually shorter than that of domestic or other captive animals used as pets, in research, at zoos or as food. Animals don't bestow rights upon their own kind as people do or attempt to treat each other "fairly" by sharing scarce resources. How can all nonhuman creatures have an equal right to life when all animals are predator, prey, or both? A significant number of wild animals is eaten shortly after birth, many more before reaching sexual maturity. This provides the indispensable food energy that the balance of nature requires. Few individuals reach old age. It would be chaotic any other way. In the natural world animals continuously face life-threatening competition, predation, cannibalism, diseases, parasitism, environmental extremes and starvation, all of which, incidentally, are usually very unpleasant.

The balance of nature would collapse without all species of animals having a natural mortality factor—nature's death ethic. This role usually involves some form of predation. In nature everything is linked together by eating and being eaten. Nature is seldom humane; in all cases either the predator goes hungry or the prey is killed and eaten. From a humane point of view, the lucky animals are unquestionably those killed by people, whether it is by slaughter, euthanasia, hunters or trappers. All animals suffer to some degree no matter how they die.

It is difficult to view wild animals objectively. Instead of being realistic about nature's death ethic, we are often categorically opposed to death. Today, many biologists and a large portion of the public think we should do all we can to ensure every animal with a long and full life, even though it is contrary to nature's death ethic. In a stable population, the number of deaths within a species is roughly equal to the number of births. Recycling from decomposers is also a part of the ethic.

How do you want the animals to die? This question needs to be answered honestly even though it may be difficult for you to do so because it forces you to recognize the brutality of natural deaths. Try to answer it!

In general, society does not accurately acknowledge the role of life and death in nature's scheme of things. Life actually depends on nature's death ethic, hence responsible (humane) killing of sentient animals that possess some degree of consciousness can still be considered a sacred act when done respectfully on behalf of nature's laws. Humans have countered nature's original death ethic for *Homo sapiens* with advances in public health, medicine, agriculture and technology. But at what cost? See what the resulting explosion of the human population has done to the environment and the welfare of other organisms. I don't want to die, even if at 87 I have utilized more than my share of nonrenewable resources by living so long.

We must not fight nature's death ethic and attempt to keep all individual animals alive in our wildlife management schemes. Some form of mortality is essential to maintaining a healthy balance of both domestic and wild animal populations in the natural scheme of things.

Since nature is not always understood, helping people to comprehend nature is one realistic change that can be made to help solve some of today's environmental concerns. Despite its harsh brutality though, nature's actions can often be viewed as a beautiful act of creation. Think of the vast diversity of fauna and flora nature's death ethic gives rise to.

As a result of the popular acceptance of anthropomorphic Bambi-ism (humans acting as if animals could speak), plus extreme environmentalism and propaganda falsehoods in the mass media, it is no wonder that our innate sensitivity keeps us from understanding the true balance of nature. Nature must be the way it is in order for species to survive. Nature's death ethic is, in reality, neither brutal nor cruel. It is a fact of life that makes life itself possible.

Any substantial human disturbance of an environment causes a marked shift in relative abundance of coexisting species and can result in a reduction of species richness and numbers. In most ecosystems we are now dealing with artificial assemblages consisting of both a different species composition of native species and an increased biological diversity of well-established exotic plants and animals. It is inevitable that our activities will alter the relationships of most organisms to the environment.

No species can live in all types of environments, and once its own particular type of habitat is destroyed most species then vanish from that area. However, habitats cannot be eliminated, only altered, with the result being the succession of species by new ones. Even our houses support many organisms. Nothing succeeds like biological succession. New and better man-made ecosystems that are ecologically and economically sound are feasible in today's world. For example, this is a goal of sustainable agriculture. The so-called "harmony" or "balance" in nature is really no more than the present degree of biological equilibrium established by the sum of interactions among all the organisms present, as each attempts to survive and reproduce under the current climatic and soil conditions in the current man-modified environments.

What is natural? Is it a process, the consequence of nonhuman-caused events? Unfortunately, it is an axiom that people, as all species do, must exploit the environment, and change the balancing components in order to survive. To sustain themselves in a balanced community, it is easy to see why animal populations must have fairly high mortality rates to prevent them from attaining excessive populations. The lack of such mortality would put a stress on most members of the population and also often permanently alter their habitat.

People, in contrast to other animals, have been highly successful in their competition with other species and in overcoming nature's original death ethic for *Homo sapiens*. Humans have become dominant over all other animals, and our technology, public health and medicine have enabled us to subdue most invertebrate pests, predators and diseases that formerly limited our survival under nature's death-ethic scheme.

Nature, in its evolutionary history, has established a great variety of effective natural mortality factors to take care of its overproduction of young—predation, starvation, territoriality, cannibalism and diseases. These factors not only provide essential food to predators, scavengers and other consumers that feed on the prey, but such mortality is necessary to prevent any species from overpopulating "naturally" and putting stress on most members of that population. This "self-limitation" is usually achieved as a result of a dramatic increase in these mortality factors or other consequences result: habitat destruction, territorial fighting, infanticide, nest abandonment and other ways that excessive populations of animals must face to ultimately limit their own densities in absence of adequate predation.

To regulate the density of hoofed herbivores requires human or natural predators. Defense of territories by ungulates is not as effective a density regulator as it is with many other species. Without predation, herbivores overpopulate, as is happening with white-tailed deer in many suburban areas and Canada geese on golf courses and in parks. Ultimately, starvation and/or disease usually become the controlling force. These self-limiting factors may have serious impacts on local habitats and regulate entire local populations of herbivores. It should be obvious that a better life results for animals in modified environments if their population densities are managed by sensible and relatively humane harvesting schemes to avoid forcing nature to impose a limit.

Natural or human-regulated mortality factors are what keep animal populations in a healthy state and prevent a severe overpopulation, triggering species-specific self-limiting forces. This is why overprotecting a population often results in "loving them to an ugly death."

In nature, all species, including *Homo sapiens*, are inherently programmed to overproduce. The successful species, notably man, have displaced their competitors, which were not as well adapted. The species that survive in altered habitats always have an impact in the changed environment, and it may be advantageous, deleterious or neutral to the welfare of many native species. Attempts to stabilize a disturbed community may have unintended consequences. However, if no action is taken—regardless of how valuable and desirable the lack of doing anything may first appear—there may still be undesirable tradeoffs.

Both birth and death rates of all species of wildlife are high. For example, if the field mice I studied for my doctorate had the same survival rates as humans, in a few years the species would be so abundant that, theoretically, it would soon cover the earth.

Any prevention of natural deaths usually leads to overpopulation, disease and starvation in wildlife species, much as it has done to many human populations or underharvested flocks and herds of domestic animals. Natural mortality factors have evolved to restrict the distribution and density of animals in natural environments so that they match the available food supply, good harborage for breeding and cover from predators and weather. It is the consequence of nature's survival-of-the-fittest principle.

"Carrying capacity" is the number of animals a habitat can support and perpetuate throughout the year without damaging the future welfare of the animals or their habitat. When wildlife numbers are not controlled by mortality factors and they exceed the carrying capacity, the excess animals eventually die. The main problem is that first they may have undesirable effects on the environment, thus affecting many other individuals of their own species as well as other species.

Many national parks are experiencing the consequences of these imbalances where some species overpopulate. This is why the reintroduction of wolves into Yellowstone National Park is considered so successful. The wolves effectively reduced the overpopulation of elk. In some of Africa's parks, elephants, rather than being endangered, have become too abundant for the limited habitat still available to them. In some parks, like Amboseli National Park in Kenya, they are permanently eliminating most of the tree species they need for food. In an excellent synopsis of the African elephantproblem, Cheri Sugal (1997) explains how the woodlands of the Serengeti-Mara ecosystem along the border of Kenya and Tanzania, which I visited in 1996, have reverted to grasslands. This is because the palatable trees have been consumed and overrun by an overpopulation of elephants, except in demonstration exclosures where the elephants have been kept out.

Rural people in much of East Africa are forced to bear the cost of living with wildlife without obtaining any significant benefit. The governments have taken over the control of large mammals and other wildlife with the consequence that benefits from wildlife (trophy hunting, ivory, meat, etc.) no longer go to local communities (Skonhoft 1995). African elephants provide unique management problems.

The most serious elephant problems have been caused by the loss of so much of their habitat and many of the migration corridors. This is due to people occupying the elephants' former range. I have observed how devastating elephants can be to tree species they like. In parts of Amboseli National Park, it looked as though a cyclone had blown over all the trees. The same phenomenon was occurring in Masai Mara National Park. In Tanzania, I witnessed similar destruction of trees by elephants in the Serengeti, Ngorongoro Crater, Lake Manyara and Tarangire National Parks.

According to one report, about 43 people are killed annually by elephants in Kenya, with another 40 being seriously injured. In India, however, elephants kill each year more than 300 people. Wildlife service experts call for lifting the hunting ban and for the profits to go to farmers, not government. Continued loss of habitat and migration corridors for elephants is to be expected due to the growth of the human population in Africa and the inevitable conflict between elephants and agriculture.

The ivory poaching problem is complicated since the past illegal poaching of elephants was principally the result of corrupt officials. One wonders whether more of the international effort should have been aimed at these political problems rather than primarily just struggling to protect elephants from poachers by banning the sale of ivory.

The main attention has been aimed at protecting elephants rather than determining how a sustained supply of ivory might be produced for the benefit of local people and for managing elephants. But maybe it was necessary for the Convention on International Trade In Endangered Species (CITIES) in 1989 to make ivory an illegal product because it was simply too difficult to deal with corrupt officials. There are many good arguments to support making ivory an illegal trade material and to justify an embargo on all ivory. Ironically, this has increased the value of ivory and, for example, in 1996 poachers in the National Park of Odzala, Congo slaughtered about 200 elephants for their ivory.

In June 1997, CITIES approved a sustainable-use limited harvesting of ivory in Zimbabwe, Namibia and Botswana, after control mechanisms were developed. This is a victory for African sovereignty. These countries had a collective ivory stockpile of 120 tons and along with South Africa are believed to be among Africa's best in managing elephants. The CITIES' vote is considered a major defeat by some animal rights and environmental organizations that oppose any elephants being killed. In 2004 many claimed it to have been a failure. What have we done in the United States? We have removed many dangerous and economically destructive animals, including mountain lions, wolves and poisonous snakes, whenever there is a threat to human life. California eliminated grizzly bears and Europe exterminated its lions.

It does seem a terrible waste of resources to have to burn ivory to convince local natives that there is no longer any value to ivory. This was done in Kenya and Zambia. Ideally it would be so much better to let ivory sales fund the preservation of elephant habitat and to pay for the hiring of wardens to protect the elephants. My colleague, Dr. Timothy Caro et al. (1998), found that tourist hunters had little positive impact on ungulate densities, presumably also elephants, even for sought-after trophy species.

With proper management, family groups of elephants could be harvested selectively and humanely, and the elephant populations kept below the carrying capacity of their habitat. The involvement and support of local communities in wildlife conservation is a prerequisite to effective and long-term conservation of African wildlife and wildlands. What is needed, Cheri Sugal (1997) points out, is what some communities in Zimbabwe have done. They manage their wildlife through the Communal Areas Management Programme For Indigenous Resources (CAMPFIRE). This program gives local bodies stewardship over natural resources, which provides an incentive for them to manage elephants and other wildlife. The program is partially funded by the U.S. Agency for International Development (USAID). The economic value of hunting elephants in state forests has been shown to be greater than the value of extractable timber. As long as the density of elephants is regulated, these economic returns will offset the negative impact of elephant damage on the timber according to Campbell et al. (1996). Many parks in Africa need community-based conservation as David Western who is in charge of Kenya's wildlife, is trying to do.

Elephants can reproduce at a surprisingly fast rate, some say even 20 percent or so a year, though 5 to 7 percent is more realistic. Therefore, there is great potential for both the conservation of elephants and the production of ivory as long as harvest rates are not excessive and ivory is also harvested from elephants that die naturally as well as those that are intentionally culled. It has been estimated that 70,000 elephants a year are needed to satisfy the ivory market

For a number of years some organizations, such as the Wildlife Conservation Society, which is the research arm of the New York Zoological Society, World Wildlife Foundation, African Wildlife Foundation, Defenders of Wildlife and others, claimed that elephants were about to become extinct. In reality, Bonner (1993) thinks most national parks have far too many elephants for them to be maintained on a sustained basis. The damage that an overpopulation of elephants can inflict on their habitat is tremendous. According to Cummings et al. (1997), some savanna woodlands have been converted to shrublands and grasslands and never again will be as good a habitat for elephants.

When elephants destroy trees much faster than the trees can regrow, the carrying capacity for elephants in such parks will never again be what it was before elephants overpopulated. However, there was considerable recovery of trees and shrubs that had been destroyed by elephants in Tsavo National Park, Kenya, as a result of large-scale poaching for ivory (Leuthold 1996). Although no reasonable person condones poaching as a way to manage elephant densities, this example shows that controlled harvesting of surplus elephants for ivory could have a beneficial effect on the environment and, perhaps, the long-term survival of the elephant population if it was not overharvested.

In national parks, such as Krugerin South Africa, the artificial development of water for game can result in excessive browsing of vegetation. I agree with Thrash et al. (1991) that in drought years the artificial water supply may enable excess game that normally would die to survive, only to further depress the drought-stressed vegetation. I observed this in Kruger National Park in 1992, at the end of a five-year drought. When elephants damage their environments by removing too many trees, however, that habitat alteration will favor other species like antelope. Fayrev-Hosken et al. (1997) point out that Kruger National Park culls a mean of 517 elephants per year, but park biologists told me that it would be many more if the public would tolerate it.

It is self-evident that humans must exploit the environment and deliberately unbalance it to survive. Native plants and animals can sometimes be used to effectively promote desirable landscapes. The "man must not meddle with nature" philosophy, after people have already modified an environment, does not apply. It is akin to denying humans the right to exist, and leaving it to nature is not desirable ecologically or humanely.

Few people realize that agricultural crops could not survive if all native mammals were treated like endangered species. In fact, most home landscaping and city parks would also be largely destroyed, at least aesthetically, if native mammals like species of deer, rabbits, squirrels and pocket gophers were allowed free range. Since these landscaping plants are mostly exotics, they have not co-evolved to withstand the feeding pressures of native mammals in their unnatural plant communities.

Andrew Neal Cohen (*Atlantic Monthly*, November 1992) points out that due to human introduction of exotic animals, habitat destruction, disruption of natural predator-prey cycles and other factors, wildlife managers now often face the choice of either eradicating an alien predator or watching some native populations plummet. Examples of conflicts between native and exotics that cause species to become endangered include introduced red foxes threatening to exterminate least terns and California clapper rails on California's coast; coyotes destroying nesting success of whooping cranes in Idaho and sandhill cranes in Oregon; common ravens preying on endangered desert tortoises in California's Mojave Desert; mountain goats, about 12 of which were released in 1925, that are destroying rare alpine plants in Washington's Olympic National Park; brown tree snakes that have exterminated nine native bird species on Guam; and cowbirds that are outcompeting native songbirds by laying eggs in their nests throughout the fragmented temperate forests of North America.

In modified environments one should only let nature take its course when willing to accept the consequences of the survival-of-the-fittest process and the loss of those species that now are unfit in the new environments. A common sequel of such management is a reduction in local diversity, and in many instances this would also cause the demise of sensitive, threatened or endangered species and their habitats. In altered environments, the choice is ours to either accept the consequences of whatever new balance develops naturally or manage the densities of populations to "humanize" nature and help protect the species we consider most desirable. Without our help, many more species would unquestionably disappear in modified environments. This is why the preservation of natural habitats wherever they may still exist is so important. The Nature Conservancy has been a leader in saving natural habitats.

Nature does not have pain pills, life-support devices, or homes for the elderly. Pain and trauma, however, are essential to evolution and the survival-of-the-fittest process. Pain is necessary to train young animals how to survive. The lack of such training is part of the reason most domestic animals die when set free. However, even though we are part of nature, we do not have a license to wantonly inflict unnecessary pain and distress. When, as a predator, we assist nature in human-modified environments and harvest the surplus population of animals that otherwise would damage the environment and the species' own welfare, we should make the lethal management tools we use as humane as possible.

## Transplanting Animals

Helping animals is not simple. A coyote, skunk, or raccoon forced to leave its normal habitat for another chance at life might be translocated by a well-meaning person to an unfamiliar site where that species is abundant. Compassionate stewardship might more wisely, however, dictate humanely taking the animal's life because translocated displaced mammals frequently, but not always, die while searching in vain for their original home. They have little chance of finding a vacant niche and a mate unless the species is below carrying capacity at the release site. They were probably forced out of their original home range because they were surplus. Translocated mammals also cause additional fighting with their own kind before their almost inevitable early demise. Research with radio telemetry on released displaced mammals confirms this high mortality for many species of mammals.

Relocation of wildlife species into unoccupied suitable habitats by wildlife professionals, however, after appropriate analysis of the sites and with appropriate care and handling can prove highly successful. It remains a basic and essential technique for restoring wildlife populations, such as wolves in Yellowstone National Park. However, being released into an unfamiliar environment still causes much stress, and many of the released animals die. Frequently, with many species the translocates must initially be protected from native predators. Capturing and releasing unwanted, displaced mammals is not a compassionate act and should be prohibited by law unless it is the reintroduction of a native species designed to reestablish a viable population.

Wild animals, unlike pets and domestic livestock, must be constantly vigilant to avoid being injured or killed by other animals. In nature, wild animals usually do not die suddenly or without trauma. Most small rodents can easily live 5 to 10 years in a laboratory, whereas in nature's food web I found only a very small percentage of prairie deer mice that I (Howard 1949) was studying attained one year of age.

Nature is not composed of species compassionate to one another; it is a battlefield where often-bizarre types of cruelty are inflicted on animals. Most predators are not humane in their killing methods. Coyotes often partially consume sheep that are still alive. Coyotes wait for sheep to run, then usually attack at the neck, crushing the trachea, thus causing the sheep to suffocate. After a sheep becomes short of oxygen, a coyote can then throw to the ground a sheep that is much larger than itself. Then, commonly, the coyotes immediately start feeding on the still-alive sheep's small intestines. To avoid being repeatedly and painfully attacked in the neck, the live sheep typically lies silent and motionless, although fully conscious, while the coyote consumes its small intestine, which many coyotes seem to relish.

On two personal occasions, when a coyote was observed feeding on the small intestines of what all the students with me were positive was a dead sheep, upon flushing the coyote, the sheep immediately stood up and cried loudly before we put it out of its misery. The sheep's suffering would have lasted until the coyote fed on the heart and other vital organs if the coyote had not been frightened away.

Predators often play with injured prey or use them to teach their offspring how to kill, as cats often do with captured birds and mice. In Argentina I learned that female mountain lions also known as pumas or cougarsoften kill 15 or so sheep in one night when training their cubs how to kill, but carry away only one for food. The same surplus killing of goats by mountain lions has also been observed in California. Dr. Dan Fagre (1981) has shown that coyotes also get into killing frenzies, especially with chickens, where one coyote can kill over 100 chickens in one night. Wolves also engage in surplus killing.

Every organism in nature, humans included, considers itself number one and fights tenaciously, even unconsciously, for its right to live. An important function of any organism, other than its need to do whatever is necessary to live and reproduce, is that it will probably become food for another, usually a different, species. Humans, as predators who must operate under regulations, can play a vital role in the harmonious functioning of an animal community even though some wildlife will be killed in the process. To maintain balance, nature's death ethic requires a mortality factor that includes carnivores.

It is frequently stated that humans have upset the balance of nature. Is nature no longer in balance? Is it bad for humans to influence nature? Bad for whom or for what? Even devastating floods, lightning, fires, earthquakes, hurricanes and volcanic explosions are acts of nature.

The alteration of an environment by people does not mean the ecosystem will no longer be healthy. Humans do not eliminate balances; they merely alter them and initiate new balances. This is why we must carefully manage populations of fauna and flora. Whether the new balances are better or worse often depend upon one's viewpoint, one's ethic. Some people consider any death in the wild, no matter how brutal, to be acceptable if it was "natural." When the suffering is the consequence of the environment being modified, the burden of responsibility swings in our direction and a humane alternative becomes clear.

Humans cannot make advancements in the world without gaining some measure of control over nature and manipulating it to their advantage. How to utilize natural resources, as people must, while preserving nature's original balance is not easy in a world dominated by an economic scheme that requires growth for progress.

People's different philosophies on this subject appear to center around whether "natural" (original) stability should prevail. What was present prior to the invasion by people is generally considered "in balance." A basic question is what type of "balance" should be our goal? What role should humankind have in both adjusting that balance and in controlling perturbations that may alter the original balance, as often happens when species are overprotected and become too abundant? No national park is large enough to include an entire ecosystem or provide adequate space for dispersing surplus large mammals. Elk grizzly bears and wolves require more space than exists within the boundaries of Yellowstone National Park.

In modified environments, nature's evolving balance may not be what we want; hence, wildlife usually must be managed or controlled. In fact, overabundant or expanding populations of native species can reduce diversity by monopolizing resources, introducing or spreading infectious diseases and parasites, changing the composition of the species and their relative abundance and even causing local extinctions of natives. If we use our knowledge of the balance of nature's processes judiciously, we can unquestionably create desirable and economically feasible communities, and even more favorable ecosystems of forests or grassland with regard to human preferences. Most of us would agree that the symbiotic interplay between nature and environmental alterations by man has generated some interesting diversified ecosystems for some extensive forested or prairie natural areas that lack diversity and can become monotonous. The beauty of home gardens and city parks is due largely to exotic plants, not native species, many of which are then considered to be "weeds."

The preservation of natural biodiversity is, of course, a credible goal, but may not be feasible in all situations. We need to know how to manage modified environments if the equation means some native species must be left out and some exotics accepted. Nonnatural biological diversity may sometimes be the goal people desire either for esthetic reasons, sport and recreation, or to provide us with food, energy and other resources. For instance, most people approve the enhancement of California's limited warm-water fishery by introducing striped bass, catfish and perch. Our species could not survive without manipulating and modifying natural environments. Thus, our only option, in the resulting human-modified environments, is to manage nature responsibly.

The potential positive opportunities for environmental compatibility in modified habitats created by man often have been disregarded by environmentalists and landscape architects. We overlook the fact that nature's frequent "natural" perturbation or other disturbance of the environment is often that which neither man nor many wildlife species would consider desirable. Just look at the destruction wrought by floods and hurricanes.

Because preventing the destruction of natural habitats is the most important way of helping existing wildlife, people often think that any unnatural modification is heresy. But no animals, including people, can avoid altering habitats. The introduction of exotic plants or animals may create new habitats that are favorable substitutes for wildlife species we may consider desirable. If so, their populations usually must be managed by hunting, fishing or by some other means.

For instance, in the Sacramento Valley home landscaping with exotic plants has made new habitats that seasonally have enriched the variety of birds that nest, spend the winter there or stop briefly during seasonal migrations. Buildings and bridges provide nesting sites for cliff swallows and the artificial irrigation of rice provides them feeding areas nearby. Rice fields create many beneficial situations for migrating waterfowl and other wildlife. I'd venture to say that without rice production, the migratory wildlife would be in a world of trouble. Due to the improved food supply and nesting sites around my house, an area which used to be only grassland, I now have breeding western robins, hummingbirds, mourning doves barn owls (aided by a nest box), Swainson hawks and others. However, in recent years the predacious scrub jay has driven away the hummingbirds, house finches, mockingbirds and mourning doves by eating either their eggs or young.

People often forget that they are part of nature, and that they should maintain closer harmony with wildlife and other natural resources. An acceptable wildlife ethic is needed so that we will never be allowed to forget that we are part of nature. There is no shortage of ecologists who know how to measure what is happening in natural environments. Badly needed, however, are more applied ecologists who can predict the cause-and-effect relationships between wildlife and environments modified by people. Some form of artificial control or manipulation of the densities of wildlife species is an important conservation tool that is necessary to protect a species from destroying itself in situations where humans have appreciably modified the environment. We can't discontinue agriculture, although there is room for improvement to reduce the dependency on so much water, chemicals, fertilizers and the high use of fossil fuels. Sustainable agriculture is the new goal.

Society's primary aim ought to be "to achieve maximum coexistence among all forms of life." But most wildlife needs water, and water brings mosquitoes. The wastes of roosting birds make sidewalks slippery and dead animals encourage flies. Another basic problem is that wildlife does not recognize property boundaries. Many species of predators in particular are wide-ranging. Few vertebrate animals have small enough territories or home ranges that they will remain in just one backyard. In my yard, western toads survived for years until they wandered onto the street.

We are so entrenched with the thought that we are competing with nature—the "man-rules-beast" philosophy—that we cannot even bring ourselves to plant part of our gardens for the wildlife we have displaced. Instead, we let ourselves be guided by esthetics, conventional wisdom and conformity. The urbanite's niche has often become a concrete and plastic domain, with about the only reference to wildlife being that of calling a pest control firm to remove a skunk from under the house, a tree squirrel or raccoon that is tearing a hole in the roof or house mice in a garage.

People's physical environment is usually molded to fit their economic and social requirements. They isolate and insulate their biological territory with little, if any, consideration of nature or wildlife. Homeowners have little patience with wild animals that become pests. They are much less tolerant than farmers, who generally like to share with wildlife, until seriously influenced by economics. In fact, modern pest control practices incorporate thresholds that essentially acknowledge the reality that farm fields are an ecosystem where some pest damage is acceptable.

When someone builds a home and establishes a garden, he or she displaces, purposely or unknowingly, nearly all the native species of wildlife and plants that had prior claim to that piece of land. People rarely try to favor wildlife with appropriate landscape plantings. Instead, they surround their homes with plants that are hardy, disease—or insect-resistant and easy to care for, and all of this is for esthetic, not economic or ecological reasons. How can you favor insectivorous birds if you kill off the insects?

Meanwhile, some think that farmers should not be allowed to reduce wildlife species even if they have become abnormally abundant because of the crop planted, and even though the species may be causing acute economic damage to the farmer's basic livelihood. Some species increase beyond their normal density as a consequence of land-use practices that provide us with food, fiber and other resource needs. Examples of potential problem species are opossums, moles, bats, meadow mice or voles, rats, ground squirrels, pocket gophers, beavers, starlings, skunks, raccoons, coyotes, deer and many others.

To protect endangered species, to manage wildlife and to control problem animals in ecosystems we have altered and to do so in the most environmentally compatible manner possible, we must thoroughly understand the role of nature's death ethic and how to manage the balance of nature in such disturbed environments. Too often people in academia and the general public oversimplify such issues and advocate letting nature take its course, as if nature always knows best. Some think it is our flawed approach to wildlife management that needs examination and revision. Of interest, Dubos (1973) pointed out that we would not have peat, coal, oil, shale and guano deposits if nature had not failed in the recycling process

When species populations are declining in an altered environment, the question should be asked: Is it better to manage the species or to let nature take its course, even at the expense of some populations? According to Ernest Thompson Seton, "life of wild animals always has a tragic ending." Because of our presence and because nature clearly does not know best, we have a moral responsibility to do what we can to maintain healthy populations of animals and to help preserve "biological diversity."

Biological diversity is the variety of life and processes that link plants, animals, soil, air and water into ecological systems. Because of human activity, it is interesting to note that the biological diversity of all continents has, surprisingly, actually been enriched, in spite of the extinctions brought about by human endeavors. Introduction of exotic and domestic species increases biological diversity, but not *natural* biological diversity. Extinction of native species, usually by habitat destruction, is what reduces "natural" biological diversity. Ecosystems are often able to cope one way or another with new species as new communities develops.

Grizzly bears now extinct in the Sacramento Valley of California, were once common. However, I have never met anyone who wished to have these carnivores roaming about freely, although many, even professional biologists, foolishly claim they should be reintroduced into all their original habitats simply because they were once there and because they are on the California State flag.

When predators maintain a natural (though involuntary) balance with their prey by thinning the prey population, the surviving prey will be less susceptible to excessive starvation, disease and the other vicissitudes of life. As a result, the prey will be in better physical condition and have a higher quality of life than would have been possible had natural predators been removed.

One way nature limits populations that have exceeded the carrying capacity is through outbreaks of plague, rabies and other diseases, with starvation often being a contributing factor. A high mortality rate in the young occurs when parents are facing starvation. A mortality factor of some kind is beneficial to eliminate the unfit to preserve a species' competitiveness for survival, although territoriality and competition generally reduce the chance for unfit animals to breed successfully.

Natural populations of wild vertebrates in relatively undisturbed communities also fluctuate in numbers, but for the most part such populations are more stable. That is, they are quite tough and their density is not delicately balanced. Native populations also have a surprising resilience to disturbances by humans. That is why the populations of most songbirds, mammals, reptiles, amphibians and fish survive. According to a review by Korpimäki and Krebs (1996), the importance of predation as a regulating factor in population cycles of small mammals still needs further experimental research.

The web of life that holds an ecosystem together is not as sensitive to disturbances as many believe, at least as far as vertebrates are concerned, unless one is dealing with a direct predator-prey or competitive relationship. For example, artificially altering the density of jackrabbits may have little or no measurable effect on most of the other species of vertebrates present in that community except for predators. The high degree of adaptability and resilience to climate fluctuations and some human-caused factors that some species display in natural communities is attributable to both extrinsic and intrinsic factors that will be discussed later.

Except for prey species being available to predators, for the most part each vertebrate species in its natural environment responds to environmental forces quite independently of other species of vertebrates, except for local situations, such as the effect beaver dams may have on fish, or the use of abandoned squirrel burrows by burrowingowls. The population density of vertebrates will vary within relatively narrow limits in any particular habitat. This ignores, of course, the rare obligate predator's dependence on availability of a specific prey species, such as black-footed ferret or prairie dogs and the occasional competition that may occur between different species for space and/or food, such as between wolves and coyotes.

Instead of a day-to-day affair, the main mechanisms that deal with competition and other population-limiting factors are largely an evolutionary event. Those species that couldn't adjust are extinct. Unsuccessful competitors were eliminated long ago; hence the very large number of fossils that exist. More recent animal extinctions, such as the European lion and the passenger pigeon, have often been the consequences of these species being unable to survive in human settlements. Vertebrate populations, except for herbivores, seldom increase much beyond the innate carrying capacity of a natural community, even if extra amounts of food, cover and all apparent needs of the species are provided artificially in what otherwise are natural habitats. This type of poorly understood population self-limitation is apparently common to species, and it prevents them from destroying their natural environment and themselves by overpopulating.

It is often a surprise to discover just how independent of each other the different vertebrate species are in a community. Humans, for example, are quite independent of other species, and their viability on this earth would be little affected even if many species were tragically exterminated. If *all* vertebrates were removed, organisms that must feed on vertebrates to live and perhaps some plants that require birds or bats for pollination are about all that would be dramatically affected. Of course, no one wants to lose any species because of their esthetic and other values. The point to emphasize is that we want to protect viable populations of all fauna and flora for ethical and moral reasons, not just because we think it's necessary to save our lives.

To show how independent vertebrate species are of each other, let's consider all species of deer, one of the most dominant wild herbivores of North America. If all species of deer in North America were suddenly removed, the effect on all other species of vertebrates would hardly be measurable for several years, except perhaps for such predators as the mountain lion, wolf and coyote, and species-specific parasites. The main environmental disturbance caused by the disappearance of such dominant herbivores would eventually be a modification of the habitat. This would be due to the lack of their browsing and grazing, which would change the composition and structure of the vegetation. This alteration of the habitat might then affect other species, including small mammals and birds. Similarly, try to speculate on what would happen if all of any particular species, such as robins or jackrabbits, were removed from North America. It's confusing!

Humankind can modify ecosystems and change the species composition a great deal without seriously affecting the basic flow of materials and energy, thus not destroying the vitality of biotic communities within these ecosystems. But major alterations over large areas, such as the destruction of most tropical and other forests, would be serious.

Virtually all of the earth's energy comes from the sun, except for deep sea vents and nuclear energy. But the current and potential greenhouse warming effect from an increase in $CO_2$, the increase of acid rain, water and air pollution, ozone depletion, soil erosion and other factors also need to be reckoned with. DDT is still a serious pollutant, and has even spread to the Arctic ecosystem.

As long as the earth has abundant producers such as green plants, even drastic changes in the species composition of most consumer organisms, whether native or exotic, will not prevent the survival of humans. We benefit when food and resource production is increased but suffer when we create deserts. The basic functions of resource recycling are necessary to preserve the earth's vitality. Fortunately, because of our conservation ethic and other values, we want to preserve as many original natural habitats as possible.

And, as Edward O. Wilson (1992) has so well explained in his book, *The Diversity of Life*, people should care about preserving natural biodiversity. It can be the source of new scientific information that could be lost. A vast potential of biological wealth would be destroyed that may give us new medicines, crops, pharmaceuticals, timber, fibers, soil-restoring vegetation and petroleum substitution, to name a few products and amenities we do not want to lose. Wilson points out a few benefits derived from nature regarding obscure bugs and weeds. It was a moth from Latin America that saved Australia's pastureland from cactus. The rosy periwinkle provided the cure for Hodgkin's disease and childhood lymphocytic leukemia. The barks of Pacific yew provided a treatment for ovarian and breast cancer. And a chemical from the saliva of leeches dissolves blood clots during surgery.

All wild and domestic animals have legitimacy and value and deserve humane treatment. Animals enrich our spirit, whether they are wild, pets or livestock, and the Endangered Species Act has done much to help justify the preservation of all types of animals. Animals deserve respect as fellow members of this planet, but it is only natural that people favor most those species they can use or enjoy. All life forms, however, have inherent worth, and we do not live independent of other forms of life. Even though people's values differ, we should strive to share similar ethical concerns about nature and try to leave to future generations a healthier environment, even though it will be significantly modified.

Yes, we need ways to sharpen people's perspectives on environmental issues. It is not easy. Once a specific paradigm has become deeply entrenched, it is very difficult to overcome our stubborn resistance to change. However, environmental consciousness has increasingly become more evident in politics and business. Ecology, environment and diversity have become buzzwords that the public recognizes and values.

A number of biological factors are responsible for determining the stability and the balance of nature. One of the most significant factors for animals is the suitability of the habitat. Animals obviously do well in their natural habitats. If they migrate or are introduced into a foreign locale where the environment provides suitable habitats for them, they might also survive. If they manage to get there and the environment is not satisfactory, they, of course, will not do well. Civilization is shrinking the size of suitable habitats, but as Beier and Noss (1998) point out, the evidence from well-designed studies suggests that preserving corridors is a valuable conservation tool to overcome the problems of isolation.

Just how animals are adapted for different types of habitat conditions is still largely unknown. We do not know the inherited behavioral traits, independent of food, cover and predation, that seem to favor the successful existence of each animal when certain types of habitat conditions are present. This field needs much more investigation.

Limiting factors in nature include many intrinsic and social factors, including variable reproductive roles, various types of stresses, cover, food supplies, predation, diseases, territoriality and aggression. If all aspects of the environment are favorable to the survival of a species, and natural interspecific mortality factors are eliminated, the ultimate break to population growth comes directly from other members of that species, by way of their own self-limiting behaviors. Changes in the conditions of the habitat merely raise or lower the upper density limits that are controlled by these regulatory feedback mechanisms. For example, animal movements are important factors affecting population densities. These movements include dispersal, which is to emigrate away from place of birth, or to immigrate by moving into new territory.

Dispersal of subdominant animals is the primary way territorial species, such as carnivores, usually control their densities. Weather, fire and other environmental perturbations also affect the carrying capacity of populations. Food is usually less significant, unless there isn't enough of it. When we add more food to the environment, we seldom see many populations of animals, other than herbivores, increasing to a density much greater than they would attain naturally in the most favorable natural habitats. When I provided surplus food all winter, to a small range-rodent population, the density increased five-fold compared to a control population. However, over a period of several years the natural population that didn't have access to the additional food fluctuated 20-fold, indicating that food availability was not the controlling factor determining the density of the population.

Many people think that predation is the main factor regulating population densities. Natural predation, of course, is very important in maintaining the balance in animal-plant communities. However, natural predators usually are not very effective in depressing the densities of rodents in favorable habitats. In fact, the carrying capacity of a population of prey species usually can be maintained at a higher level over time with the presence of predators than could be sustained if the predators were not present. When predators are removed, their principal prey species usually respond at first with an increase in population growth, but it is only temporary. Within a year or so without predation, self-limitation from disease and starvation resulting from the species overpopulating usually keeps rodent densities at a lower level than when natural predators are present.

Some new and meaningful, but confusing, phrases that have arisen are *Conservation Biology* and *Natural Biological Diversity*, where the primary goal is to keep natural populations intact and all species from becoming threatened with extinction. To achieve this goal, a sensible environmental ethic is desperately needed in the national and international conscience that is consistent with the laws of nature.

It is difficult to foster sustainability of natural biological diversity and at the same time maintains and improves human living standards. A strong moral imperative to preserve and enhance natural resource systems needs to lay at the foundation of our policy decisions in this realm. As the dominant species on this planet, we maintain a healthy environment and as much natural diversity as possible. We must learn to live within the means provided by our environment rather than savaging it, something not easy to achieve with an exploding human population.

Society needs to support strongly the objectives of the Society for Conservation Biology, The Nature Conservancy, The Wildlife Management Institute, The Wildlife Federation, and other organizations concerned with preserving and restoring biological diversity. Much more needs to be done to prevent the loss of additional species. To achieve these goals the Nature Conservancy and other organizations are striving to preserve critical natural habitats. However, insufficient attention in most of the world is being given to determining the best biological and technological ways of managing the preponderance of human-disturbed environments. We must acknowledge that the feasibility and acceptability of wildlife and other resource-management practices are limited less by technical savvy than by political and social factors.

The diversity of species is directly influenced by the variety of habitats available. With careful planning, environmental alteration can increase habitat variability, and hence local diversity. Biological systems may be viewed as hierarchical and biological diversity manifests itself at every level of that hierarchy, from molecules to ecosystems. Only a minuscule fraction of all species that have ever existed on this planet still exist today. These species successfully adapted to climatic changes and dominated over their competitors. We must not let our destruction and elimination of other species by habitat modifications accelerate because we do not want to lose species.

We rightfully fear loss of natural biological diversity, such as happens with the transformation of rain forests, yet it is not understood exactly how diversity of genes, genotypes, species and communities affects the functioning of ecosystems. One hundred years of research in genetics, systematics, evolution and ecology have produced a large body of data that points to the importance of diversity for the proper function of organisms and ecosystems, but as pointed out by Solberg (1991) we still lack a comprehensive rigorous theory of biodiversity. Introduced alien species rarely extirpate native species, although the density of some native species may be dramatically altered and even locally eliminated. Introduced game fish in California have caused the decline of native nongame fish and the introduction of exotic perch extirpated the native Sacramento perch from all its native habitats, according to my colleague, Dr. Peter B. Moyle.

The emptying of foreign ship water-ballast tanks in ports has caused disastrous ecological invasions. Examples of such invaders in saltwater ports, inland waterways and marine estuaries include the introduction of zebra mussel into the Great Lakes in the mid-1980s. In the early 1980s the North American comb jellyfish was similarly carried in ballast into the Azov Sea of the northern Black Sea. This unintentional introduction virtually wiped out the Azov Sea's anchovy fisheries, causing a major economic and social disaster, according to marine ecologist James T. Carlton. At least 212 nonindigenous species have become established in North America's "most invaded" aquatic ecosystem, the San Francisco Bay Delta.

California currently has more than 2,300 exotic species, including 1,025 plants, 42 freshwater fish, 11 mammals, 9 birds and 208 invertebrates, costing millions of dollars annually in control measures and crop damage. Exotic species are invading California now faster than at any other time in the state's history, according to Venette and Cary (1998). Peter Moyle and Light (1996) have observed that the species most likely to invade and become pests are those that maintain high rates of growth and maturation, and do so over a wide range of environmental conditions. They have a small number of genes within a cell (genomes), and are genetically related to native organisms already adapted to local climate conditions. Invasions are most likely to succeed in sites that are highly disturbed (Moyle and Light 1996).

Invasive exotic species have wrought significant damage to populations of native vertebrates, even causing many extinctions such as the cichlid fish of Lake Victoria, birds in Hawaii and Guam and many other places in the world. One of the best concise reviews of endangered species is by John Tuxill (1998). As he points out, another looming problem whose ultimate effects on biodiversity have not yet been felt is global climate change. In the evolutionary past, the ecological effects of abrupt climate shifts were somewhat cushioned as plants and animals could shift their range. Such compensatory migration is less likely today because many species are now confined to only fragmented remnants of their former ranges.

Too many species (biodiversity) are being lost in the world due to habitat destruction. Just how many total species are there on earth? Stork (1993) looked into this and said most global totals range from 5 to 15 million species. Obviously, one can only guess on how many have been named. What are the named species? In order of abundance they are mainly insects (8,000,000), fungi (1,000,000), arachnids or spiders (750,000), nematodes (500,000), viruses (500,000), bacteria (400,000) and plants (300,000). Less abundant are mollusks, algae and protozoans (200,000), crustacea (150,000) and vertebrate animals (50,000).

The earth experienced a massive loss of species from the five major extinctions of the geological past, and that accelerated the evolution of new species as new habitats were formed.

Much has been learned about local extinctions and recolonization from the 1883 volcanic eruption of Indonesia's Krakatoa, the 1980 eruption of Mount St. Helens in southwest Washington and pre-industrial human-caused extinctions (e.g., loss of moas by the Maoris in New Zealand and lions in Europe).

Current extinctions are occurring at a rate unprecedented since the end of the Cretaceous period 65 million years ago. Since the 1600s, scientists have documented 484 animal species and 654 plant species that have vanished, and 5,366 animal and 26,101 plant species that are at significant risk of meeting the same fate, mainly because of human activities, according to an international biodiversity conference at Jakarta, Indonesia, in November 1995. The current *rate* of species depletion cannot be counter-balanced by speciation or evolution, which requires a very long time. The creation of new species environments is a slow, unpredictable process.

We do not have a license to exterminate any species, and we should embrace stewardship of this fragile planet with greater humility. Too often we succumb to greed and narrow self-preservation. Concern for other species is a hopeful sign that we humans have retained the capacity to adapt new behaviorisms that may serve prospects for our long-term survival. With regard to human-caused extinctions, 29-33 percent of America's endangered and threatened species are the result of water development, 23-26 percent from recreation activities, 19-22 percent from livestock grazing, 14-17 percent from logging and 4-6% from hard-rock mining (Losos et al. 1995).

It may be technically true that society does not "need" any endangered species to survive; however, the environment also does not need you or me. Economic and social advances made in the current civilization compel us to treat all animals humanely and ethically. If indeed we are genuinely concerned about their ultimate survival, then we must act decisively and sometimes counterintuitively.

We cannot afford to wait until a species is on the brink of extinction before we try to save it. A risky and expensive proposition. It is much better to take preventive action before a species declines to a dangerously low level. Many natural plant communities may no longer be adapted locally because of climate change. Once disturbed by people, as in some tropical African forests, the vegetation may not have the ability to return to its former community status due to changes in microclimate or other factors caused by deforestation. Little attention has been given to controlling overabundant or expanding native species that then negatively affect other native species (Garrot et al. 1993).

The Endangered Species Act (ESA) of 1973 is extremely important. No one can deny that it has done wonders for conservation biology by preserving native habitats and by protecting native fauna and flora threatened with extinction, usually as a result of people exploiting natural resources. In fact, with today's rapid utilization of resources, the Act is absolutely essential.

Originally, the Act was intended to identify "threatened" species to spur measures to ensure they did not become endangered. This could occur when the number of individuals of such a species was so low or limited in distribution that they were vulnerable to being wiped out if some catastrophic phenomenon or sudden habitat loss occurred. But the ESA was abused when a judge in Minnesota misinterpreted the Act and classified threatened wolves as having almost the same protection as if they were fully endangered and the U.S. Fish and Wildlife Service let the ruling stand unchallenged. Many problems have since developed with the subspecies category of "threatened" fish, amphibians, reptiles, birds and mammals. Several environmental groups and their lawyers discovered how easy it is to misinterpret the original intent of the Endangered Species Act and now use it to stop all sorts of resource utilization not really affecting endangered species. Sometimes this is done by using the ESA to protect newly described subspecies, a classification less significant than species, regardless of the economic impact, or by classifying an organism as being threatened or endangered without adequate study or citizen input.

At the time of this writing (2004) discussion is underway in Congress to make the ESA more realistic. Let's hope it will be corrected, not weakened. There is concern, especially in terms of the economic impact that may occur if an endangered species or

WALTER E. HOWARD

subspecies should be on private property. Scott Norris, a freelance writer, does a good job of summing up problems with the ESA. "Critics claim the ESA is taxonomically biased, insufficiently funded and overwhelmed by litigation. It fails to provide adequate incentives or enforcement, and sometimes punishes good deeds. It is subject to conflicting political, legal and regulatory mandates and is completely intractable as a conservation mechanism on private land. It impedes economic development and imposes costs and obligations unfairly. It maintains but seldom recovers species, and it does nothing to prevent species from becoming threatened in the first place." Over 1300 species have been listed, but only 18 delisted. The good news is that relatively few of the listed species have gone extinct and more are stable or increasing rather than declining.

Examples of misclassified species include a small fish known as the snail darter, which was used to close the Tellico Dam on Little Tennessee River in September 1979, and the northern spotted owlwhich caused the closure of many lumber mills in northwestern states in the early 1990s. A balance is needed concerning resource utilization and our moral obligation to protect nature.

Should peer review by both scientists and the public be required before a species is listed by the U.S. Fish and Wildlife Service as fully endangered? Should a committee that includes both public and private representation prepare recovery plans? Landowner participation is clearly needed. Today, the listing of a species is often political with pressure from environmental organizations, businesses and Congress. The recovery plan should give economic impacts and private property more consideration than in the past, yet designate and protect critical habitats.

When a species is declared "endangered" based on findings of scientists, the U.S. Fish and Wildlife Service is then effectively locked into returning the species to good health. This has become a liability to private property owners unlucky enough to host such species. However, the U.S. Supreme Court ruled unanimously on March 19, 1997, that private property owners could sue the federal government for actions taken under the ESA. In balance, conservationists with no legal "interest" can sue when government action results in less protection for endangered species.

The spotted owl wars in the Northwest are blamed or credited, depending on one's viewpoint, for what were inevitable changes coming in the logging industry. By the late 1980s, some wood-product businesses had been heading for a fall due to overcutting done in the 1940s and 1950s. Instead of a financial crisis in Oregon, high-tech jobs have exceeded the wood-industry jobs. This is not to say that many in the logging industry were not seriously and unjustly hurt.

Another misuse of ESA is the use of the gray wolf to get livestock off federal lands. Even though it is desirable to set aside suitable federal land for wolves and grizzly bears, we must recognize that surplus populations of these species will surely develop. If the habitats are favorable, populations of wolves and bears will inevitably exceed carrying capacity. When these territorial animals force the surplus subdominant wolves and grizzlies to disperse beyond the boundaries of their defined habitats, such individuals should immediately lose all endangered status and fall under that state's game and depredation laws. This type of displaced animal should not be captured and translocated back into its former habitat. This is cruel for they seldom remain where released.

Another problem with ESA is that exaggerated historical records have been used to inflate the size of the land areas claimed to be endangered species habitat. This resulted in unsuitable space for the species being locked up just to stop agriculture or other development. Currently, the process to declassify an endangered species is difficult and much too slow. For example, until the mid-20th century the California gray whale was listed as endangered, even though the government knew for some time that the population had become as abundant as ever.

The federal Marine Mammal Protection Act (MMPA) of 1972, which classifies marine mammals as endangered species, has been effective, but today it runs the risk of being prejudiced because it forbids the importation of the byproducts of marine mammals (except for fur seals killed in Alaska's Pribilof Islands). The original intent of the MMPA was to benefit dolphins, to encourage fisherman to develop ways for dolphins to escape from their nets and to protect seals and whales from extinction and inhumane killing methods. Now, many species of seals and whales do not need such inflexible, extreme protection.

A few years ago the International Whaling Commission's technical scientific committee reported that moderate take of Minke whales by Norway would have no effect on their total population. However, people in the Green Movement are opposed to killing any whale, even if there are more than a million minke whales. Furthermore, only for emotional reasons can one object to the Japanese harvesting for food a moderate number of whales of a species that are abundant.

People are not very different from animals in their struggle for survival in the balance of nature. Unfortunately, people rarely spend much energy or funds to help animals for purely ethical considerations. There is no feasible way to reduce today's drive toward economic growth and industrialization since, for the present generation, higher standards of living mean a higher quality of life. It is not just those in poverty who want to raise their living standards—everyone does. It's part of human nature. However, most people are willing to make some sacrifice to prevent species from becoming extinct, and many people in the world now have time available to become activists.

As far as diversity of animals is concerned, what we want is the diversity of species that were present before humans disturbed things. Due to the wholesale shift in earth's biota caused by the current spasm of extinction, the real threat to biodiversity is "not a decline in species *per se*, but a long-term erosion in the variety of biological characteristics and functions that grace the natural world" (Levin and Levin 2001).

Today, whether we like it or not, many more kinds of animals inhabit all of the continents of the world (other than the North and South Poles) than would have occurred naturally. This increased richness in species variety is due to our creating new habitats and intentionally or accidentally introducing many kinds of birds (both songbirds and game species), mammals (rats, mice and a great number of game species), fish (practically all the species of warm-water game fish in California are exotics), pets, livestock and some other breeding programs. Some of these species, such as the house mouse, rat and starling, may not be considered desirable, but the same could be said of some native species that homeowners and farmers regard as pests.

Intuition cannot be relied on for any theory of environmental ethics. Ethics are rooted in person-to-person relations, and thus human ethics serve as the basis for expanded animal welfare standards. Animals cannot act morally, cannot be held accountable for what they do and cannot form judgments about right or wrong. A mountain lion biting the neck of a deer and killing it is neither good nor bad, it is just manifesting the natural behavior of a lion, and a functional part of an ecosystem. Sportsmen, who operate under many regulations, can perform the same predatory role, although more humanely.

People have many ways of experiencing and enjoying nature. Wilderness means different things to different people. The backpacker dislikes horses; the saddle-sitter disapproves of the four-wheeler; the cross-country skier frowns on the snowmobiler; the motorist objects to the hazards of cyclists; and mothers protest hunters in adjacent forests. We all see the world a bit differently. Thus the balance of nature is a relative term, one that we should not hide behind to defend our preferences. The only place where environmental problems do not exist is in a truly undisturbed natural area, where no environmental problems exist since everything unaffected by people is considered to be in a pristine state. Efforts to save wilderness have evolved beyond esthetic and recreational arguments. Wilderness is being defended for its own sake to ensure that native wildlife species have a home.

I find it gratifying that there is a growing concern about nature conservation among those of a religious or spiritual calling. Even greater progress could be made with more emphasis on the values of wilderness. It is difficult to grow the world's economy and still have natural species diversity and heritage survive. But they don't have to be mutually exclusive. Developing countries cannot risk retarded economic growth just to protect the environment, so the energy-environmental collision continues. Everyone wants more amenities. Unfortunately, from striving to live in a modern world, developing countries are essentially forced to degrade their environment to keep abreast of their growing population and to produce exportable goods to help pay off their enormous financial debts. Statistics show that the rich are getting richer, the poor, poorer in much of the world. The share of global economy of the richest 20 percent of countries in the world is constantly rising, whereas the share of the global income of the poorest 20 percent is falling.

Without an ecological foundation, economic policy is blind and unsustainable, making ecological policy impractical. This is the view of the International Society for Ecological Economics. If the value of ecosystem services—that is, the life-support systems that sustain us—were actually paid for, global economics would be very different from what they are today. Costanza et al. (1997) are right that the price of commodities using ecosystem services directly or indirectly would be much greater. Economic growth is immediate and blind to considerations that can no longer be ignored. Habitat integrity often conflicts with economic progress.

It might be helpful if the politics of species preservation were shifted to being the politics of "habitat and ecosystem" preservation. For example, as others have pointed out, it is difficult to assign a value to the mammals of Africa, the redwood trees of the western United States or the Antarctic penguins, or to quantify the cultural significance of the American bald eagle all of which have value far beyond the purely biological ones. Their existence, moreover, makes their habitats more valuable, but economics rule the world, so multiple uses of federal lands are often governed more by economics than environmental needs.

Conservationists have rightly claimed that the federal government has mismanaged much of the public domain for decades, especially some of the land in the West, which is administered by the Bureau of Land Management and the U.S. Forest Service. Public land policy has failed to keep pace with changing societal perspectives about the environment and human impact on wildlife, soil and forage. Unfortunately, much of the now identified environmental damage, such as overgrazing, will be difficult to correct.

The land disturbances and pollution from mining, overgrazing and improper logging are well-known issues. But when human survival is at stake, conservation and preservation take a back seat. For example, I was shocked to find many bare, steep rocky hillsides in Mexico that are caused by removing the brush and trees so as to cultivate food for humans. As a consequence of removing the woody vegetation that held the soil, the soil was soon lost due to erosion. Much of this hillside farming practice in Mexico has occurred in my lifetime. In fact, a few years ago I witnessed government demonstrations in Mexico showing how to remove the natural vegetation from steep slopes. The instructor admitted to me that the soil often lasts only for a couple of years. I have also seen this type of soil erosion in Haiti and elsewhere.

In addition to saving precious soil, large areas need to be saved because of the nature of environmental systems and related wildlife issues. For posterity, it is also justified to save areas that have unusual natural, cultural and historical value.

The World Bank's policy of making environmental analysis a central factor in evaluating development loans to Third World nations has been very helpful. The Nature Conservancy in Costa Rica and Conservation International in Bolivia were the first to arrange some very effective "debt-for-nature" swaps. These enable nations in financial debt to be forgiven all or a portion of their foreign debt in return for a commitment to protect needed habitats in tropical forests, grasslands or river basins. The World Wildlife Fund and other organizations are similarly participating.

To protect endangered species, manage wildlife and control problem animals in ecosystems altered by people, and to do so in an environmentally acceptable manner, it is essential that we thoroughly understand how different species of fauna and flora interact in disturbed environments. Conservation used to mean the wise use of natural resources for the good of mankind, but now conservation is more wisely viewed as being beneficial for all wildlife species and preserving biological diversity as well.

Wildlife management is—or should be—the science of managing wildlife and its habitat, including people, for the benefit of the entire biota, not just for "ecology of modified environments." Sportsmen have been the main consumptive users of game animals. The time has come for a new management discipline that focuses on the ecology of modified environments. We must give sportsmen credit, for they have been a tremendous force in preserving wildlife habitat for waterfowl, mountain (bighorn) sheep, while-tailed deer, elk or wapiti, tule elk, wild turkey and other game species.

Providing harmony and stability in modified environments requires people to do all they can to assist nature in maintaining new and acceptable balances, not pristine ones. Since every development or preservation decision will involve trade-offs, social and political issues inevitably emerge. When habitats are modified, it often produces ecological misfits out of some native species that can then be saved only through careful follow-up management schemes. Substitution is often possible to replace keystone species or critical-link species.

The arrival of an exotic species usually does not cause a net loss in number of resident species, although it does happen, but introductions of exotics should be made only after a careful analysis of their effect. When only a small population remains after habitat alterations, they are vulnerable to genetic drift and inbreeding, as well as human or climatic changes.

Nature is not "ending" due to man's activities, as predicted by McKibben (1989) in *The New Yorker*, but it is certainly heading for some drastic changes that we surely do not want to happen. He correctly notes in his book, *The End of Nature*, that man's influence on nature is leading to imposition of an artificial world in place of the broken natural one. Let's hope we manage it properly and remember that whenever habitats are modified, many species are affected deleteriously and may even disappear.

How can we bring ourselves to limit our own population, our desire for amenities and our ambitions for progress so that nature can sustain a healthy, independent cycle? Only then will the biosphere be able to regulate (balance) environments by the natural means of an ecological feedback process that results from the interactions of microbial, fungal, plant and animal communities. We have a great opportunity to reshape and synthesize new ecosystems in environments we occupy—if we can accept management and overcome the "hands-off" philosophy, since we are already dealing with human-modified environments. The best solution for fish and wildlife conservation is to concentrate on the management of watersheds—the soil, the vegetation and water. This approach has recently been recognized by several states.

To obtain the best possible natural resource and conservation decisions, it is essential to have the confidence of the public and to obtain community support, and integrate the inevitable continual growth of the human population with habitat loss. A harmonious relationship between people and the land that has accountability should be the goal. Also, the development of habitat conservation plans (HCP) has been an encouraging step.

The reader should now have a better grasp and appreciation of nature's life-death ethic in environments that have been modified to some extent by people, and recognize why it is essential for us to help nature manage a new predator-prey balance.

CHAPTER 2

# An Ecology Primer

This chapter will include some definitions of ecological terms. It will explain what ecology is all about, how the environment functions, some of man's influences on ecosystem complexity and stability, the meaning of some biological principles, the role and concepts of wildlife management and also animal predation. The chapter is designed to especially help the uninitiated biologists to better understand the basic terminology about the ecology of our environment. (A German scientist, E. Haekel, who wrote two volumes on the morphology of organisms, coined the term "ecology" in 1866. It is derived from the Greek word "oikos," which means household, home or place to live. "Logos" is the "study of.")

"Ecosystem" was first defined by G. Tansley in 1935 as "nature's household system." It is concerned with the interacting system comprised of both living things and their nonliving habitat. It is an organizational level that is larger than that of the community, explained later.

*The environment* includes all the surroundings of plants, animals and other organisms, all of which can be modified by each other. An animal's environment is the sum of all substances and forces external to it that influences its very existence. Thus ecology might well be considered as how an environment functions.

*Habitat* is that part of the environment where an organism exists. An individual's or species' habitat consists of certain environmental conditions that enable an animal to survive, including such factors as food and cover.

48

*A biotic community* exists only as a part of the total environment surrounding it. For example, a forest cannot be separated from the air that surrounds it or the water and minerals in the forest soil, since there is a constant interplay among all of these components. The forest changes the composition of the air; the air changes the physical and chemical composition of the forest.

An organism apart from its physical environment is an abstraction. It becomes incapable of reproducing, swept away from its moorings in nature. Life needs this connection to sustain its continuum.

How does an ecosystem function? Energy enters the environment in the form of solar radiation. The sun's energy is captured by the producer organisms of the system, primarily green plants. They convert the sun's energy to storable chemical energy or to food energy.

This food energy then becomes available to the consumer organisms, such as the animals that feed on the green plants. All consumers rely on this stored energy for their energy demands.

Food energy passes through many levels—through herbivores that eat plants, through carnivores that eat herbivores, through larger carnivores that eat smaller carnivores and through microorganisms that bring the process full circle. These different trophic levels or food chains form the web of life.

When energy is transferred from one body to another, some is lost from the ecosystem in the form of heat. This energy can only be replaced to the system by solar radiation from the sun. The beef we eat provides only about 10-29 percent of the food energy of the vegetation eaten by a cow, as 80-90 percent is lost to metabolic heat.

The ecosystem is a storehouse of energy, with its plant and animal life preventing complete degradation of the energy into atmospheric heat.

We use this energy stored in ecosystems for food, to raise domestic animals or as fossil fuel to run the engines of commerce.

The only nonorganic sources of energy for man are hydroelectric power, solar power, nuclear power, tides and thermal power, plus lightning and cosmic radiation, which are important in fixing free atmospheric nitrogen to be incorporated into chemical compounds by plants.

Chemical raw materials containing various elements also are components of ecosystems. They enter the producers, the green plants, and, like energy, move in food chains through various levels of consumers. Unlike energy, however, these nonorganic substances are never lost to the system, only changed as they are transformed into different chemical compounds.

When a consumer organism dies and is not eaten by a scavenger, it is broken down (decayed) by reducer organisms that return the chemicals to soil, water and air, where they again become available to circulate through food chains.

Chemicals in an ecosystem thus move continually through circular pathways (cycles), whereas heat energy follows a one-way route into and out of the system and is then lost forever.

Of interest, why don't trees get taller? The tallest redwood is 370 feet. This is near the theoretical maximum height. As trees get taller, the water pressure inside leaf capillaries drops as water rises in a tree. When water stops reaching the leaves, photosynthesis becomes impossible, preventing any further growth in height.

*Niche:* Each individual animal or plant survives in nature only to the extent that it can find and occupy a suitable habitat in the environment; known as its ecological niche. Niche is one of those concepts in which ecology is rich. It breaks down or becomes confusing upon close examination. It defies objective definition and measurement yet is a crucial concept to understand.

A niche is an individual species' place in a biotic community where it can perpetuate itself. It is defined both in terms of the surrounding environment, the habitat and the role played by the organisms within it. Niches can be either generalized in nature or specialized.

Are there "vacant" niches? The answer is frequently disputed, depending upon one's definition of niche. This applies to all exotic and invasive species, which of course may alter (but not necessarily displace) the niche of other species.

The "natural law" of this world, if there is one, is constant change, not permanent stability. Deforestation and soil erosion may be undesirable, but they do not "eliminate" all habitats; they merely change the type of habitats that will be present. For example, many organisms even live on the pavement of a street.

## Influence of Man on Ecosystem Complexity and Stability

One of the major ecological influences humans have had on the environment is to simplify the world's ecosystems. Agriculture, which is the applied management of food chains, fosters simplified systems that reduce species diversity. In addition to cutting forests, we have plowed the prairie, thus locally eliminating a vast number of native herbs and grasses, and substituted for them stands of wheat, corn, soybeans and alfalfa. This increases the efficiency and productivity for man, but at the expense of increased ecological vulnerability, e.g., from disease, and instability of the nonnatural environment. For example, a pure stand of wheat has the risk of catastrophic collapse should some pathogen (such as wheat rust) or a herbivore (such as grasshoppers or locusts) sweep in suddenly and decimate the entire system. Usually it is not as dramatic with vertebrate pests as it is with insects, which have short life cycles and high rates of reproduction. Chemicals, i.e., pesticides, are often—for good or bad—used to ensure high productivity of a crop by preventing such hazards. Genetic changes also make plants immune to some pests, as will be discussed in the chapter on agriculture.

In many instances humans have stripped away the native complexity of animal populations and replaced it with an oversimplified system of farm and ranch animals. For example, the ungulate fauna of Africa and India, each consisting of many species of wild antelope, wild buffalo and other ungulates, have been replaced with domestic cattle. This has had a drastic damaging effect on the native grasslands and forests, although early or mid-serial conditions of rangelands are often beneficial to many wildlife species. It has also produced exaggerated disease epidemics, such as rinderpest and foot-and-mouth disease. We clearly pay a price for oversimplifying ecosystems, and we will continue to do so because monoculture is much more efficient, thus enabling the growth of the human population. This is what underlines the need to practice more and more monoculture, supported with fertilizer, pesticides and introduction of genetic resistance to reduce need for pesticides to satisfy people's demand for blemish-free fruit, bug-free vegetables and more economical food.

Six broad types of ecosystems are oceans and coasts, fresh water, forests, grass and shrublands, farmland and urban and suburban areas. The concerns Americans have about the condition of our natural resources is high, but we need more strategic indicators to provide feedback on the state of these ecosystems similar to those we have concerning the condition of our economy. There is intrinsic ecological value in heterogeneity at multiple levels of ecological organization. In most human-disturbed environments, it is futile to attempt to restore an elusive and ill-defined past that cannot be replaced. It is better for us to look to the challenge of the biocomplexity of modified ecosystems. Since insignificant species may become important after other species go extinct, we need a whole-ecosystem approach for the conservation of biodiversity.

## Biological Principles

To better understand man's position in the universe and how he affects the environment, a number of terms and principles need to be understood.

*Ecosystem homeostasis* is a technical term for the balance of nature. A homeostatic condition within an ecosystem implies that all aspects of ecosystem function are in balance, that there is a high degree of uniformity in functions of an organism or interactions of individuals in a population or community under changing conditions. Thus, there would be a balance, i.e., capability to make adjustments between production, consumption and decomposition, as well as between all species within the system. Technically, a static balance does not occur because changes are continually occurring.

The concept of homeostasis within individuals has been a valuable tool in physiology. It shows the interplay of nervous and hormonal regulation in growth, reproduction and behavior, and has contributed much to our understanding of health and disease. People are healthy when they function without evidence of disease or abnormality.

In many ways a comparable concept of homeostasis at the ecosystem level helps us to understand the processes of regulation within plant and animal communities. It pinpoints areas where more research is needed to clarify control mechanisms and routes of interaction between components of ecosystems.

The concept of intrinsic regulation or feedback helps us understand homeostasis, but we must recognize that in disturbed environments as a consequence of homeostasis new and different sets of conditions are produced (i.e., a different balance of nature than occurred before).

*Shelford's Law of Tolerance* states that the population density (abundance) or distribution of an organism can be regulated by any factor that comes into play when the population exceeds the *maximum or minimum level of tolerance* for that organism. This focuses upon the ecological requirements of plants and animals in terms of climatic, topographic and biological factors. Thus a species might be limited by numerous factors when its levels appear above that which sustains the organism—too much of something, too little of something else. There might be too much light, or not enough; too much moisture, or not enough; too many dissolved minerals in the soil, or not enough; too many predators, or too little protective cover; too little food, or improper balances in the types of food; too many pathogenic diseases; etc. If water is removed from a lake, the fish will certainly die.

In some instances, one or more factors might be critical, or various factors, such as weather and food supply, might work in combination in determining the resulting balance. For example, there might be adequate food in the summer to support feral house mice in the forests of Maryland. They can certainly withstand cold temperatures such as those of a typical Maryland winter—if they have adequate food. But the "combination" of winter temperatures and reduced winter food can act together to prevent forest-dwelling house mice in Maryland from surviving. On the other hand, the native white-footed wood mouse fares well in the Maryland woods throughout the year because the species has learned to store a winter food supply, whereas house mice do not store food, hence are usually limited to barns and human dwellings in the winter in Maryland.

*Cold-weather starvation.* I found that deer mice can withstand freezing temperatures as long as they have ample food available. But if food is not available, deer mice are so small that they are unable to maintain their body temperature overnight and will succumb at temperatures of 60 or so degrees Fahrenheit.

*Liebig's Law of the Minimum.* Simply put, this concept means not enough of some required ingredient to survive. Liebig, a botanist, noted that essential materials nearing a critical minimum would tend to be limiting. That is, a chain is no stronger than the link with the weakest strength. Since Liebig thought primarily in terms of light, temperature, nutrients and essential elements, he sought to explain such common observations as the lack of vegetation above certain altitudes in the Alps, or the lack of some plants in shaded areas. Thus, he found explanations of plant distribution in terms of insufficient light, insufficient warmth or insufficient nutrients. He did not, however, develop at length the corollary that there might be too much of these factors as well.

The principles elaborated above by Liebig and Shelford are valuable concepts to guide analysis of plant and animal abundance. The practical search for limiting factors can be an intriguing mystery and is one of the most important aspects of applied ecology and wildlife management.

Animals differ greatly from plants in their range of tolerance to different environmental factors. Some animals, such as the starling, are exceedingly adaptable and are able to exist in a wide range of habitats and climates. Since their first introduction into the United States in 1872, starlings have successfully spread from New York to California and from Alaska to Mexico. Feral populations became established in the United States about 1890-91. They were first seen in California in 1942. They are found in cities, farmlands and coniferous forests of the far north and deserts of the Southwest. Rats and mice are another example of species that are adaptable to a wide variety of habitats.

The systematic study of tolerance levels and limiting factors forms a logical interdisciplinary bridge between physiology, ecology and biogeography. We do not know the tolerance levels of many species and the wide range of environmental influences that impinge upon them. Some key factors involved in the adaptability or lack of adaptability of different species to habitat changes other than adequate food, cover and protection from predators still need to be analyzed. For example, why are black-footed ferrets so dependent upon prairie dogs for food when there are many other species of rodents and other food items?

Tolerance levels become key in the evaluation of pollution. What are the tolerance levels of different aquatic organisms to different man-made pollutants in the water? What is the tolerance level of different species to a shortage of dissolved oxygen? How much acidity or alkalinity can zooplankton tolerate? How susceptible are clams and oysters to copper, chromium, mercury, lead and other trace metals in water? In human terms, how many contaminants and pollutants in our air and water can we tolerate before harmful effects begin to appear? What is the effect of hot water from a nuclear reactor or other pollutants on coral?

We know so little about the tolerance levels of the various components of ecosystems to various types of insults and stimuli that too often we don't seem to discover the damage until it is too late.

It is important to know tolerance levels of whole ecosystems, as well as individual organisms. The ecosystem is more complex, possibly more resilient, but its alteration or destruction can be just as fatal as the death of an individual, even though a new and different ecosystem will be formed (e.g., deforestation can result in grassland).

When an ecosystem is modified, inevitably destroying many habitats, it becomes a different ecosystem, whether we like it or not.

*Indicator organism* refers to plants, animals or microbes whose presence or condition indicates what the current ecological conditions are. Their reliability as indicators is generally inversely proportional to their tolerance. Thus the narrower the tolerance, the greater the accuracy in indicating the occurrence of specific ecological condition. For example, if an aquatic organism grows only at a pH from 8.0 to 9.0, its presence would be a field indicator of the alkalinity of that site. Like the proverbial canary in a coal mine, mosquito fish can be used to identify the presence of many toxicants.

Ecological indicators may also provide evidence of former land-use practices. Some plants, such as bull thistle (*Cirsium lanceolatum*) are graze-resistant and often flourish in pastures where competing plants are removed by cattle grazing. In Argentina, I observed that year-round grazing with sheep results in the loss of native palatable plants.

A skilled plant ecologist can frequently "read the landscape" with remarkable accuracy, describing past land-use events by a critical analysis of the present-day plant and animal community. In California, the native grasses have been largely eliminated and replaced with exotic annuals as a result of grazing.

Sometimes the examination of species as indicators is on a grand scale. Why are tigers in India and not in Africa? The answers are related to the geological history of continents and the facts of evolution. "Biogeography" thus goes far beyond the question of limiting factors and tolerance levels.

In the course of geologic history and evolution, each continent has evolved its own characteristic flora and fauna. Over the last 500 years, however, humans have done much to intermix these biotic communities with alien organisms.

It would be misleading to imply that all plant and animal introductions are invariably harmful, although the perceivable degree of favorability will vary among people. There certainly are some desirable and beneficial ones. The ring-necked pheasant, a prized game bird to many in the United States, was deliberately introduced from Asia in 1880 and the Hungarian partridge, that many also consider a desirable game bird, was introduced from eastern Europe in 1908. The striped bass of the Atlantic coast was introduced to the Pacific coast, and is now an economically important species in the West. Most of the fresh-water game fish in California, such as small and large-mouth bass, catfish, perch and both brown and eastern brook trout are nonnatives.

Unfortunately, it is very difficult to find compelling arguments for preserving natural biodiversity. Too many people use "utilitarian values" as the justification of not doing so. The best justification, however, is our love of nature and our ethical concerns about the welfare of nature. Fortunately, most people have a strong feeling that it is wrong to wreak havoc with our environment and cause the extinction of any species with which we share the biosphere.

We spend a great deal of time criticizing what mankind has done to the environment (often with justification), but we seldom constructively recognize the significance of humans, for better or worse, in the global ecosystem. To better understand the complex ecological communities we are dealing with, and the importance of including several significant factors in our attempts, we need to understand the ecology of the environment.

If we are going to contribute substantively to building more sustainable ecosystems, I suggest we include two facts in our "management" schemes. First, many exotic species are now permanently established, and must be included in any hoped-for solution to preserving what we can of the original natural biological diversity. Second, we must recognize that we face an ever-growing human population. People are here and are not going to go away, so they must be included in management schemes. For example, feeding and housing a growing population must be dealt with.

We cannot leave nature to its own devices. We must "manage" the structure of communities, since all environments have been modified to some degree and nature cannot recreate what was originally present.

A good question is "Why should we conserve?" People sometimes conserve out of necessity, but I hope it is part of their personal "ethics." Conservation of natural resources is important to ensure the survival of humans, as well as native species. It's not easy to overcome human desires from what should be done. What value do endangered species really have since there are so few individuals left that for the most part they are no longer ecologically viable? Here one's ethics become important. One could also agree that biological diversity has actually increased on all continents—due to introductions and genetically bred animals. Some of these exotics are beneficial, whereas others are not only pests but destructive of original habitats we want to preserve. However, I strongly believe we need Aldo Leopold's land ethic and that we help develop a deeper reverence for all life. Old animals are rare in nature. To maintain the balance in a modified environment with the current information and technology revolution is not easy and requires careful management. We should show respect for nature by developing a suitable conservation ethic and responsible use of the soil, the water, the air, the minerals, the plant life and the wildlife. Conditions are going to vary in different societies, since people have drastically modified most habitats in different ways. And, unfortunately, society usually lacks the collective institutional and political will to practice the needed land ethic.

## Principles and Concepts of Wildlife Management

Below are listed a number of applicable principles and concepts that summarize the many aspects of the subject to help you understand the role of wildlife management.

1. Wildlife management is the science of managing wildlife, their habitat and the role of people for the benefit of the entire biota.
2. Conservation is wise use of resources, whereas preservation usually implies nonuse.
3. Carrying capacity is the average number of animals that a habitat can support (i.e., the optimum ecological density of the species).
4. Where wildlife numbers exceed the carrying capacity, the excess animals become unhealthy and many will die.
5. When plant succession in a forest or on rangeland is set back to an intermediate stage, the resulting earlier successional plant species usually produce more palatable foliage for herbivorous animals, and also more readily disposable litter.

6. Both the birth and death rates of most species of wildlife are high.

7. The suitability of habitat is the key to survival of wildlife.

8. Predator control practices usually are not necessary to maintain healthy wildlife populations if their habitat is good.

9. Proper laws are essential to achieve effective wildlife management.

10. The main goal of a wildlife refuge is to provide for or to preserve good wildlife habitat.

11. The most important thing you can do to help wildlife is to prevent the loss or destruction of their habitat.

12. Stocking (the releasing of individuals of a species) is usually unnecessary in good wildlife habitat, but may be done to increase harvest (e.g., of fish or pheasants).

13. Many introduced exotic animals find their new habitats unsuitable and disappear soon after release. A few profit from their new habitat and may become pests.

14. In the United States sport hunting is used as a management tool (e.g., as a surrogate predator to remove excess animals in a population without damaging the breeding stock).

15. Wildlife management programs for game and nongame wildlife in the United States are financed almost entirely by sportsmen. Sportsmen are the greatest contributors of money used to preserve natural habitats.

16. Sport hunting has never led to the extinction of a wildlife species or caused any species to become rare or endangered.

17. Wildlife management programs must have adequate public support in order to succeed.

18. Integrated pest management (IPM) is usually practiced in the control of wildlife pests. First, control methods include such nonlethal approaches as sound and visual frightening devices; biological control with predators or habitat manipulation; repellents, construction of barriers, etc. Lethal methods—shooting, traps and poisons—are the last resort.

19. Potential biological methods of controlling animal damage include encouraging predators of the pest, making the habitat

unsuitable for the pest to survive, introducing or augmenting epizootics (i.e., outbreaks of diseases that affect them), using chemosterilants to keep pest population numbers in check and introducing genetic traits that will make the populations of the pest species less successful.

20. Habitat manipulation should not be employed *a priori* to control vertebrate pests because it will frequently be disrupting to nontarget wildlife. Yet, there are times when this type of biological control is the wisest solution, such as removing the food and/or cover for rattlesnakes or rats.

21. Most vertebrate pests are pests are highly adaptable to existing habitats. Their resilience enables them to promptly recover from control efforts.

22. More research is needed to improve the use of natural predators in vertebrate pest control to approach similar success with that of weed and insect control.

23. The intentional creation of disease epizootics in populations of pests has not been useful this far, with the exception of the myxoma virus, introduced to control European rabbits in Australia. Diseases that might be used for animal control may pose threats to desirable species or cause zoonosis (i.e., transmitted from animals to man). Even the most virulent diseases of wildlife are usually only local in their effect, such as outbreaks of plague in rodents.

24. So far neither chemosterilants nor genetic control have been very successful in abating animal damage problems.

25. The removal of populations of specific species from local areas usually does not cause adverse ecological effects on other animals in the community or, for that matter, on humans.

26. The suitability of habitat is the key to how well both wildlife and livestock will prosper. Habitats cannot be eliminated, only altered. If a forest is clear-cut and then badly overgrazed with goats so that desertification occurs, we won't like it, but desert-adapted organisms will certainly find the new habitats to their liking.

27. It is seldom recognized that most of the lethal animal-damage control methods used today nearly always treat wildlife more humanely than nature does with "natural" deaths. However, when animals are controlled, their life span is shortened.

28. There is a tendency for some environmentalists to erroneously consider everything "chemical" as unnatural and bad, while everything "biological" is intrinsically desirable. Neither is correct.

29. It is tragic how many ver0tebrate species have been exterminated by human beings, especially in the past few centuries; however, because of introductions of game species, domestic livestock, pets and animals that have escaped captivity, most major land masses today have a more diverse fauna than occurred hundreds of years ago.

30. Humans have a moral obligation to both manage and control nature once we disrupt an environment. Nature usually does not know best in human-modified environments. Wildlife damage control proactively helps establish a new harmony in altered environments.

31. Nature exacts a high death rate in wildlife populations. Modern animal control practices can do part of this humanely.

32. Humans are the only humane predator.

33. People kill under many regulations designed to make the lethal act as humane as is feasible in contrast to nature's tooth-and-claw blood bath.

34. Only people express compassion for prey; natural predators do not.

## Predation

Since predation is such a significant part of the balance of nature, it is important we have a thorough understanding of the principles of predation.

1. Predators kill living prey because they have evolved such behavior.

2. Predators are not humane in their killing methods, and will even partially consume prey while it is still alive.

3.  Those who think predators are inhumane should remember that all living things feed on something else and in turn are eaten. Death is a necessary part of life, and predators in nature are a part of this wholeness of life.

4.  If man domesticates livestock and alters the genetic makeup of animals so they lose their ability to escape from predators, doesn't man then have a moral responsibility to protect these animals from coyotes and other predators?

5.  Most carnivores appear to be extremely cunning predators, yet are actually very inefficient in reducing native prey to low levels of density as they can with domestic animals. Of course, to do otherwise would be self-destructive.

6.  Natural predators actually help to maintain a maximum, sustained carrying capacity in their prey species.

7.  The fact that most carnivores are at the top of the food chain means they are not as important ecologically in the food web as are the primary producers and consumers.

8.  Most carnivores contribute far more carrion to an ecosystem than they consume.

9.  When native predators are artificially removed, there may be a prompt but temporary increase in their natural prey, as is the case with rodents and deer.

10. If native predators are removed, the resulting increased prey species will actually decline to a lower density than before because of self-limiting factors caused by overpopulation.

11. Predators are much like an animal husbandryman. If a livestock operator does not harvest his surplus livestock, the flocks will temporarily increase, and then the population will decline far below the former carrying capacity of the managed herd or flock.

12. When herbivores overpopulate either because humans have stopped harvesting them or their natural predators have been removed, the carrying capacity for these animals will be greatly reduced because they will overgraze or overbrowse their habitat.

13. The beliefs and attitudes people hold about the beneficial or detrimental values of livestock predators and other wild animals are greatly influenced by the manner in which the animals affect their livelihood and personal safety.

14. Predators do not recognize property boundaries; they are wide-ranging.

CHAPTER 3

# Managing Wildlife and Pests

Wildlife management is the science of taking proper care of wildlife and its habitat on a sustained basis for the benefit of the entire biota. When wildlife becomes too abundant or a pest, it needs to be "controlled." Pest control is done either to benefit the species being controlled, to protect other species or resources, for public health reasons or because an individual animal or population is currently unwanted by someone. This may occur whether or not animals are actually doing damage, such as skunks or rattlesnakes under the back porch. Society tends to avoid using the terms "death" or "kill." Instead, pests are either removed, harvested, destroyed, dispatched, slain, put down, put to sleep or euthanized.

Few people realize that agricultural crops and most landscaping of homes, all of which create unnatural plant communities would be largely destroyed if native animals were given free range. No one will tolerate a pocket gopher or mole in the garden or a rat in the garage even if it happens to be an endangered species.

It is important to understand how proper animal control activities not only reduce conflicts but can also create a more harmonious relationship between people and animals. By definition, we can only have pests where people are involved. Vertebrate animals become pests when humans attempt to use a habitat while it is still occupied by wildlife, or for food, fiber, other resources, a desired lifestyle, to avoid danger or for public health problems. Habitat modification makes some species no longer adapted to new environmental conditions, while others may be stimulated to overpopulate new habitats. Animal damage control (ADC) thus becomes an integral part of establishing new and tolerable balances for a variety of reasons.

Some people insist that growers should not poison or otherwise control pest rodents until they can show that a serious problem has developed. Consequently, this forces growers to wait to conduct control programs until after a high population of voles, field mice, rats, ground squirrels, pocket gophers or other rodents has developed. By the time the crop nears maturity and rodents start feeding aggressively, it becomes much more difficult to control them. Also, this could result in excessive amounts of poison being used for the control, greater than would have been needed in a preventive control operation to thwart a population buildup. Also, preventive control done earlier is the best ecological solution.

Yes, it is environmentally disruptive to allow species of field rodents in intensive agricultural areas to build up to serious economic densities before they are controlled. Not only are much larger amounts of rodenticides needed, but also this affects the predator populations. Their population may have increased that season as a result of the high rodent food base. After the control operation, predators will be left with inadequate prey for their offspring, unless they happen to be provided by, say, a farmer's poultry or livestock. Such artificial cycling of predator and prey populations is inhumane and environmentally unsound. In these situations, it is preferable to locally eradicate the pest or hold it at very low numbers so control operations are reduced to just monitoring to check for new arrivals.

Some people and groups may not condone the use of poisons, even when biologically desirable. This may be in part because abuses have occurred. However, some organizations protest the use of poison because they want to use the issue to make emotional appeals to raise money. With this no-poison philosophy, a large number of wildlife may die unnecessarily and the environment also suffers.

People can become disturbed about the extermination of local animal populations, even exotic species. It's as if such "local" eradication would have devastating consequences on nature's balance. This is unfortunate because in intense agriculture and urban situations the elimination of serious pests is often the most desirable goal from a humane, environmental and balance-of-nature standpoint. Most homeowners will tolerate very few wild species. Large game animals and large carnivores usually have to be eliminated from intensively settled and farmed areas. It is, of course, more preferable to physically exclude rodents and other pests from your home or crops than to periodically keep killing them.

With some rodent pests, their presence can sometimes be successfully monitored with nontoxic bait. When a pest animal moves in, toxic baiting is required only on a limited basis to control invading individuals, as large populations would not have had time to develop. This method is called "preventive control."

When their predators are removed, deer and other herbivores tend to overpopulate and then overgraze and overbrowse. This overutilization of their food supply then becomes the main mortality factor limiting the population. Such overutilization of the vegetation will result in a less productive animal-plant system. An example of this currently exists in the eastern United States with white-tailed deer.

With the presence of wolves, mountain lions, coyotes and black bear deer numbers can be sustained over time, if the habitat is favorable. Usually it will be at a higher density than would occur without predation by wild carnivores or man. This is necessary to prevent deer from overpopulating, destroying the habitat and lowering the carrying capacity. In modified environments, if habitat conditions are not the best for deer, there may be some competition for the deer between both hunters and natural predators. Examples of these imbalances occur in Alaska between populations of wolves and both caribou and moose, and with wolves and caribou in northwestern Canada. Boertje et al. (1996) explain how populations of moose, caribou and wolves all increased over a 20-year period of wolf control in Alaska. Another example is how excessive populations of protected mountain lions have depressed populations of deer in California where the habitat is no longer very good for deer. Territoriality prevents local mountain lion populations from becoming too excessive.

When a predator population tilts the balance toward excessive abundance, it may be necessary to control that population to prevent an undesirable overutilization of prey. In favorable habitats, deer and other big game can usually support the needs of both large predators and hunters. Beauchamp et al. (1996) and Garrettson (1996) claim that most predator control operations done to increase game are not as beneficial to wildlife as many expect. There are many exceptions, however, when predator control is done to increase a game population, such as controlling foxes and skunks in a restricted waterfowl breeding area. Also, predator control can protect endangered species or other species that have become highly vulnerable due to habitat destruction.

If the habitat for deer is quite good and they are abundant, territoriality among mountain lions will prevent the population of lions from seriously depressing the deer population. But where deer habitat is poor or mediocre with few deer present, lions can become numerous enough to depress a deer herd, since each lion can take nearly two deer a week.

The reintroduction of extirpated populations into a favorable habitat can be successful, but it may be desirable to first temporarily control its predators. On the other hand, the artificial introduction of vertebrate predators for biological control purposes, such as releasing snakes to control rodents, is seldom justified or effective. However, the introduction of *exotic* insects to control invertebrate pests and exotic weeds is common and successful. This approach with mammals is usually unsuccessful, except on small islands where an introduced predator is not allowed to breed and can later be removed.

One reason coyotes and other livestock predators become troublesome is that humans provide them with easy prey species— sheep, cattle and poultry—all of which have lost their predatory defenses through domestication. Unlike grizzly bears, wolves or bison, which cannot be tolerated in areas of dense human populations, coyotes can and do live in large cities (e.g., Los Angeles) and this creates problems. They feed on garbage, cats, small dogs and fruit. Attacks on children are not uncommon, although I only know of one child being killed by a coyote in California.

There is no record of wolves killing people in North America (Zaidle 1997). However, in 2000 a six-year-old boy at a logging camp in Alaska was attacked but saved as the wolf tried to drag him into the woods. During World War II, after the fur trappers in northern Russia had all gone to war, the resulting high wolf population became very threatening, and wolves caused many human deaths, especially when accompanied with outbreaks of rabies. Will N. Graves, a former U.S. Department of State official, documented these human mortalities. He learned the language while he was stationed in Russia. In some villages no one dared venture outdoors after dark. However, domestic dogs are actually a bigger threat to people than wolves in the United States. Each year, with 60 million dogs in the U.S., nearly 5 million people are bitten annually, causing about 800,000 injuries that require medical care, according to U.S. Public Health Service Centers for Disease Control and Prevention.

Human mortalities from wolves can and do occur when the density of wolves becomes excessive in localities settled by humans. Fortunately, today in the United States, wolf numbers adjacent to human populations rarely reach high densities. In 1996 wolf packs in a densely wooded area in the Karelia region of northern Russia bordering Finland killed at least one person, and so terrorized the villagers that a major hunt was organized with a prize of US $2,000 for the person who killed the most wolves. In 1996, 33 children were reported killed by wolves in Banbirpur, India. The worst disaster from wolves that I know of was in 1878, when British officers recorded 624 humans killed in India by wolves. I assume rabies was probably involved.

It is frequently stated, although I believe erroneously so, that there are few, if any, empty niches in nature, and that an exotic plant or animal can be introduced only at the total loss of a species already present. That a native species will always be displaced does not seem to be the case, for most countries today have a more enriched ecological diversity of fauna and flora than would be present naturally due to introductions or escapes. Even though exotic introductions into the environment are not always degrading, this does not mean they can be made with impunity. There have been many sad mistakes with an ensuing impact on native species. For example, the introduction of native trout into glacial lakes in the high Sierra Mountains in California, where the species was not found before, has endangered the native black-legged frog.

The biological price of introducing nonnative mammals may be very high if the introduced vertebrate species has no near-taxonomic relatives already present. New Zealand, which originally had no land mammals except for two kinds of bats, is a good example. Since its unique endemic vegetation evolved in the absence of any grazing or browsing mammals, environmental instability quickly resulted when Europeans introduced European rabbits, hares, nine species of deer, goats, pigs and other domestic animals, all of which became feral (Howard 1965). As a consequence, in New Zealand today the species composition and density of plants in many of their national parks and forests have been permanently altered. A few sensitive plants, including some large species of trees, have been completely eliminated in many of the national forests and parks. However, if most of these same animals were introduced into the temperate regions of the United States, very little instability would result because we have many other species of animals already present that are quite similar biologically to those introduced into New Zealand.

The many genera of now-extinct flightless moas in New Zealand were all browsers and grazers, so the vegetation was adapted to being fed upon by these giant birds as well as a few other browsing and grazing birds, but the flora was not adapted to attacks by mammals. Atkinson and Cameron (1993) report that New Zealand has averaged 11 new species of exotic plants per year since European settlement in 1840.

The Island of Guam has a serious problem with introduced brown tree snakes, a species native to New Guinea and Australia, that is thought to have been accidentally introduced by a shipment of logs in 1949. This snake is exterminating unique native birds, nine species of which have become extinct by 2004. There is concern that airplanes might spread these snakes to other places. At least nine snakes have been confiscated at Oahu, and they are now found on the island of Saipan. Dogs are employed at many airports to detect snakes. There are many other examples for which the only way to protect endangered wildlife from predation by introduced wildlife or even native species in modified habitats is by controlling the offenders.

Forests and wildlife are renewable resources but, of course, natural forests and other natural environments cannot at the same time be utilized by us and still be kept in their exact natural state. Any use by humans modifies the environment, and it takes very little change in habitat conditions to affect the distribution and density of various species. When any natural environment is modified, most of the native vertebrate species tend not to fare as well as they did in their original habitat. However, some species of small rodents, such as the white-footed deer mouse seem able to adapt to new environmental conditions within a year or two following logging, with their numbers becoming much more abundant.

There is much we don't understand about habitat conditions. For instance, the greatest variety and density of small rodents in the United States is found in the West under desert conditions. Such rodents exist there only because they have an adequate food supply, and plants are the basis of their food web. Interestingly, desert habitats support few plants. But when people bring water for agriculture, they unwittingly can produce hundreds of times as much primary rodent food—palatable plants—as would occur naturally.

Even though many of these new plants prove to be nutritious to the various species of rodents in laboratory tests, many of the native rodent species still tend to decline or disappear following the increase in food supply. It seems they are genetically and behaviorally "adapted" to desert habitat conditions and natural predators, and that ample food supply, or adequate cover for safe breeding, does not control their numbers. Other factors that are not understood must also be operating.

Wild vertebrates learn by experience. Yet many of their behavioral traits are genetically based. For example, studies have shown that coyotes inherit the trait of primarily attacking fleeing sheep by the neck. They do not have to be taught such behavior, whereas those in the cat family seem to train their offspring on how to be effective predators. With few exceptions, coyotes, rodents, birds and other wildlife species are not like links in a chain where the loss of one species will have deleterious effects on all the others.

The principal predators of livestock in the United States are the coyote, domestic dog, bobcat golden eaglered fox, gray fox and, less commonly, grizzly bear, black bear, mountain lion (cougar or puma), jaguar, gray wolf, Canada lynx ocelot and feral pig.

A report by the General Accounting Office (GAO) in 2001 reported that "In fiscal year 2000, predators (primarily coyotes) killed nearly half a million livestock—mostly lambs and calves—valued at about $70 million. Accidents involving automobiles and deer result in over $1 billion in damage annually, and deer consume a wide variety of landscape, garden and forestry shrubs, plants and trees." The Insurance Institute for Highway Safety estimated there were 1.5 million traffic accidents nationally involving deer in 2002, with 150 fatalities. In 2000, GAO found reports of about 6,000 collisions between aircraft and wildlife.

Rodents, rabbits and hares (jackrabbits) are the major wildlife competitors of livestock for pasture or range forage. In the United States, these include pocket gophers, ground squirrels, prairies dogs, woodchuck, kangaroo Rats, meadow mice or voles, cotton rats, hares or jackrabbits, rabbits, moles and many others of lesser importance.

Due to increased restrictions on vertebrate pest control methods and materials, especially banning the use of 1080 (sodium monofluoroacetate) in baits for coyote control, it has become more difficult to protect domestic livestock from predators (MacIntyre 1982, Howard 1983, Howard and Schmidt 1984). Many woolgrowers were forced out of business.

Whereas wildlife management is largely based on use objectives, wildlife control is more a consequence of health and economic survival, or for the protection of endangered species. A common expression used is animal damage control (ADC). The USDA's ADC branch in Animal, Plant and Health Inspection Services (APHIS) in 1997 was appropriately renamed Wildlife Services.

The term "animal damage" is used to emphasize that it is the damage, not necessarily the offending animals, that need to be taken care of. Rather than the use of word "control," Schmidt (1994) prefers "wildlife damage management." An objective of management is to ensure that each species survives in adequate numbers to play its role in maintaining the health and stability of the ecosystem. Hunting and trapping of the problem species may serve as a control option if the objective is to reduce the density of the species. Management is complex, with a need to understand and estimate proper carrying capacities. Control is usually designed to prevent damage, which may or may not require the reduction of a local population to a tolerable level.

When vertebrates are *managed*, the main objective is the well-being of local populations of the species in question, whereas a vertebrate control operation has primary benefit factors other than the individual or species being controlled. Rat control, in a home or elsewhere, is not concerned with the welfare of rats. The main objective of deer control in a forest plantation is to protect new trees, although the control procedure adopted may incorporate deer management considerations. As pointed out by Hobbs (1996), "ungulates are important agents of change in ecosystems, acting to create spatial heterogeneity, modulate successional processes, and control the switching of ecosystems between alternative states." However, when too many deer inhabit a forest plantation, wildlife managers may want fewer deer for the welfare of the deer, whereas at the same time the forester may want the deer controlled to protect the forest. In these situations, the same action—increased hunting— can be taken to satisfy both management and control needs.

Wildlife is a resource that belongs to the public, and the need for more environmental sensitivity today is obvious. Recent progress along this line indicates the success of the environmental movement but also is due in part to the animal rights movement. People have always exploited animals and had conflicts with wildlife, and this issue is currently undergoing a dramatic period of transition. In human-disturbed environments wildlife must be managed and often controlled. We cannot let nature take its course unfettered, since it is impossible to reestablish original habitat conditions and fauna.

Some wildlife populations in modified environments, in addition to competing with us for food, destroying the products of our labor or becoming a nuisance, may also cause zoonoses, transmitting diseases to us. Nature has waged germ warfare against humans since the beginning of time. Even with proper sanitary facilities, safe water and other public health precautions such as inoculations, people and animals are still highly vulnerable to many debilitating and deadly microbes and parasites for which animals serve either as vectors (carriers) or reservoirs (homes) of the disease.

Animals are considered a reservoir if they enable pathogenic organisms to survive and either perpetuate or benefit by having a portion of their life cycle spent in, on or around them. This portion of the life cycle of a disease may be spent in the bloodstream or saliva of the animal, within internal or external parasites of the animal or in the animal's feces or urine. Sometimes it is only of academic interest whether an animal is serving as a vector or a true reservoir of the disease.

Lyme (tick) disease is now the most commonly reported vector-borne infectious disease in the United States, with more than 100,000 cases in the United States. It was first noted in 1975 at Old Lyme, Connecticut, but now is reported in 48 states. It illustrates well how a disease may be transmitted. Lyme disease (see Ostfeld 1997) is an infectious illness transmitted by the bite of certain species of small ticks—deer ticks and the western black-legged tick. The disease is caused by a spirochete (a spiral-shaped bacterium, *Borrelia burgdorferi*) that, if not properly diagnosed and treated with antibiotics, may persist in the body for years. Early symptoms are a characteristic circular spreading rash ("bull's-eye rash") and flu-like symptoms. I do not know why the incidence of Lyme disease has spread so far, but Borchert (2002) is a good reference about the disease.

Approximately 15 to 30 percent of the cases of Lyme disease are asymptomatic and may progress to a late-stage Lyme disease years later. Fever and arthritic aches are the most common long-term symptoms. The reservoirs of the disease are deer and certain small rodents, and even lizards have been implicated. The larval and nymphal ticks acquire the spirochetes when feeding on the blood of infected mammals. The tick must be removed within 36 hours of biting to reduce infection. A vaccine to prevent Lyme disease has been approved by the Food and Drug Administration.

Sylvatic (silvanus, wooded or forest) or bubonic plague, also called Black Death, is a highly infectious disease caused by a bacterium. The initial symptoms of plague include fever, chills, headache, muscle aches, weakness and, commonly, swollen tender lymph nodes named buboes; hence at that stage, the disease is called bubonic plague. It is curable with antibiotics, but only if a doctor recognizes the disease soon enough. Fortunately, correct identification usually occurs if the doctor knows that the patient has been exposed either in the outdoors or to infected animals, including infected people, within the past seven days.

If not treated in time, plague is fatal. Bubonic or sylvatic plague can sometimes progress to pneumonic plague and/or to a rarer form of septicemic plague (bloodstream infection). When pneumonic plague infection occurs, it can then be transmitted through the air directly from infected pets or people to others, who may die within three to five days. The nursery rhyme "Ring Around the Rosy, Pocket Full of Posies, Ashes, Ashes, All Fall Down" stems from the high rate at which people dropped dead from Black Death (pneumonic plague) that ravaged Europe first in the sixth century (the plague of Justinian). This pandemic probably began in Africa, but was first recorded in Egypt in 541 AD. Probably carried by black rats on grain ships, the disease entered Constantinople (now called Istanbul), the capital of the Eastern Roman Empire. It eventually spread across Europe, depopulating towns and whole regions during the ensuing 50 to 60 years.

The next huge outbreak of plague known as the Black Death erupted in the mid-1330s. It started in central Asia and spread through India and China. Genoese traders introduced the disease into Italy in 1348. It then spread rapidly through Europe, with local epidemics continuing for 400 years. The Great Plague of London occurred in 1664 and is said to have taken 100,000 lives.

The third or Modern Plague started in Asia in the 1850s and lasted for many years, affecting most of the world. In North America, plague-infected rats arrived in 1899 in San Francisco from Hong Kong. Even though the ship was certified to be rat-free, infected rats probably came ashore, because in 1900 plague broke out in San Francisco, lasting for five years with 126 cases, 122 of them fatal. One year after the great earthquake and fire of 1906, the disease appeared again in San Francisco.

Plague was found in the California ground squirrel in 1908. The disease has now become endemic in rodents in a number of states, with New Mexico usually having the most human cases. Arizona had a fatal case in 1996.

Certain species of small rodents now serve as the reservoir for plague. "Despite >30 years of study of plague in prairie dogs, the mechanism by which it moves among colonies and persists between epizootics remain a mystery" (Stopp et al.). Even though not completely understood, when conditions are right, susceptible species, called amplifying hosts, such as ground squirrels, chipmunks and woodrats, become infected. Once infected, local populations of these susceptible species may die off. The danger to humans occurs when fleas on these dead animals search for a live host.

For example, several years ago golden-mantled ground squirrels died off near Lake Tahoe in California. A domestic cat carried the carcass of one of the infected squirrels to where the cat lived. The woman who owned the cat took care of children of working parents during the day. Apparently infected fleas got on the cat, but not liking the cat very much, they jumped off and attacked the woman when she had the cat on her lap. Fortunately, when she became ill her doctor suspected and correctly diagnosed plague. The woman was able to provide the names of the 80 or so people she had contacted, and they were all successfully treated with antibiotics to prevent the disease. Unfortunately, it was too late to save her life.

In California all plague outbreaks have occurred when the susceptible rodent species grow to an unusually high density. This is one reason why excessive populations should not be allowed in campgrounds. California Public Health Service stopped supporting ground squirrel control in city parks in the mid-1980s.

The editor of *Postgraduate Medical Journal* in London asked me to write an article on the serious potential for a major outbreak of plague in the Los Angeles area as a result of this policy. I did not write the article, however, because a later change of policy occurred and excessive populations of squirrels in urban areas are now controlled, hence that time bomb for a pneumonic plague holocaust no longer exists. Consider, however, what could have happened. Squirrels within a heavily human-populated area suddenly die from plague. Cats, dogs and rats, investigating the carcass or burrows of the dead rodents, pick up infected fleas. Remember, pneumonic plague kills people in three to five days; it would spread like wildlife with today's mobile human population.

Rabies (a neurotrophic virus) is another dangerous disease that sometimes appears when a mammal carrier species becomes abundant. The most frequently reported rabid wild animals are raccoons, skunks, bats and foxes. The U.S. Public Health Service Centers for Disease Control and Prevention (CDC) reported 8,509 cases in 1997 in nonhuman animals and 4 cases in humans. At least 11 people died in 2000 from rabid dogs in Jakarta. CDC reported in 2000 that during the past 20 years there had been 37 human fatalities from rabies. The reason there are few human cases in the United States is due to dog vaccination campaigns, educational programs and a very efficient public health infrastructure. Among animals, in just one year, raccoons accounted for 4,300 cases of rabies; skunks, 2,000; bats, 958; foxes, 448; cats, 300; dogs, 126 and cattle, 122 (Krebs et al. 1998).

There seems to be considerable doubt among wildlife professionals that reducing the population of carriers such as foxes and skunks is a viable method for rabies control. Trapping and hunting can assist in control efforts. In one study the incidence of rabies and the density of skunks were not affected by rabies control in a skunk population (Schubert et al. 1998). The scattering of oral baits to vaccinate animals has been successful in Europe for some time.

Government control of coyotes by the U.S. Biological Survey started in northeastern California in December 1915 because of an outbreak of rabies in coyotes that threatened people and livestock. This was the beginning of current government predator-control activities because it proved so beneficial to the livestock industry.

Another rodent-borne viral disease, which appeared in the Southwest in 1993, is hantavirus. Four types have been identified in America. The genus is the family Bunyavividae, and all are susceptible to most disinfectants. Officials at CDC reported 18 suspected or confirmed cases during the first five months of 2000. The mortality rate is about 40 to 50 percent.

Hantavirus is a zoonotic agent maintained in rodent reservoirs and transmitted to humans via infectious virus shed in the urine, feces or saliva of a host rodent. It made an abrupt appearance in May, 1993, when it killed Navajo Indians in the Four Corners area (Arizona, Colorado, New Mexico and Utah) of the Southwest. It is found in the "fresh" urine, feces and saliva of the omnipresent, ubiquitous deer mouse Only a few people catch the disease. CDC believes that those at highest risk of infection are persons who have very close contact with deer mice, resulting in direct physical contact or by breathing aerosol or dust of the animal's fresh urine or feces. This is especially the case if in close proximity to a live animal. Rodents should not be permitted to live in people's houses or summer homes, as this is a terrifying illness.

Hantavirus may be a long-present viral disease that previously went unnoticed. After contracting the disease, death may occur in 12 to 35 days. Strains identified in the United States seem to differ from hantavirus strains in Asia and Europe, which cause hemorrhagic fever along with kidney disease. The lethal U.S. variants primarily attack the lungs. A common strain of hemorrhagic fever in China annually infects about 100,000 people, killing about 10 percent of them. U.S. soldiers were infected during the Korean War.

Life is not without risk. To determine a proper risk-to-benefit ratio is difficult. Few people stop to think what they consider an acceptable risk in the food they eat, the medicines they take and the lifestyle they choose. One scientist estimated that Americans consume about 10,000 times as much natural pesticide as they do from agricultural pesticides in grocery store produce. It is only natural that we are more concerned about involuntary risks than those we take voluntarily. Participating in sports, driving a car, using gas and electricity and taking public transportation are all risks we usually leave to fate. Also, we must remember that environmental solutions have trade-offs. For example, the removal of prairie dogs through control operations can affect the food supply of black-tailed ferrets.

Economic strength in today's world is tied directly to growth and development. But no matter how responsible we are with economic growth, it cannot continue unabated without seriously affecting the environment, especially if we don't do a better job of managing the wildlife. The bounty of the earth is not limitless, and it is being depleted too rapidly with deleterious effects on wildlife. For example, mercury has been recognized as a very serious health problem and is a major environmental issue not well understood. Dr. Franz Slemr and his colleagues at Germany's Max Planck Institute for Chemistry point out how mercury is a global threat to human health. Studies have shown how smog and other air pollutants can convert gaseous mercury to a water-soluble form. Mercury, PCBs and other pollutants are contaminating many of our food fish species.

The daily loss of soil is a great tragedy. Some economists may think most environmental problems are manageable, but most ecologists don't. According to Lester R. Brown of the Worldwatch Institute, "Every major indicator shows a deterioration in natural systems: forests are shrinking, deserts are expanding, croplands are losing topsoil, the stratospheric ozone layer continues to thin, greenhouse gases are accumulating, the number of plant and animal species is diminishing, air pollution has reached health-threatening levels in hundreds of cities." Hands-off management will not do. We must intervene, using the best information available toward carefully identified goals. Science needs to give us the best alternative solutions and their consequences, even though science cannot answer many policy questions.

We need to appraise the changing attitudes that affect animal control, including both beneficial and detrimental viewpoints, and to analyze what action can be taken to constructively modify some of the mistaken negative attitudes about animal control. If we are going to save our wildlife heritage in a growing human population, where people are going to continue to markedly alter the environment, we must assume the responsibility of preserving biological diversity and of managing and controlling wildlife in a responsible manner rather than leaving their fate to the whims of nature. Only by managing and controlling wildlife numbers and their distribution can we establish true harmony between people and the fauna in human-modified environments.

It is so easy to be overly idealistic about wildlife management. With our technological advantages, we have unwittingly created an *environmental battlefield* for many species, so we must exercise far greater care in choosing how we treat animals and the environment in disturbed ecosystems.

Sustainable development, the ultimate goal, still eludes most societies for a variety of economic, political and other reasons. Sustainable development occurs when current exploitation of resources and the environment do not jeopardize the potential support of future generations. As discussed earlier, the Endangered Species Act (ESA) of 1973 is a useful tool that has been abused. However, the ESA is the consequence of environmental abuses perpetrated by those who have profited at the expense of the environment. Attempts to delete, not modify, the ESA should not be allowed just because some ranchers, agricultural corporations, land developers and others object to environmental obstacles such as preserving wetlands or endangered species that happen to prevent their economic gains. But the ESA is not perfect and does need to be modified concerning private land and how endangered species become listed and delisted.

The bounty of the earth is not limitless, and its soil, vegetation and fauna can be and are being depleted. The gross domestic product

(GDP) and gross national product (GNP) does not warn us whether we are cashing out our natural resources at the expense of future generations. Rather, the GNP actually records the rate of consumption of raw materials and the exploitation of natural resources as assets in the natural economy's accounting system, thus ignoring environmental harm.

Give a person a fish and you feed him for a day, but as the Chinese proverb goes, teach a man to fish and you feed him for a lifetime. However, modern fishing is exhausting the supply. Industrial fishing has killed off 90 percent of the world's largest and most valuable fish species. Marine life has been thinned to where it is only a fraction of its former base. Once overfished, populations replenish themselves slowly. What is needed is a sustainable fishing goal. We must find ways of eliminating overfishing, of reducing the bycatch of unwanted species and of protecting and improving the habitat for fish.

Some resource exploitation is essential for people to survive, but such action must be taken responsibly. Economic strength in the world today is unfortunately tied directly to growth and development. No matter how responsibly such growth is achieved, it cannot continue unabated without deleterious effects on the environment. Environmental issues are inseparable from economic impacts.

A new experiment has been tried in California to increase wetlands and help waterfowl. One solution being tested after harvest is to flood fallow rice fields and work the stubble into the mud with a giant roller. Bacteria and fungi in the soil then cause the straw to decompose. Labor-saving mechanical harvesting leaves considerable waste rice (300 pounds per acre) for waterfowl to feed on, and the flooding provides abundant wetlands for wintering waterfowl and other birds. In spring, when new crops are to be planted, the stubble will have decomposed and most of the waterfowl will have migrated to the north for nesting, as they always have done.

It looks like this approach will also prove to be beneficial to the state's rice growers and end some of the air pollution problems resulting from open field burning, a practice that developed to control diseases like stem rot and aggregate sheath spot. The reason the straw can't be left in the field is that rice straw floats when the field is flooded in spring and smothers newly planted rice. If there were pathogen-destructive organisms that could thrive in straw-incorporated soils, the straw could be plowed under after harvest. New procedures are also being developed to find ways of disking and rolling the straw rather than flooding. Rice straw that can no longer be burned is also baled.

Perhaps no more vivid illustration of how and why people must assist nature exists than the 30 million or so unwanted cats, dogs and other animals that must be euthanized every year in our city and county pounds or humane organizations. If this were not done, think of the additional animal suffering that would occur, as many of these surplus animals would also be reproducing, as it is not practical to capture and sterilize them all.

Obviously it is necessary to regulate the density of cattle, sheep and deer for their own welfare, because the results are devastating when they are forced to self-limit. Overgrazing affects the entire population, not just surplus individuals. What happens when foxes, skunks or raccoons get too numerous? Nature often uses rabies or other diseases as a cruel population regulator.

If wildlife needs to be managed and controlled in an altered environment, one may legitimately ask: "How much should we manage?" Sometimes in wilderness areas and remote regions of national parks the best management plan may be to do nothing. According to Greg Wright of the Yellowstone Association Institute, in 1988 in Yellowstone National Park there was a combination of 51 separate fires—42 lightning-caused and 9 human-caused—that were allowed to burn 36 percent (793,880 acres) of the park. Leaving it to nature can be the best management scheme in situations where we are willing to accept the consequences of nature's survival-of-the-fittest struggle in establishing a new balance. In Yellowstone lodgepole pine is regenerating in most of the burned area. However, the result still will not be the same original wilderness balance that existed before human intervention.

A century or so ago the wolf's wild prey of deer and other ungulates had been greatly reduced by people. This occurred before hunters got organized to protect diminishing deer herds and pronghorn antelope. Most environmentalists overlook the fact that sustained and regulated control, not elimination, of wolves by people can preserve an optimum density of *both* the ungulate prey and wolf populations in modified environments. But management may be needed to neutralize extreme population fluctuations that occur in predator-prey relationships and also to permit the human hunter, who pays for the care of these animals, to have a role as predator.

In much of the West, livestock grazing is part of the multiple use of public lands and this creates problems. Strychnine was brought to the United States by European pioneers to poison wolves. Wherever wolves are to be encouraged, a management scheme of hunting and trapping is essential to prevent them from exceeding the carrying capacity of their designated habitat and being forced into areas where they are not wanted and may feed on livestock. Actually, wolf populations can be sustained fairly close to livestock if there are ample deer or other natural prey available and surplus wolf numbers prevented. Wolves and grizzly bears could be reintroduced into some of their former habitat, but this should be done only after satisfactory plans have been developed to prevent the species from overpopulating the areas reserved for them and to deal with the *inevitable dispersing* wolves and bears when they do overpopulate. When people overprotect wild animals, the surplus populations must disperse or develop diseases, starve or attack their own kind. Often, the result is similar to what would happen if humans contracted highly infectious and contagious diseases and the infected people were forced to commingle.

People ask why displaced and surplus animals shouldn't be captured alive and released elsewhere away from people where the species is known to exist. Many well-meaning people want to translocate surplus or displaced animals, rather than kill them, to give them another chance. Doing so is often at the expense of the animal. If members of that species already occupy all the suitable habitats in that area, an early and tragic death of translocated mammals is almost guaranteed.

It is very cruel to translocate animals, mammals in particular, into a *strange* locality. They seldom survive. They probably were surplus animals to begin with. When released into a strange area, they desperately search for familiar landmarks, and when they enter the territories of established individuals of the same species, territorial fights ensue. For animals that are a nuisance, most suitable habitats are already occupied. Most die while searching for their original home and few find a suitable new home site and mate. The National Nuisance Wildlife Control Operators Association advises its members not to translocate animals that may cause damage at a release site or spread disease, if the new habitat or weather conditions make it inhumane.

Bears, lions, wolves, coyotes, foxes, tree squirrels and other mammals that have had radio transmitters attached before they were released confirm the high mortality experienced by translocated mammals. Of course, some individuals do survive, but no one has determined the amount of suffering such surviving translocated animals experience before eventually dying.

Most agricultural and landscape plants are exotic, and they have yet to evolve to where they can cohabit with native browsing and grazing mammals. For instance, nowhere can agricultural crops be successfully grown if all native mammals are present. One exception may be kelp, a plant found in oceans, which is harvested for iodine and fertilizer. It does appear that if we had all the seals and sea otters that used to be present on the West Coast, there would probably be fewer sea urchins, hence more giant kelp to be harvested. Kelp forests are readily deforested by herbivorous sea urchins when sea otters are absent.

Most wild grazing and browsing herbivores are kept out of agricultural crops and people's gardens for obvious reasons. Thus wildlife damage control is an integral part of life in many modified environments, for it can help establish a better harmony between man and wildlife. But the control practices used should follow life-sparing approaches whenever feasible.

One aspect of single-crop monoculture that is usually not recognized is that far fewer species of *vertebrate* pests can live in monoculture than are found in diversified agriculture, even though biological diversification results in greater stabilization of nonagricultural environments. Many ecologists rightfully complain that monocultures break down the normal balances of ecological systems and may produce disastrous populations of insects and other pests, as occurred in 1848 with the potato blight in Ireland. This concern has to be qualified, however, when referring to wild species of vertebrate animals.

Very few vertebrate species can live in monocultural agriculture. Many of these can feed in single-species crops seasonally or for short periods of their daily routine, but few can live exclusively in monocultural fields. In the Sacramento and San Joaquin Valleys of California, for example, if alfalfa is planted over very large areas, the only native mammals that can thrive in these modified habitats are voles (meadow mice) and pocket gophers. Dozens of rodent species and other mammals like black-tailed jackrabbits and deer that originally lived there are also excluded from permanent residence. Either voles or pocket gophers, if not controlled, may become more abundant per-unit area in alfalfa fields than the combination of all the other species of rodents and other mammals that may have occupied that same terrain under natural vegetation.

Many zoologists have erroneously claimed that the reason agriculture has rodent problems is because farmers have abused the land. Growing nitrogen-fixing alfalfa certainly cannot be called land abuse. It is just that these species of rodents are favored by the habitat changes created by agricultural practices.

Self-regulatory feedback mechanisms in nature tend to ensure the sustenance, adaptiveness and perpetuation of a *greater* variety of vertebrates in varied habitats, thus making their control more difficult in diversified agriculture. Hedge rows and riparian vegetation along ditches can create many agricultural problems by favoring animals such as rabbits. For instance, in Australia, New Zealand and the United Kingdom, these hedgerows provide suitable habitat for rabbits between plantings of annual crops when the habitat is unsuitable for rabbits. Plowed fields do not provide sufficient food or cover for most of these animals.

The conversion of natural habitats to agricultural crops eliminates many species of vertebrates locally, although a few species may profit by the new habitats and become unusually abundant, as occurs with voles and pocket gophers in alfalfa fields. However, artificially controlling these species will still be simpler than trying to control the many kinds of animals that might be present if, instead of there being large monocultural fields, there were numerous small fields of diversified agriculture separated by hedge rows. The same may not be true with insect pests.

No predator control method—in fact, no animal damage control as now practiced in the United States—significantly affects the basic flow of ecological processes in the environment or threatens the survival of a species. Modern vertebrate pest control operations do not damage the welfare of wildlife communities in modified environments. In fact, implementing a well-regulated human-caused mortality factor often helps create a more favorable balance in modified environments. Sometimes, it is difficult to assess economic and environmental trade-offs because one person's pest may be another's preference or livelihood. For example, I love to watch coyotes and hear them howl, but not so with a sheepman. Homeowners in particular find many mammal species objectionable, even though others may at enjoy the same animals.

The fact that most carnivores are at the top of nature's food chains means they are *not* as important ecologically in the food web as primary producers and consumers. But carnivores are extremely important in maintaining natural balances of nature. As for carnivores cleaning up the environment, most carnivores actually contribute far more carrion to an ecosystem from the uneaten remains of their kills than they consume from feeding on dead carcasses they find. Also, regulated hunters and trappers, in a biological sense, can be an effective and relatively humane predator, and thereby compensate for the loss of large carnivores.

Since nature demands the presence of predators to maintain the balance of nature, it should be obvious that in human-modified environments, where "natural" predation is absent or diminished, people must assist nature to help restore balance.

Even though most carnivores appear to be extremely cunning predators, they are amazingly inefficient at reducing "native" prey to threateningly low levels in natural environments as they can domestic animals. Of course, for predators to be too successful and overconsume their prey would be self-destructive. Any predator that is too successful in capturing its major prey species is now extinct as a result of destroying its food supply, hence the reason for so many fossils.

Humans are unlikely to be attacked in typical mountain lion habitat in the West unless the lions are overprotected and overpopulated. This is especially the case if mountain lions (also called cougar, puma, panther, painter, catamount) are classified as a game animal and legal hunting is allowed to help regulate their density and create in them their more natural fear of people. Lions are naturally wild, secretive animals. Human conflict comes mostly when food, such as deer, is scarce or, more commonly, from subdominant lions that have been driven out of remaining good habitat by dominant lions. Nature's natural mortality factor for lions is an evolved mechanism that prevents excessive populations from developing with the concomitant destruction of their food supply. It is territoriality, where subdominants will be killed and often cannibalized if they don't flee.

Today the typical territorial behavior of lions does not function as well as it used to. Many subdominant surplus lions that need to escape dominant lions are unable to successfully do so without coming into conflict with people. When an environment changes so that it supports fewer deer, the ratio of lions to deer may increase because territoriality among the lions might not result in a proportionate increase in the size of lion territories to adjust for the fewer deer.

No legal hunting of mountain lions has taken place in California since 1971. From 1972 to 2002, the California Department of Fish and Game issued 4,321 depredation permits to destroy problem lions, of which 1,405 were killed. Without an ample supply of their preferred food (deer) being available, lions have to scrounge for rodents, rabbits, livestock, dogs, cats and the like to supplement their normal diet. Under these conditions even people become vulnerable, especially children. A five-year-old girl and a six-year-old boy were mauled seriously by lions in 1987. Another child was attacked in 1992, three in 1993 and two in 1998. In Montana a five-year-old boy was killed near his home by a mountain lion. Lions are dangerous predators when territoriality or lack of sufficient deer forces surplus individuals to venture out of the remaining suitable habitat.

Lions also attack adults. While jogging about a mile from a school in Idaho Springs, Colorado on January 14, 1991, an 18-year-old youth was killed and partly eaten. On April 23, 1994, while jogging near Cool, California, a 40-year old woman was killed and fed on. A second woman was also killed in California in 1994 while hiking. In 2004 a man was killed and a woman badly injured in California. Dr. E. Lee Fitzhugh, a wildlife extension specialist at UC-Davis, has documented a total of 11 fatal attacks by lions in the United States and 6 in Canada as of May 2004.

Even coyotes can be dangerous. Since 1975, in the Los Angeles area, coyotes have attacked more than a dozen children, but with only one fatality that I am aware of. Lions are much more dangerous than coyotes.

Surplus lions can no longer disperse from occupied lion habitat to search for a mate and suitable habitat to avoid being cannibalized. Now, when they are forced to disperse from what remains as favorable lion habitat, they encounter people, who either kill them or force such dispersing lions to return to the overcrowded lion habitat, where they are not accepted. It is no wonder that so many normally, very secretive lions have become a serious threat and are now being seen, even in shopping centers, as they seek food and sanctuary.

Some in California claim that the problem is that people have invaded the lion's territory. Of course, everyone in Sacramento has also invaded the grizzly bear's territory, as well as that of poisonous spiders and snakes. What is needed is a reasonable plan of cohabitation between different species of animals and people, in the inevitable modified environments present today and expected in the future.

The conflict between lions, the public and livestock operators in California has become more serious since the moratorium against hunting lions appeared in 1972. For instance, in 1996, the California Department of Fish and Game issued a record 281 depredation permits to remove offending lions, and 103 lions were found and destroyed. Starting in 1907 and lasting until 1969, a bounty was paid by California Department of Fish and Game for lions taken by hunters and trappers, but these actions did not overharvest the lion population or bring their numbers to a dangerously low level. Even though in 1932, when there were nine Department of Fish and Game State predator trappers, lions have never been an endangered or threatened species in California.

The present high lion population in many places in the West is undesirable. A population of lions is considered to be healthy when many of the offspring have a reasonable chance of living to maturity and the adults do not overharvest their natural food supply. With lions, this occurs when they feed principally on deer (at times nearly two per week per lion) rather than livestock, pets and rodents, and when lions do not exceed the carrying capacity of the remaining lion habitat. The Round Valley deer herd study by the Department of Fish and Game in Owens Valley, California (Torres 1996), found that 51 percent of deer deaths came from lions. Other causes of death of deer were coyote (22 percent), road kill (14 percent), hunters (7 percent) and others (6 percent).

How can the lion population in California be reduced to a healthier state? Since lions are now forced to live in a restricted environment that people have markedly altered, what should we do? Lions, like other large native carnivores, require several hundred square miles of land that is relatively inaccessible to humans. Lions are no different than livestock or pets. They naturally overproduce and nature's death ethic requires a mechanism that culls or harvests the surplus individuals. In modified environments the best and only viable method is sport hunting.

Hunters provide considerable and badly needed funds so the state can employ game wardens to protect the lions, biologists to ensure that the lion populations are not overharvested and funds to help preserve and acquire lion habitat. In 1994 the Montana Department of Fish, Wildlife and Parks harvested 566 lions for a total income from sportsmen of $155,620. They charged a $50 trophy fee for all successful hunters. California could raise several times that amount if lions were a game species. Hunting with dogs is a humane solution to lion management, because after the dogs tree a lion, the hunter will have time to make a clean kill.

In Malaysia tigers frequently attacked herders when they were bringing their cattle into the village for the night. As with mountain lions, they attack people from behind. Someone in Malaysia, following my discussion with the people about the problem, came up with the brilliant idea of wearing a face mask on the back of the head, which makes the back of the head look like your face. I wish I had thought of the idea. I have been told that it has greatly reduced the tiger attacks.

We have come a long way from the days of the popular adage, "A good coyote or wolf is a dead one," which many livestock men used to claim. As before, however, some extremism still flourishes on both sides, and inadequate attention is given to nature's life-death ethic. The public is confused. The first European settlers of the United States quickly learned that economic ranching often was impossible without wolf control and that all forms of agricultural production, even home landscaping, required protection from many species of wildlife. The same is true today.

Healthy reproducing populations of bears, mountain lions and wolves cannot be tolerated in human communities any more than domestic livestock can cohabit with high numbers of these carnivores. Reintroducing or encouraging recolonization of grizzly bears or other large carnivores will probably be successful if it is into their former range. This ensures that they will be successful in reproducing, hence these introduced animals will inevitably multiply beyond the carrying capacity of the available habitat as occurs with all species. Due to territoriality amongst carnivores, the dominant animals will force the surplus animals to disperse unless people remove them. This will take them into areas where they are not wanted.

Much more research will be needed before any use of natural predators will become practical for abating most types of animal damage. This is true because before most pest species cease to be a problem, they must be reduced to a density lower than what natural predators achieve with natural prey. Most predators are not species-specific in their prey selection. They are opportunists and even small numbers of some surviving prey may be considered a serious pest under some circumstances—like a pocket gopher or a mole in your lawn or garden, for example.

Even though eliminating coyotes would probably have no undesirable ecological consequences, no one proposes their extermination any more. The objective of those who suffer livestock losses from coyotes is to stop coyote depredations of fairly helpless domestic animals. Whenever guard dogs, fences or other ways of frightening coyotes away works, they are often used. But in many areas, traps, snares, toxic baits and shooting are still required for effective control of coyotes. Sometimes even the complete eradication of a small number of local coyotes is the best solution. In our experiments, when we removed the usual "killer" coyote, another of the small group of coyotes involved immediately became the killer. However, other field research has shown that the removal of a killer coyote, at least temporarily, does reduce further kills. Sheep killing increases when coyotes have pups and sheep have lambs.

Since people dominate over all wild species and have some control over nature, what is our moral and ethical responsibility with wildlife populations that have been adversely affected by our intrusions into the environment? Should we let them be governed as much as possible by existing natural forces, even if it inflicts unusual suffering to the animals? Or should we manage the population as best we can to keep them in as healthy and natural a reproducing state as possible? It would seem that we should nearly always use our dominion over nature to manage and control populations of wildlife for their welfare.

Wildlife management programs, for game and nongame wildlife in the United States, are financed mostly by sportsmen's license fees and excise taxes on the sporting equipment they use. Predator control by USDA's Wildlife Services receives government subsidies. Sport hunting in recent decades has not led to the extinction of a single wild species, nor has it caused any to become rare or endangered; instead, sport hunting provides money for their protection. More on hunting will be found in Chapter 4.

When managing wildlife the question arises, "Should people *use* animals for food, fiber, and pleasure?" Isn't it the "natural" thing to do? All life utilizes other life. The difference between how humans use other kinds of life and how wild animals use other animals is that man possesses a conscience and has, or should have, moral concerns about the exploitation of sentient animals. Consequently, we should not inflict unnecessary pain on animals any more than we should with other humans. The common ground will be the fundamental search for an ethic of the land and its living components that embraces both science and human considerations (Kellert 1982).

In 1972 India passed a wildlife protection act, making it illegal to kill any animal. This is overprotection. Tigers and elephants, like all animals, do not recognize property lines. As the populations increase in national parks and tiger reserves, more and more tigers and elephants are forced by dominant members of their own kind to forage outside the parks. Consequently, both tigers and elephants often do a lot of damage and kill villagers.

In 1982, when I was with the head wardens from all of India's tiger preserves and national parks for three weeks, the wardens calculated for me that about 150 villagers had been killed by surplus tigers during the past year. In 1995, I was told that more recently only about 50 lives are lost per year. Elephants kill even more people. Of course, tiger predation against humans is not an effective or desirable way to regulate human population densities as several extreme protectionists in my audiences have suggested. Without guns, pesticides and other modern ways of controlling troublesome pests, the world could never have attained its current density of people.

One of the game wardens, at our three-week training program in Kanha National Park, Madhya Pradesh Province, in India, had a badly scarred face. After we became well acquainted, he asked me to come out into the forest with him so he could explain what

91

happened to him. We had all had assumed he had been attacked by a tiger. However, he told me that he had driven outside the park with three of his staff to look at a boundary problem. Upon their return to the national park, they stopped in a village, which happened to be market day, for some items they all wanted. They rarely went to a village. When the villagers realized that none of the four were armed, because of their *hate* toward the park and because they were displaced and not allowed to collect wood or honey, they did their best to kill the park officials. When the police arrived, the warden's heart was still beating and his life was saved. But the three staff members were not so lucky. It is tragic that people surrounding many of India's national parks hate the park authority so much that the wardens and other officials are unable to venture outside their boundaries without armed guards or with weapons themselves, and then only because the villagers do not have guns.

Foolish overprotection of wolves, grizzly bears or mountain lions could create similar resentment from many people in the United States. Environmentalists must recognize that large populations of people cannot successfully cohabit with some of our carnivores any more than the Indians can with tigers and elephants. Thus, once wolves, lions or bears—if locally classified as an endangered or threatened species or otherwise protected from hunting—leave their geographic sanctuary, they should then no longer be afforded special protection. Such animals must be removed.

Wildlife managers also frequently must decide whether to sacrifice one species to save another. For example, to save habitat for three species of terns in Maine, both the dominant black-backed gulls and herring gulls had to be poisoned. Gulls were also killed in Massachusetts for the same reason, to benefit puffin and tern colonies (Cohen 1992). Garbage dumps in reachable feeding areas enabled the gulls to extend their nesting range into these habitats. Such populations of wildlife in modified environments often must be managed to protect other native species, not left alone.

The U.S. Fish and Wildlife Service also has had to control introduced red foxes preying on endangered least tern and clapper rails, the introduced arctic foxes preying on Aleutian Canada geese and other birds, coyotes killing San Joaquin kit foxes and black-footed ferrets, coyotes preying on both whooping cranes in Idaho and greater sandhill cranes in Oregon and ravens killing desert tortoises. All of these were the result of human activity.

It seems fairly clear that modern civilization could not coexist with saber-toothed tigers and mammoths, unless these animals were confined in parks or wilderness areas. Likewise, how could the former huge freely migrating herds of American bison be tolerated today with fences and agricultural development? In the interior valleys of California, too many people and too much essential agriculture is present to attempt large-scale reestablishment of tule elk, pronghorn antelope, mule deer, grizzly bears and beaver in their former haunts.

Even though the loss of a species is not like removing the support from under a bridge, and the disappearance of certain species might seem like "good riddance" to some, I think it is fortunate that most people do not want to see the complete loss of any biological information that is inherent to each species, or to lose a species that may not seem to have any value. However, social attitudes that lead to extreme overprotection of wildlife must be dispelled. The density of animal populations must be regulated for their own welfare, as well as for the benefit of other wildlife species, and also man.

Wildlife conservation in fact, the wildlife profession—is in trouble. There seems to be a steadily growing percentage of the public, as well as too many biologists, who no longer understand the basic biological principles responsible for the so-called "balance of nature." Objectivity suffers when wildlife biologists preach with impassioned zeal instead of stimulating others to think critically. Many anti-hunters ignore the laws of nature and use too many generic, emotional statements, with few facts to back up their contentions. It is much better to negotiate and reach consensus than to litigate. We must be honest about the inevitable trade-offs of any environmental issue if we hope to gain the confidence of the general public.

There is a need to discuss nature and animal welfare issues in human-modified environments objectively, not emotionally. When a conservation organization uses an emotional issue for raising funds, it runs the risk of creating more disharmony in the environment than would otherwise be the case. In addition to being critical watchdogs, it would behoove these organizations to take a more positive approach of seeking and actively funding more humane and environmentally suitable alternative methods of dealing with troublesome animals, which they rarely do. Conservationists must look to hard science for enduring blocks on which to build more realistic philosophies about the inescapable need for animal damage control.

A more balanced and positive approach to the control and management of wildlife in altered ecosystems is essential to developing a healthy and moral ethic about the environment and an authentic respect for all fauna.

Once a species becomes a legal game animal, the populations of those species usually live healthier lives because of the licensing regulations paid for by sportsmen. Where hunting is permitted, it is often a good animal damage control option. Wild animals are adversely affected far more by other human activities than they are by hunting or trapping. Too many people don't realize that shooting and trapping are more humane than leaving the regulation of surplus populations to cannibalism, starvation and disease.

In modified environments the choice is ours: either let a survival-of-the-fittest new balance evolve or help nature by managing both the species and the habitat. The latter requires humans to serve as surrogate predators to replace those that have been displaced by our intrusion into wildlife habitat. Intensive predator control is as old as livestock husbandry. Fortunately, extinction of pest species is no longer the goal. The control of predators is a means of increasing the harvest of fur and game species, and as a sport. Only recently has the public begun to recognize the benefits derived from natural predators. Still, some people reject the idea that predator control sometimes may be necessary to benefit endangered species and domestic animals.

Most native vertebrates that have become pests are well adapted to a wide range of modified habitats. They usually have high resilience, and their populations will promptly recover if control operations are discontinued. It is important to note that many animals that may be a serious pest to one person may at the same time have an esthetic or other value to someone else. For example, black bears are enjoyed by many, but when other food is scarce, a bear with its sharp claws can rip the bark off of as many as 50 timber trees a day in the Northwest to feed on the exposed sugar-rich sap wood (phloem). Invariably this leads to the death of all such trees.

Ranchers, in particular, are acquainted with the gruesome sight of a two-day-old calf with its hindquarters eaten away, yet still alive, or a sheep lying motionless and silent to avoid being repeatedly attacked while a coyote consumes its small intestines. However, many people also feel that public lands are theirs, and that the public should decide whether they want predators managed on those lands or whether they want those lands managed for the benefit of ranchers. So far Congress recognizes livestock as one of the original decreed multiple uses of the federal rangelands, hence the current practices.

A zealous "animal protectionist ethic is usually unsound biologically. Conservationists, to achieve their goals, need a wildlife management ethic, based not on emotionalism but on the laws of nature, which include animal management and damage control. Animal damage control has been and will be for the foreseeable future an integral part of people's lives. It is as much a part of the true harmony between man and nature as has been man's exploitation of animals and plants for food.

Since animal damage control involves applied ecology, the approaches used must be varied, often involving frightening devices, barriers and cultural methods, as well as the use of repellents or various types of biological control. Lethal methods, such as shooting, kill-trapping and toxic chemicals, are also used for reducing pest populations. Sometimes they are the only economical and practical solutions, especially with many species of rodents, some livestock predators and some crop and fish-eating birds. Animal damage control personnel are frequently called in to help save endangered species such as the whooping crane, desert tortoise, San Joaquin kit fox, California least tern and peregrine falcon

The public has a right to demand from animal control experts the highest standards of humane and responsible wildlife management and conservation. As the first animal control specialist in government, Jack Berryman (1994) stated regarding animal damage control, "We can develop improved policies, develop new technologies and improve program administration. But, if we fail to enjoy public support, it will all be for naught."

Many people have worked very hard since the 1970s to find an alternative to leg-hold (foot-hold, to be correct) traps for controlling coyotes. A better alternative is still needed, including safer and highly selective ways of poisoning coyotes. The vocal opponents to traps are not just against traps. Many are opposed to any procedure that takes the life of an animal, no matter how surplus or dangerous the animal may be or how humane the method may be. To such folks it is not how the coyotes are taken, but that they are taken at all.

Coyotes are highly adaptable animals and great survivors. They are clever and cunning. With my students I have raised more than 300 coyotes. Unfortunately, until an acceptable alternative control method can be found, in many situations the current padded off-set jaw, spring-tension trigger steel trap is still required. None of the alternative "humane" traps have proven adequate for coyotes, including the Aldrich Footsnare, Ezyonew Legsnare, Swedish Legsnare, Novac Legsnare, Victor Power Snare or the completely hopeless live cage traps. Experiments at the University of California, Davis—with observers in blinds—showed that coyotes are very hesitant to enter cage traps. Even the padded-jaw trap needs refinement since some coyotes escape. The public does not realize that a person can set off a modern coyote steel trap without it damaging their fingers. Many furbearers are, or used to be, trapped with these humane leg-hold traps when a state conservation department wanted to relocate them. Some European countries have banned the use of leg—or foot-hold traps, but they do not have coyotes or need of such traps, and this prohibition occurred before more humane traps were developed.

Since the average size of a coyote litter may increase slightly when a population is well below carrying capacity, some biologists have mistakenly claimed that government control programs are making predation of livestock by coyotes worse. They incorrectly reason that these slightly larger litters will actually over time increase the total density of coyotes. They overlook the fact that a slight increase in litter size can in no way offset the greatly reduced number of coyote bitches left to breed. When a coyote population is being controlled, the total annual production of young is of course less, regardless of average litter size. In any case, the objective of coyote control efforts by Wildlife Services of USDA is not to eliminate coyotes, but to reduce the damage they may be causing.

Many consider everything "chemical" as unnatural and bad, while everything "biological" is thought to be intrinsically desirable. Both claims are false. What is "natural" sounds desirable but is not necessarily the best. Earthquakes, volcanic eruptions, hurricanes, poisonous mushrooms, even ants in the kitchen are natural but few people welcome them.

Some people like to think that wild animals have a right to live where they want to—until the animals become a pest. In nature many animals are possessive and prevent other individual animals of different and even the same species from also occupying their habitat, the same way people do. That is nature's survival-of-the-fittest struggle in action. Maybe that explains road rage.

What is our role in the balance of nature? Should we be willing to share our agricultural crops with wild animals, insects and weeds, thus requiring that much more land be devoted to food production? If we indiscriminately shared our agricultural crops with wildlife, we would soon discover that there is insufficient arable land available to feed ourselves. The food surpluses would soon disappear and food prices would rise sharply. Consumers in the United States now have access to the cheapest and most abundant food ever. For agriculture in the United States to retain its domestic markets and expand its foreign exports, it must be able to lower production costs and hence share less of the crops with pests. This is basic economics.

In developing countries it's not unusual to lose more than half the crops to wildlife pests in the field and in storage. In some instances they can't grow certain crops because of uncontrollable pests. For example, the prime minister of Western Samoa once told me that because of Polynesian rats they were unable to grow potatoes, peanuts and many other nonnative food items that their diet and economy desperately needed.

Once a habitat changes, ignoring necessary control measures to keep certain vertebrate species in balance invites ecological disharmony. To try to protect all vertebrates in the interest of conservation may be counterproductive. In the West, many logged-over coniferous forests have reverted to brush because broadcast conifer seed was not treated to repel deer mice and other seed-eating rodents, or the mice were not kept at low levels with poisons until a new stand of seedlings became established. Now, following logging or wildfires, so regeneration can be established because of these rodent problems, seedlings are usually planted. To ensure successful regeneration, the problem now has become one of protecting seedlings from deer, rabbits, porcupines, pocket gophers and other rodents. Damage by wild animals costs the U.S. Forest Service $30 million to $60 million per year.

Feral animals often become troublesome. The definition of "feral" wildlife is an animal that has been held in captivity for many generations or has been domesticated and then escaped into the wild. However, the breadth of this definition depends on how the words captivity, escape and established are used. Any introduced exotic species—that is, any species that has been successfully released into a new environment—would first be held in captivity to be transported. If it later escapes from its new location, the new species may then be considered feral. Any formerly domesticated species that is now living and breeding, as a wild creature without food or protection being provided by man, is truly feral. Wild boar is a good example. They are really nothing more than feral pigs.

Under common usage, feral also often has a derogatory implication among many biologists. Some may speak of "wild" horses and burros and do not use feral, even though they are feral mammals. When someone considers an introduced or exotic species undesirable, it is commonly called feral to signify that it is a misfit that doesn't belong there. Fortunately, however, most people use the term feral in its more proper ecological meaning.

What is meant by the word "established" is also not clearly defined. Can a single animal escape and be considered as feral for the rest of its life, or must a breeding population exist before the species can be considered established? It is useful to have the term "feral" apply to both single individuals and populations because both situations are common.

With some species it is not known whether they were intentionally released, had escaped or whether both types of introductions occurred. A few examples of feral mammals will be discussed.

## Dogs

A statewide survey by the California Department of Fish and Game of the "dog problem" to wildlife (especially deer but also to colonies of nesting birds and livestock) showed that depredations by true feral dogs appear to constitute only a fraction of the animal losses attributed to dogs. It is the unrestrained vagrant domestic dogs that do most of the damage. They are also the result of both an overpopulation of pet dogs and owner irresponsibility. The consensus among animal control officers, game wardens and biologists is that to abate the uncontrolled dog problem requires better enforcement of current laws, stricter judicial action and better public awareness of existing laws and responsibilities of dog ownership. I am not aware of anyone suggesting that there is a desirable ecological niche for wild dogs

## Cats

All cats, especially males, seem to be natural wanderers. Urban feral cat are quite social and do not defend large territories. Except at sites where man provides garbage or other food, true nonurban feral cats are largely solitary hunters of rodents, rabbits, ground-nesting birds, reptiles, fishes trapped in shallow pools and insects. Vagrant-to-truly-feral cats seem to be scattered throughout agricultural regions, often preying on ring-necked pheasants and quail, and in recreational and urban areas. Some people unwisely feed them. Native carnivores, coyotes in particular, probably prevent cats from being common in any of the wilder regions. Wild coyotes, which are now found living in urban areas, also like to eat cats.

To illustrate that cats hunt for sport as well as food, look at the frequency with which the well-fed house cat brings back to the house uneaten rodents and birds it has successfully killed. Cats are clearly opportunistic predators capable of exploiting a wide variety of foods and can have a serious impact on populations of small mammals, lizards and, especially, birds. They are, for example, responsible for exterminating some species of small marsupials in Australia.

The difference between the capture-neuter-and-release method of handling the feral cat problem and euthanasia of unwanted cats is whether you prefer that the cats die a slow, painful, more natural death or have their lives shortened by a merciful, quick death. The neuter-and-release of feral cats is not considered a humane solution. It cannot be recommended except for one possible exception. Zaunbrecher and Smith (1993) believe such releases may be workable at institutions like veterinary schools, where trained help is available, even though it is not a pleasant experience for such cats. However, it will still be difficult to stop people from feeding the sterilized cats. Thus, releasing sterile cats mainly perpetuates the ultimate suffering by such animals due to starvation, being hit by a car, dying from a disease or some other tragic death.

Further, for each temporary survivor there is a huge number of birds and small mammals (mostly field rodents) that will fall victim to these nonnative feline predators, whether sterile or not. When food is put out for feral cats it is often also taken by raccoons, skunks and opossums, which then increase beyond their normal density and raise the potential for disease transmission, including rabies. Feral cats do not fit into nature's balance-of-nature scheme, except possibly in places like a farm where, even though they cannot eliminate rodent pests, cats do help keep rat and mouse populations down to a more tolerable level determined by the amount of safe harborage that exists. Sometimes feral cats can be controlled if the shelter they need is removed.

## Horses, Burros and Asses

Wild horses and burros (here commonly called wild instead of feral have been present in America since the 1850s. They represent the last vestiges of the American West and are one of the most complex problems of contemporary wildlife management in the western United States. Under the protection afforded them by the Wild Free-Roaming Horse and Burro Act (Public Law 92-195) enacted December 15, 1971, populations have increased rapidly. It is estimated there are about 48,000 in ten western states. About 25,000 of the wild horses are found on public lands in Nevada, but other states with nearly a thousand or more individuals are California, Colorado, Idaho, Montana, Oregon, Utah and Wyoming. Most of the wild burros usually occupy an area encompassing public lands in western Arizona, southeastern California, southern Nevada and southern Utah.

Some Americans see wild horses and burros as artifacts left by Spanish conquistadors and ancient Indian tribes, an important link to our heritage. Because of their use by explorers, American Indians and settlers, the domesticated ancestors of these animals played a significant role in the history of the West. Many are from U.S. Cavalry, farmers and ranchers who turned them loose. The image of Indian wars, the cowboy and the early prospectors is indelibly stamped with the presence of a horse or burro. It was the Spanish conquistadors who introduced both horses and burros to America in the 1500s. Horses that escaped during the Spanish expeditions out of Mexico are presumed to be the nucleus of the first wild horse herds in North America. Others escaped from wagon trains and were also turned loose by sympathetic farmers and ranchers, especially during droughts when they no longer needed them.

The burros were brought to the West by Jesuit missionaries and were later used by prospectors or miners, who often let them escape or abandoned them. In Death Valley National Monument and other places, wild burros have seriously affected native flora and fauna. They have caused soil damage, accelerated erosion, destroyed vegetation, mutilated springs and water holes and competed with mountain sheep and other native wildlife for food, water and open space.

The main controversy about these feral animals developed after the Second World War when a commercial demand for horsemeat to use in pet food made harvesting of these animals profitable. Horsemeat was also popular with people in some countries, especially France. The way the wild horses were captured and slaughtered was considered inhumane, hence resulted in Mrs. Velma B. Johnston's getting the Wild Horse Annie Act of 1959 passed. This was the first federal law to recognize the existence of wild horses and burros. It prohibited the use of motorized vehicles and aircraft in harassing or capturing the animals on public lands. Under state or local law they could still be captured by other means.

The federal legislation involving the management of both wild horses and burros is based more on emotionalism than on scientific facts and shows no concern for the ecology of the West. Most supporters of this legislation don't want animals taken no matter how humanely it is done. They do not realize that feral horses, like all species, must have a mortality factor. To sway legislators, those wanting to protect these animals enticed thousands of school children to write to their congressmen. As with many controversial issues, the news media in their coverage undoubtedly had a strong influence on the outcome.

As a result of this nationwide crusade, Congress passed the Wild Free-Roaming Horse and Burro Act of 1971. The law provides that even those animals that stray onto private property can be removed only by a federal agency. Helicopters are still legal for capturing (driving) the animals. The Act now also authorizes the removal of excess animals to protect the range. However, the removal of any horses is often met with opposition from vocal segments of the public. As a consequence, there are still too many animals remaining.

In 1976 the U.S. Bureau of Land Management established the Adopt-A-Horse (or burro) Program nationwide to find suitable homes (up to four animals per person per year) for the surplus animals. After proof that you have provided good care of your animal for one year you can receive ownership title to the animals. The animals to be adopted are freeze-branded with a permanent numbering scheme. I think the peak year for adoption of 11,621 horses was 1987; for 2,495 burros, it was 1981. Around 100,000 horses have been adopted. This adoption scheme is costly and does not remove enough animals. For example, between 1984 and 1993, $137 million was spent to remove 77,200 feral horses and burros from Bureau of Land Management lands, which is about $1,775 per animal according to W. E. Jones, *Journal of Equine Veterinary Science* (1993). In the fiscal year ending September 30, 2003, one way or another BLM removed about 7,000 horses.

Wildlife biologists, game managers and landowners are not satisfied with the current management of the feral horses and burros, because the remaining populations are too high. Wild horses can increase their population by 18 percent annually. Attempts are being made to sterilize animals to help check their numbers. More on this approach will be discussed later.

Pigs or Wild Boar

Feral hogs or pigs have been recognized as a problem in the United States since the 1700s. Settlers started hunting feral hogs in the 1880s. Later it became common to release one's hogs to fatten on acorns, which led to escapes. Wild pigs have crossed with introduced European wild boar and have become an important game animal in some states. Because of their numbers, they are now the number one big game species taken in California. Some commercial hog hunting management programs on private lands are quite successful. Qualified hunting guides are the keys to success in such a scheme in order to manage for trophies and to properly harvest tender or young pork to control population numbers and sex ratio. If not controlled by man or large predators, pigs can multiply rapidly and do considerable local environmental damage by their rooting. They are by far the most prolific, large free-living mammals in the United States. In some areas the pig causes considerable concern as a disease reservoir for swine brucellosis (*Brucella suis*) and pseudorabies.

## Goats

Feral goatsare found primarily on islands that lack coyotes, mountain lions or other large carnivores. These goats are nearly always considered undesirable from an ecological viewpoint. They are implicated in habitat destruction and the alteration of plant species composition of many sensitive insular ecosystems. Their removal has led to rapid recovery of suppressed vegetation. Herds of goats that are not properly managed or controlled by predators are like a slow bulldozer, eventually causing severe erosion and even desertification. Goats are not easily captured, but with much effort large numbers of goats can be driven into traps with net-wing fences. Shooting from the ground with or without dogs and also from the air is often employed.

Integrated pest management (IPM), which keeps the use of toxic chemicals to a minimum, is practiced in the control of wildlife pests. When possible, it is often cheaper and simpler to use some type of nonlethal control method. Usually nonlethal IPM (Integrated Pest Management) animal control methods are tried. They include sound, visual frightening devices, encouraging biological control with predators or disease, planting resistant cultivars, fertility control and habitat manipulations. Also employed are changes in crop phonology to discourage pests chemically, by using naturally occurring repellents, and construction of barriers. Lethal methods, such as shooting, trapping, and poisoning, involve many regulations and restrictions, which discourages their use unless they are absolutely necessary.

Examples of methods of biological control of animal damage include (a) encouraging predators of the pest (this may help but usually is not a solution with animals except on islands); (b) using fences to keep them out; (c) altering the habitat so it is unsuitable for the species (whenever habitats are altered, it affects other species); (d) introducing or augmenting host-specific diseases (epizootics) against the pest; (e) using chemosterilants and immunocontraceptives to check the reproductive success of pest populations; and (f) introducing genetic traits that make the pest species less successful.

Ultrasonic devices mounted on automobiles to frighten deer and other animals and ultrasonic devices to use in homes and warehouses to control rats and mice, or on collars to control fleas on cats, do not work. Mammals quickly get used to the ultrasonic sounds and fleas don't hear them. No one has been able to prove they control rodents. Those who claim they work say that at the same time you must also use poisons and traps and structurally exclude them. However, in all these situations, control will be just as good if the sound units are never turned on. Because these devices do not work, the Federal Trade Commission (FTC) and EPA have been trying for years to prohibit the sale of ultrasonic pest control devices in the United States. They are difficult to ban because these ultrasound devices do not "hurt" people or animals.

Both the public and animal control personnel would like to have some form of fertility control available to use in place of poisoning, shooting, trapping, biological control, habitat manipulation and exclusion. One difficulty is that the main management objective of control is usually to mitigate damage rather than only lower reproductive success. Also, large populations of nonbreeding individuals are usually still unacceptable. Of course, fertility control would slow the rate of recovery after a pest population has first been reduced by conventional methods of poisoning, shooting or trapping. One reason contraception is considered acceptable by the public is because humans practice birth control to regulate their family size.

A successful fertility control program requires satisfying a number of conditions. Fertility control methods must be:

a. Cost-effective
b. Satisfactory in damage mitigation
c. Humane and nontoxic
d. Specific for the target species
e. Easily administered to wild animals
f. Environmentally acceptable

My colleague Rex E. Marsh and I first published research on fertility control of mammals in 1967. Our goal was to prevent rapid recovery of a controlled population of rodents. We recognized that no one would be willing to have a single rat in his or her house, even if it was sterile. We also hoped to be able to slow the springtime population growth of chipmunks, squirrels and mice in Sierra Nevada campgrounds to prevent plague from developing. The presence of some rodents is part of the camping experience, but when their population numbers become excessive plague develops, endangering humans and forcing the closure of the campgrounds until public health workers can perform flea control. Such closures can be economically disastrous for adjacent small businesses that cater to vacationers.

Research is currently underway in the United States to find practical ways of sterilizing pets, wild horses and deer (Kirkpatrick et al. 1997), and field animals, including birds. No practical way of administering drugs to wild horses and deer have been found. In Australia, an orally delivered immunocontraceptive for European red fox is available (Bradley et al. 1997). Hugh Tyndale-Biscoe is investigating ways of developing immunocontraception by genetic engineering so that the individuals will still remain sexually active, even though sterilized, and retain or improve their status in the social hierarchy of the population. Whereas anti-gonadal agents, which interfere with the pituitary-gonadal axis, must be delivered by bait, dart or bullet, it is important to target the gametogenic function of the gonad so as to render the animal infertile but not impotent. Active research is also underway in Australia to find a safe, effective recombinant myxoma virus that could be used as a disseminating agent to induce infertility in wild rabbits (Robinson et al. 1997). Lowell A. Miller (1997) discusses methods of delivering immunocontraceptive vaccines for wildlife.

Current research seeks to find microorganisms that express species-specific gamete antigens to be spread through the target population by sexual transmission, by contagion or by arthropod vector. Nettles (1997) reviews the potential consequences and problems with wildlife contraceptives. The use of infectious agents as vectors to deliver immunocontraceptives is not considered wise animal health management because the product will be a new reproductive disease that might be difficult to contain within the target population. Earlier studies designed to introduce lethal genes into rat populations in the United States were finally abandoned. A species-specific form of something like AIDS for humans is needed to control pest rodents, such as exotic house mice and rats.

The introduction of diseases has been an effective way of controlling the European rabbit in Australia. The first success came with Myxomatosis, carried by intentionally introduced rabbit fleas. Progress towards using recombinant myxoma virus as a vector for fertility control in rabbits is underway in Australia (Robinson et al. 1997). In 1996, the Australian government authorized the release of a previously escaped, deadly calicivirus virus. Rabbits had acquired some genetic immunity to the myxoma virus. Tests with native animals were first carried out to ensure the safety of the calicivirus. For a review article, see Chasey (1996). The virus is now also in New Zealand.

Many, including myself, have wondered whether the encouragement of raptors, such as hawks and owls, could help in controlling troublesome rodents in agriculture and forestry. When we tested this hypothesis over a period of years, we could never prove that artificial perches helped check the adjacent rodent populations (Hall et al. 1981). We realize that evolution has resulted in predators having evolved a predator-prey relationship under natural conditions that ensures an optimum density of prey will be maintained. Both predators and prey need each other. It does, however, seem logical that in environments modified by agricultural practices, it might be possible to provide perches for raptors so that these birds could then prevent rodents from becoming well established early in the season of an annual crop before that crop had matured enough to provide good escape cover. We reasoned that if raptors could prevent rodents from becoming well established until ample cover had developed in early summer, the rodents might not have sufficient time to reach a density where they would become a serious economic pest.

Hawks and owls promptly used our artificial perches in fields where natural perches did not exist. But we never could prove that the perches had any effect on the local populations of pocket gophers. The birds did little hunting by sighting prey while on the perches. Instead, the raptors apparently hunted elsewhere and came to the perches as a comfortable place to eat their prey or to rest. The tests were a great disappointment.

It may come as a surprise to learn that habitat modification should not be employed *a priori* to control wildlife pests, even though it can be very effective since the suitability of the habitat is key to survival. Making the environment unsuitable seems like a nice, humane way to address pest problems, but we need to recognize that artificially altering habitats so a pest can no longer live there may be an undesirable form of biological control to use against vertebrates because it can harm other species. However, top dressing with fertilizer made pastures in New Zealand unsuitable for European rabbits. They cannot survive in dense forage.

Even lethal control of an unwanted animal or population is usually more ecologically advisable. Habitat manipulation may be more disruptive to other species of nontarget wildlife than even callous use of lethal control methods. Whenever a habitat is modified, most of the species of vertebrates living there tend to suffer unless they can behaviorally or genetically adapt to the new conditions. The suitability of habitats determines how well a species thrives, and any modification will usually make the habitat less suitable for most other native vertebrates that occupy the area.

By now the reader should have a better appreciation concerning the problem of, and need for, managing wildlife and controlling populations of pest animals in an economically oriented society and in human-modified environments. Many animal-borne diseases, such as plague and rabies, are often a consequence of habitat modifications by people, which then permits an overpopulation of certain rodents to develop. Even though agricultural practices and home landscaping cannot coexist with "free-ranging" native mammals, many of us fail to come to grips with how we want such problem animals to die. The control of animal damage should be guided by applied wildlife ecology. It is obvious that agricultural crops, home landscaping and reforestation cannot be successful if native mammals and many species of birds are not controlled. Therefore, in human-modified environments, it is essential to manage and control wildlife populations to preserve the life-death ethic of the balance of nature as best we can for both the sake of wildlife and ourselves. Without a doubt, the best way to preserve healthy populations of native wildlife is to assist nature's life-death ethic. To do otherwise is to turn our backs on scientifically sound stewardship practices.

CHAPTER 4

# Hunting and Trapping

The origin of human culture can be traced to a time when hunting and gathering were the sole means of subsistence. It was physiologically impossible for people to be strict vegetarians and live off the limited types of vegetation available. In a historical context, it has been only recently that agriculture and husbandry have been developed. Hunting is thus an old practice of humans. It is more ritual than sport and establishes an indelible bond between people and animals.

In a pamphlet on "Placing Hunting in Perspective," the Wildlife Management Institute points out that the "thrill of the chase" is the foremost lure of hunting, combining anticipation, mental alertness, tension and physical exertion—all of which provide excitement and intrigue, challenge and fulfillment. It is the pursuit of an animal with the intent of taking it, but hunting neither begins nor ends with killing. It is more a sport than a necessity.

According to Ted Kerasote (1996):

By and large all those people who by dint of geography
or sentiment are distanced from nature tend to hold sentientist
values while outdoor people, especially hunters and anglers,
cling to ecosystemic values, sometimes with a strong leaning
toward self-interest, expressed by a utilitarian
view of nature . . .

Unfortunately, the gulf between sentientists and deep ecologists will continue to widen, not because one of the most outspoken subgroups of the sentientists, the animal rightists, are winning the day (I don't believe they are), nor because outdoor ethics programs are totally failing (they aren't), but because the values of the uncommitted public—people who eat mesquite-grilled tuna but flinch at the thought of bopping a trout over the head—are shifting, slowly, inexorably and without all that much prodding from special-interest groups, toward a code of ethics in which utilitarian beliefs are being replaced by a respect for individual animals.

Many highly civilized countries have now developed a complex hunting culture. Yet in just such countries we find especially rich wildlife populations today, because the game species are "wanted" by the hunters. Trophies were common even in the Stone Age.

No one knows how many species of animals were exterminated by early man's hunting for food and, especially, self-protection, as was the case with lions in Europe. The Maoris of New Zealand eliminated all the genera of the flightless moa for food and their feathers. The largest of these birds stood close to three meters (about 10 feet). In modern times, extermination or the threat of extermination has mainly come from habitat destruction, certainly not from organized noncommercial hunters.

Hunting regulations in the United States came about because sportsmen recognized that "unrestricted" hunting—especially market hunting—clearly threatened many species of mammals and birds. Today such overharvesting is no longer a problem because, should it occur, state game or conservation organizations, financed largely by sportsmen, will close the season for as long as necessary to allow populations to recover. Sportsmen are the main providers of funds used to purchase habitats required to help many species thrive.

We must practice conservation the wise and effective use of natural resources. Such conservation measures are the only way to sustain natural biodiversity of many plant and animal species, which naturally occupy the same habitats as game species. It may not be necessary for sportsmen to hunt or trap some populations of game animals to maintain a healthy balance, but the additional habitat they provide can improve the lives of other species of animals that live in the same area as game animals. *The limiting negative impacts on wildlife today are not from hunting and trapping but from urbanization, roads, picnickers, hikers, campers, aquatic recreation and other human activities that further limit the availability of suitable and essential wildlife habitat.*

Due to the unprecedented exposure of nature on television lately, it has become more difficult to convey any utilitarian use of animals, regardless of the benefits to the ecosystems at large or the welfare of any specific animal population. The more charismatic the birds or mammals involved, the more likely there will be opposition to such utilitarian activities as hunting and trapping.

Poaching and other illegal harvesting of wildlife are a problem—albeit a comparatively minor one—due in part because the license fees that hunters and trappers pay for the privilege of hunting and trapping enable wardens to be hired to prevent poaching as well as to enforce the state bag limits. Additional public funds are needed so the number of wardens can be increased. The emphasis here is on hunting because fishing is not as controversial, but most of the principles discussed apply equally to hunting, trapping and fishing.

Overall there has been a fairly happy marriage between the hunting fraternity and conservation-management agencies, with both helping to ensure the survival of game species and their habitats. Because of public pressure, state fish and game conservation agencies are actually quite conservative in their game management and wildlife protection regulations, sometimes too much so for the best health of the species being protected. The public must be informed that it is the hunters' money that makes conservation efforts possible as sportsmen directly support wildlife conservation efforts in many ways. In 2000 they contributed 65.4 percent of the funds used for wildlife conservation. Other forms of support include state general funds and a lengthy list of federal legislation, including the Lacey Act of 1900, American Game Policy of 1930, Migratory Bird Hunting Stamp Act of 1934 (the duck stamps have raised over $400 million), Pittman-Robertson (P-R) Federal Aid in Wildlife Restoration Act of 1937 (10 percent excise tax, which has generated over $400 million to help purchase and maintain millions of acres of wildlife habitat), Dingle-Johnson Act of 1950 (excise tax), Multiple-Use Sustained Yield Act of 1960, Dingle-Hart Act (10 percent tax on handguns), Goodling-Moss Act of 1972 (11 percent excise tax on archery equipment), Resources Planning Act of 1974, Federal Land Policy and Management Act of 1976, National Forest Planning Act of 1976, Alaska Lands Act of 1980, Wallop-Breaux Act of 1984 (sport fisheries), Food Security Act of 1985 (initiated the Conservation Reserve Program), North American Wetlands Preservation Act of 1989 (which funds the North American Waterfowl Management Plan) and the Magnuson-Stevens Fishery Conservation and Management Act of 1996 (which helps eliminate overfishing, rebuild depleted populations, reduce bycatch and improve fish habitat). Some of this funding has been around for more than a hundred years—a strong indication of a long-standing commitment to the betterment of wildlife in America.

About $200 million is collected annually by federal excise taxes that sportsmen pay (11 percent for shotguns, rifles, ammunition and archery equipment; 10 percent for handguns). State wildlife agencies received about $400 million, for example, in 1996 to support wildlife restoration and recreation. The Wildlife Diversity Funding Initiative, known as "Teaming for Wildlife—a Natural Investment," is an act that provides an excise tax not to exceed 5 percent on outdoor equipment such as binoculars, bird feeding supplies, mountain bikes, canoes, recreation vehicles and sleeping bags. The above P-R excise tax has generated well over $3 million to help purchase and maintain around 5 million acres of wildlife habitat. By 2002 Ducks Unlimited had raised $1 billion to conserve 10 million acres of wetland habitat.

In contrast, the organizations, with annual budgets of hundreds of millions of dollars, provide *no* support for biological diversity or wildlife conservation. Most state conservation agencies rely largely or completely on user-derived funds. If these funds are eliminated by organizations opposed to hunting and fishing, no one seems to know from where other sources of revenue would come to support conservation agencies. Those opposed to hunting are not offering to contribute to finance the needed wardens and biologists or provide funding for habitat purchases.

The American Humane Association (AHA), which is a conscientious humane organization and which should not be confused with the Humane Society of the United States, is opposed to the hunting of any living creature for fun, for food (except by indigenous people), as a trophy or simply for sport. The AHA and other responsible humane organizations believe that sport hunting is a form of exploitation of animals for the entertainment of the hunter and that hunting is contrary to their values of compassion and respect for all life, and is hence a violation of the inherent integrity of animals. They also incorrectly claim that it is disruptive of the natural balance of the environment. They do agree, however, that on occasions when all other avenues have been exhausted and a need to kill some wildlife can be demonstrated that responsible officials, not sport hunters, should perform it. Calling hunting a sport raises a red flag. Also, the methods utilized must result in instantaneous and humane death.

Even though nature requires that animal populations be harvested by some form of predator or other mortality factor in order for the species population to remain healthy, it is not an easy sell. Avid hunters and fishermen avoid unnecessary cruelty or suffering by striving for a clean and quick kill. That is an act of compassion.

The interest that ethical hunters have in pursuing game has been the principal factor in nurturing conservation of wildlife and other resources. Many species of birds and mammals have survived surprisingly well in North America because they are game species. Current hunting of game species in developed countries is done ethically with regulations that prevent species depletion and inhumane treatment of the wildlife resource. Hunters have proven they will support conservation and self-regulation when a species is threatened with loss of habitat or other factors that threaten its existence. Sportsmen are much more active in organized wildlife conservation efforts than nonhunters. They also are the prime supporters of wildlife research and enforcement of wildlife laws.

Is hunting brutal, sadistic and primitive, as it is often claimed to be? Or is it a biologically sound, effective and relatively humane way of helping nature cull surplus animals in order to maintain healthy populations? Economically, the best way to manage the population density of game animals is by hunting or trapping. This is especially true in people-altered environments. To ban all hunting and trapping would bring about the elimination of many game species and their habitats. Within any biological community, killing is the basic activity of maintaining nature's food webs; hence, regulated hunting is a morally desirable choice.

The anti-hunting sentiment so prevalent today has been nourished by animated talking-Bambi wildlife and by making the hunter, instead of the poacher, the villain. And sportsmen have been slow in speaking out. I respect an individual's right not to hunt if he or she personally opposes killing. It is easy for me to understand why someone may be opposed to others taking the life of another animal. But such a view indicates that the laws of nature are not understood and neglects the necessity of humans assisting nature responsibly in disturbed environments.

Effective communication strategies are needed to inform the public that the hunting and trapping of animal populations are regulated and game populations benefit as result. The public does not realize that America's wildlife is thriving, and that most game species are more abundant today than at any time during the past 100 years. There are more than 70 million American hunters, anglers and trappers and they are the great conservationists, footing a bill of more than $2 million per year.

Not everyone needs to hunt and many are opposed to hunting. Most areas probably have too many hunters now for the amount of game and habitat available. Many nonhunters like to eat chicken, turkey, fish, lamb and beef, as long as they do not have to kill the animals. And they relish fresh crab as long as they don't have to drop the live crab into boiling water.

A simplistic way to look at hunting is to ask how anyone can morally justify and enjoy killing wild birds or mammals. First of all, "Hunting" is not equivalent to "Hunters." Hunting is as much a state of mind as it is an activity. The motives of hunters vary widely. The human hunter and the animal predator have much the same interaction with the prey, except people kill under numerous regulations designed to ensure that animals are killed as humanely as feasible and not by nature's no-holds-barred, survival-of-the-fittest predation. When killing is done with the proper respect, regulated hunting and trapping are appropriate actions—even though it may cause some pain and distress.

People do not hunt just because it is called a sport. Rather, they hunt to find themselves and to experience nature in a visceral way. It is a spiritual event to those hunters who have the proper attitude. As Shane P. Mahoney of Newfoundland suggests, the term sport hunting should be discarded and hunters should refer to themselves as "hunter-naturalists." Hunters are naturalists and not just out to kill something. They are hunter-conservationists. They have an unfair public image. When forest trees are cut illegally, we do not say "foresters" did it. "Hunters" are not the ones that shoot signs, livestock, water tanks, etc. Punks with guns do these things. To comprehend hunting, one must understand nature and man's role in nature.

Hunting is intertwined in Native Americans' lives and customs. This country was founded on a hunting and trapping tradition. When the facts become clear and the conservation principles are understood, informed publics will more likely support hunting and trapping. For the hunter or trapper, the challenge and anticipation of a successful conclusion lures a pursuer on, yet an unsuccessful "kill" does not mean the outing or chase was not appreciated.

Hunting is not for everyone, but nonhunters need to understand nature's life-death ethic, especially the role that hunting plays in humanizing nature in environments that are no longer natural. Hunter's participation and their funds help regulate animal population densities. The nonhunter nature lover or wildlife photographer cannot understand the full excitement of a potential "kill," with its anticipation and often uncomfortable waiting and pursuit of the prey. By using portable heart monitors, Dr. Susan Hapaniemi of William Beaumont Hospital in Royal Oak, Michigan, found that due to the excitement of deer hunting from a tree stand, one hunter's heart rate soared from 78 beats per minute to 168. No wonder some say hunting can be a cardiac hazard.

Hunting, fishing and trapping are long-standing, legitimate American traditions. In fact, they are privileges that were recognized at the beginning of this country, even though they are not constitutional rights.

People like to hunt, trap and fish for many of the same reasons people like to climb mountains, hike and go camping. All are done because of the challenge and our respect for, and love of, nature. People's desire to hunt may be inexplicable, but hunting is actually as much conservation as it is recreation, and conservation is not synonymous with providing complete protection of animals.

The purposeful harvesting of wildlife resources can be very important in both preserving natural biological diversity and enabling other animals to live. Sportsmen or their state wildlife organizations often underharvest game rather than risk overharvesting them.

Responsible hunting and trapping are a good outdoor expression of our heritage and they are defensible from ethical, moral, economic, legal and ecological points of view. No one has to be a hunter, trapper or fisherman if he/she doesn't want to, since the personal justification of hunting and trapping depends upon one's ethics. It would clearly be hypocritical for an animal rightist to hunt, trap, fish or eat meat, but not so for those who understand, accept and wish to respect nature's life-death ethic.

Hunting and trapping pose no threat to nonhunters who can enjoy the same resources. Hunters don't go on hiking trails and shoot guns to harass hikers, but the sound of gunshots in the distance can be annoying to nonhunters. Animal rights activists nevertheless have no right to unlawfully harass hunters on public lands as has happened. Hunters have shown admirable restraint toward such harassment by anti-hunter activists.

Hunters find great satisfaction in the roles they play with nature by preserving the basic population, managing a sustained form of production and utilizing some of the natural recruitment of offspring. When game animals of managed populations are sacrificed for a hunter's pleasure, such action usually then makes it possible for others of that species to live. Hunters harvest selectively and support insurance of a sustained yield. Laws regulate the seasons, set quotas, close seasons when necessary and regulate the methodology used in taking game and the care and disposal of the animal's byproducts. However, even though hunters are part of nature, they still do not have a license to inflict unnecessary distress; hunters should make their tools as humane as they can. Hunters and trappers often assist nature in modified environments by harvesting the surplus that otherwise would damage the environment and the species' own welfare.

Interestingly, most people condone the brazen brutality of nature's predators cruelly feeding upon helpless prey, yet cannot defend their nonhunting philosophy. They object to hunters humanizing the predator, even when the increased exposure of a prey species to natural predators is the consequence of the environment having been modified.

Sport hunting has played a significant role in bringing about substantial increases in many species of wildlife that were headed toward extinction. For example, in 1920 the wood duck was nearly extinct and now it is the most common breeding waterfowl in the eastern United States. In 1935 there were only 73 trumpeter swans; now there are more than 16,000. Around a century ago only about 12,000 pronghorn antelope remained, whereas there are now over 1 million. In the early 1900s there were fewer than 500,000 white-tailed deer while today's population approaches 20 million. In 1907 Rocky Mountain and Roosevelt elk were down to about 41,000, whereas now there are more than 800,000. Most dramatic of all, wild turkeys were nearly extinct in 1890 but now there are between 4 and 5 million and they have become a game bird in many states. It was once estimated that fewer than 1,000 American bison (buffalo) remained, including both captive and free animals, whereas today there are over 120,000, the limiting factor being availability of suitable range to support more. Since buffalo steaks are becoming common, the breed now is even more secure.

Hunters today provide a sustainable use of wildlife populations and habitat preservation through conservative hunting. They produce a utilizable population increase by protecting or conserving the basic breeding stock. Use and preservation are inseparably intertwined. Depending on many external factors, the ratio of the level of use and the basic population may change from year to year. When the authority for the take of animals is flexible, hunting and trapping can have a compensatory effect on population density.

It may be difficult to appreciate the humaneness of wildlife management or the harvest or the regulation of these animal populations through hunting and trapping. Yet public opposition seems to come primarily from vested interests, personal philosophy or emotion, rather than being based on biological facts and sound reasoning. Many game species would be extinct or nearly so, if sportsmen's organizations had not saved them.

When wildlife exceed the carrying capacity, as they frequently do, the excess animals will die. The greatest impact on wildlife comes from the effects of urbanization, roads, boating, water-skiing, camping, hiking, picnicking and other human social activities. Regulated hunting, trapping and fishing on the other hand actually produce much less, if any, negative impact on wildlife.

Deer management in many states is now governed too much by politicians and judges, rather than by biologists supporting both the best interests of the game and resource conservation. Consequently, each year a number of deer herds suffer tragically from starvation and disease. In some states a great many more game animals are killed by cars than by hunters. Female deer as well as bucks must be harvested just like natural predators do in nature. The ones that most often do not survive in nature are the young of both sexes.

Now that hunting and trapping are regulated in North America, Europe and most other parts of the world, most desired species and their habitats are sustained and protected. Many species of birds and mammals have survived surprisingly well in North America, primarily because they are game species.

Hunting accidents, although uncommon, receive an unfair amount of publicity. They are uncommon. More deaths occur from fishing than from hunting, but of course more people fish than hunt. Accidents related to hunting are about 8 per 100,000 participants, whereas it is 104 with golf and over 2,000 with both baseball and football. The accidental death rate for hunters is 0.82 per 100,000, whereas the death rate from accidents in homes is 8.6 and 18.6 from automobiles. The National Safety Council says hunting has fewer injuries (7.06 per 100,000) than participating in football (3,313 per 100,000). Ping-pong averages twice as many injuries as hunters. The main reason hunting accidents occur so infrequently is that most states require the applicant to complete safety courses before a hunting license is issued.

In contrast to wild species in nature, most people show great respect for the animals they kill. And hunters have proven they will support conservation and self-regulation when game species are threatened with loss of habitat or other factors threatening their continued existence. If the endangered whooping crane had been declared a game animal 50 years ago, hunters would have closed the hunting seasons until the populations had recovered, which would have made them common today.

Sometimes hunters do not respond quickly enough politically. They and the wildlife profession were slow in pushing for adoption of the current less toxic shot regulations for the hunting of waterfowl to eliminate lead poison hazards to game birds and their predators, including bald eagles. The wildlife profession should have regulated itself sooner by responding to this deadly waterfowl hazard in which lead shot is ingested or embedded in the birds' flesh. When such delays occur, there is a danger that Congress will impose restrictions and that the professionals will not be respected and will lose control of the outcomes.

A concern voiced by some environmental groups is that wildlife managers do tend to manage for "artificially" high populations of some animals to benefit hunting, even though such management may also be beneficial to many nongame species. I applaud the sincerity of these groups, but as long as the take by sportsmen is regulated, destructive artificially high populations do not develop. This is easier to recognize by comparing the sporadic planting of fish done to increase the take throughout the season in locations where the habitat cannot produce a bountiful supply, such as trout in the Sierra Nevada Mountains. Whenever fish are caught or game taken, space becomes available for additional individuals, whether supplied naturally or artificially. Wildlife managers are often politically forced to let game species overpopulate.

Deer herds are a good example. When they greatly exceed the carrying capacity of their habitats, the survival rate of fawns may be very low. Also, the adults often succumb to starvation and disease or become a local pest and greatly overbrowse their habitat. Research has shown that nearly all does have twin fetuses following mating, but in areas where the vegetation is overbrowsed or predation exceptionally high, the average fawn crop may be as low as ¼ fawn per doe. However, in a healthy herd it may average 1½ fawns per doe. For example, in an overpopulated herd of 50 does, where only about 12 fawns would survive, if the herd had been reduced to, say 30 does, these fewer does might then produce 1½ fawns each, or 45 fawns. The "missing" fawns either die before they are born or soon after birth from malnutrition and/or diseases of their mothers. Sometimes the mortality is from excessive predation by coyotes, mountain lions or other predators.

Due to regulations, we now have little fear of hunter overkill. No species is going to be depleted by hunting, but prolonged trophy hunting may cause a loss of desirable genetic (trophy) traits. Mounting evidence seems to indicate that harvesting the largest animals, whether it be fish or big game, may be causing "contemporary evolution," i.e., forcing genetic changes that result in smaller racks in, for example, deer, elk, bighorns and smaller fish when only the large ones are kept. As Donald Walker, a professor of biology and environmental studies at the University of Wisconsin illustrates, the Atlantic cod populations around southern Labrador and Newfoundland's Grand Banks plummeted about 99.9 percent between the early 1960s and the early 1990s. The remaining cod are smaller, mature at a younger age, spawn much earlier and yield weaker offspring than they used to.

Some care is needed to preserve desirable bloodlines of genetic diversity to continuously produce trophy animals, although nutrition is usually the key to large ungulate racks in wild populations. When a trophy hunter bags an old buck on stag, it usually occurs after that season's breeding period. One might think that old stags should probably be removed anyway to reduce inbreeding and that trophy animals have had ample time to breed and pass on their genes during their lifetime. But evidence indicates such a Darwinian shift in our selection of size of animals could have unwanted consequences.

Game trophies enhance the awareness of and appreciation for these great animals. Trophy hunting is not a frivolous, wanton pleasure of the rich, for every hunter has an equal opportunity and is overjoyed if he or she can take a trophy animal. Financially, trophy hunters contribute significantly toward the preservation of native habitats.

For wildlife conservation to succeed in developing countries, people who live in or near protected areas must receive benefits that offset the costs of their having less access to natural resources. International trophy hunting must be properly managed to generate significant economic benefits for residents of game management areas (Lewis and Alpert 1997). These authors recommend an international system of certification for trophy-hunting operations.

Hunters do their best to achieve clean kills to ensure recovery of the prey. Anyone with first-hand experience observing the feeding behavior of predators in nature will certainly understand the difference between killing by predators and killing by hunters. Unfortunately, both ways sometimes only wound the prey.

How about bowhunting? Is it cruel? The Fund for Animals claims that 80 percent of deer shot with an arrow are wounded and die later. This statement has no data to support it. The data show that nonlethal broadhead wounds are quite clean, free of contusion and normally, but not always, heal without complications. Studies show that puncture wounds in male deer and bull elk resulting from fighting are common; they often receive 20-30 such wounds per year.

Some states have difficulty passing laws that permit bear or mountain lion (cougar) hunters to use dogs. Nonhunters sometimes condemn shooting a treed bear. A state wildlife organization's director once publicly claimed that it was "morally" wrong to shoot a bear in a tree. This occurred shortly after his department had produced a 483-page environmental report confirming that good science and biological data were used when they recommended the use of hounds as an acceptable wildlife management option to regulate bear numbers. This shows how easy it is to become emotionally aroused.

In the rugged mountains of California, bear or lion hunting with hounds is probably the most strenuous of all hunting sports: a pack of excited predators, the dogs, pursue another predator, a bear. Bears have learned how to flee from natural predators, although many bears are killed when they fail to escape from dominant bears or other tree-climbing predators like mountain lions (puma, cougar). Using bear or lion hounds is like using dogs to hunt pheasants, quail and other game, except it is more strenuous. If a bear or lion cannot elude the dogs, it climbs a tree, where it thinks it is safe from the predators howling below.

Eventually, the exhausted hunters reach the scene of the howling dogs. Instead of having to take a quick shot at a fleeing bear or lion and possibly only wounding it, they have time to assess the prey to see whether it is pregnant or nursing. For many reasons they may leave it alone. Sometimes for the hunter, especially if only training the dogs, the chase is then over. But if the bear is to be bagged, a well-placed clean shot or arrow can then kill it. No other game animals are taken so humanely. The bear's or lion's death also means another bear or lion now has territorial space available. Under natural conditions, few bears or lions become very old.

Hunters with dogs account for two-thirds of bears taken in California, which has a healthy population of between 17,000 and 24,000 bears. In some states it is not possible to adequately harvest bears to keep them from overpopulating.

When bear numbers exceed the carrying capacity of their territory, many will be forced to leave the area. That's when they create problems for people. The quality of life for excessive numbers of bears deteriorates rapidly when the population exceeds a healthy density. Disease, starvation, territoriality and cannibalism become more pronounced. As public affection for these large charismatic predators continues, we must not lose sight of the fact that these animals are always potentially dangerous. They are, after all, *wild* animals. We may one day see the pendulum swing the other way if there are human injuries or death resulting from encounters with bears and other predators. Proper wildlife population balances are hard to achieve politically.

Except for professional wildlifers, few people may realize it was people who like to fish and hunt that originally saved the American wilderness. Between 1901 and 1909, President Theodore Roosevelt, with support from hunters, protected 230,000,000 acres of the United States' most majestic wildlands by designating 150 national forests and grasslands, 51 national wildlife refuges, 4 national game preserves and 5 national parks. Now, conservation organizations are also helping. For every dollar the government spends on wildlife programs in the United States, 75 cents comes from sportsmen.

In a balanced ecosystem, the species in surplus must be harvested each year, one way or another, on a sustained basis. In modified environments, people provide this needed service through hunting and fishing. States with wildlife management programs that include intensive hunting have dramatically improved the health of deer and other game populations. Even though wetlands are in short supply in North America, the conservation of wetlands would have fared much worse without waterfowl hunters and organizations like Ducks Unlimited.

Most nonhunters do not understand the difference between hunting at a well-managed commercial hunting resort and open hunting on public or private farms or timberland. A private landowner who charges an access fee for upland game hunting will leave the cover needed to support many birds after crops are harvested. Private shooting preserves also do this. Commercial hunting preserves include good wildlife habitat and escape cover, thus making the hunting experience more challenging. Shooting preserves have evolved past the days when many only charged for dead birds bagged. That didn't seem like good sportsmanship. In game preserves the ring-necked pheasants, chukar partridges and other exotic birds are regularly restocked as needed to increase the total take by hunters, just as is often done with fish.

The U.S. National Wildlife Refuge System, a federal land system managed primarily for the benefit of wildlife, had its origins in 1869 with the Pribilof Reservation off Alaska to protect the northern fur seal

However, federal wildlife refuges were not officially created until 1903. President Theodore Roosevelt, a hunter, established 2.5-acre Pelican Island in Florida as the first national wildlife refuge to stop market hunters from devastating the breeding populations of brown pelicans, white ibises, egrets, herons and other species exploited to supply plumes to the fashion trade. Now more than 500 refuges cover almost 4 percent of the United States—more than that of the National Park Service.

In contrast to national parks, refuges were originally established to provide a protected area for wildlife, with other compatible uses being secondary. Livestock grazing was often permitted as a concession to purchase the land and many wildlife managers consider proper grazing as beneficial to some wildlife species. Hunting became ensconced in refuges in 1949. Legislation raised the Duck Stamp charge to hunters from one to two dollars and opened 25 percent of the refuges to hunting (Curtin 1993). An amendment in 1958 increased the open area to 40 percent. These moves provided more hunter support and funding for refuges. Even though refuges are to be managed on biological grounds, according to Curtin, a 1989 General Accounting Office report states that harmful activities were occurring on 60 percent of the refuges, indicating that real problems still exist. Many anti-hunting groups oppose hunting on refuges.

Is it ethical for hunters not to offer humane assistance to wildlife? Where do we draw the line? For example, when weather conditions cause pronghorn antelope or deer to starve, as happens periodically in deep snow, someone must decide whether we should interfere with nature and feed them, let them die naturally or have the surplus taken by hunters. In contrast to hunting, feeding starving deer frequently creates worse problems later on.

When should we mercifully apply euthanasia to suffering animals? I believe we have an obligation to prevent needless suffering when we can. But we should do so only after careful analysis of the long-range consequences to the ecosystem.

Trappers, hunters and fishermen will inevitably cause some distress to animals, but unlike in the natural world sportsmen do what they can to avoid inflicting unnecessary cruelty upon their prey. Even trappers and people who love to wear fur oppose furbearers being unnecessarily mistreated. In sharp contrast to natural predators, trappers show compassion toward prey species. Most trappers, like hunters, love the outdoors and the species they take. They do not want to cause any more distress to the furbearers in the way they are taken than is necessary.

The primary goal of better management practices for trapping furbearers is to improve the welfare of individual animals caught in traps, not just to improve traps and trapping. There are many benefits derived from trapping animals—protecting migratory species, providing cultural and subsistence uses of wildlife, protecting wildlife habitat, providing economic and lifestyle benefits to native and rural people, enhancing wildlife populations, controlling unwanted predation and producing valuable fur.

Trap and fur organizations have donated considerable funds to developing more humane catching devices because many sportsmen and rural people believe it is morally and ethically correct for society to trap animals and to wear fur, as long as the animals are treated as humanely as trapping technology permits. In contrast, opponent organizations flatly refuse to fund any humaneness gestures because they detest traps. Also, they do not fund animal welfare activities, except for some support in neutering feral cats.

Of course no furbearer enjoys being caught in a trap and such trauma should be minimized as much as possible. Animals may suffer more traumas captured in a live trap than in a modern soft-catch leghold trap. Furthermore, furbearers may suffer far more when short of food, sick, being attacked by another predator or involved in a lethal territorial battle. Natural deaths are nearly always ugly and horrible and are usually much worse than being trapped. Of course, the fact that leghold traps may not be as cruel as nature does not in itself justify the use of traps if such distress can be avoided.

The controversy about the leghold (foothold) animal trap and the wearing of fur is widespread, especially in Europe and North America. Lobbying against leghold traps and wearing fur has been fierce. In contrast little has been written to justify this method of taking furbearers and of recycling their skins. Thus in October 1983, Europe banned the import of white-coat seal pelts because the animals were being clubbed to death, even though this method causes instant unconsciousness.

The European Union has tried (may have succeeded) to ban all imports of fur from any country that uses leghold traps. About 70 percent of America's fur ends up in Europe. However, European countries that need traps to control muskrats and nutria (a South American muskrat-like rodent now in the United States) are making exceptions for the control of these troublesome animals. The pressure to give in to animal rightists and ban leghold traps is too great when there is no fur trade or any serious furbearer pest to serve as a counterbalance.

It is hypocritical for a European country to ban the importation of fur when they sanction trapping of pest muskrats, nutria and European lynx. In 1990, leghold traps were banned only in the United Kingdom, Ireland, Germany, Denmark and Greece. The United Kingdom used them until they had resolved their problem with nutria, muskrat and mink. As of 1998, Holland was using $35 million per year of taxpayers' money to trap and discard muskrats.

Leghold traps are relatively inexpensive and quite efficient for catching furbearers and these traps are easier to transport than bulky live traps. However, older models of leghold traps do have a history of causing injuries including loss of the trapped foot, especially when an inexperienced trapper uses too large a trap without a tension spring. Trapped animals also experience pain when a predator attacks them or when a trap causes a broken bone, flesh cuts or abrasions, which still happens. But it is not nearly as common as it was with previous traps.

The International Standards Organization (ISO TC191) from 13 countries has been trying to develop humane animal killing and restraining devices since 1987. The American National Standards Institute is the United States member to ISO and it gets advice from technical advisory groups (TAGs), which include members of the American Veterinary Medical Association, animal welfare organizations, conservation groups, trap manufacturers and academia.

A fur trapper must check his traps frequently or risk losing his catch or having fur quality damaged by predators and scavengers. Regulations now govern the size of traps to be used for different species as well as where and how leghold and conibear (instant-kill, body-gripping) traps are set in order to provide humaneness and species selectivity. Spring-mounted anchor chains and drags must be used to provide some give when trapped animals try to escape. Conibear kill-traps are probably more humane whenever they can be used. Since they kill any subject, nontarget animals cannot be released as can be done with leghold traps.

The out-of-date and outlawed, jagged-tooth, nonoffset steel-jawed leghold trap probably earned more money for opponents to traps than it ever did trappers. These traps were often used in highly emotionally staged photographs even after they were no longer being used in America.

Whether a furbearer or an unwanted predator, all animals taken by trappers are regulated by bag limits, seasons of harvest, open and closed zones and other considerations. The financial support provided by trappers further assures careful monitoring of the welfare of furbearers and actions by trappers to ensure healthy, sustainable populations. Capture regulations may specify types of traps and snares, size of trap, offset jaws, padded jaws, frequency of visitation by trappers, placement, location and type of baits or attractants used. All of these regulations are intended to improve the selectivity of the species trapped and to increase humaneness.

The question shouldn't be whether leghold traps ought to be banned but, rather, what are the most effective and humane ways that different species of furbearers can be managed? If a government wildlife agency wants to reintroduce foxes, coyotes, wolves, mink or other furbearers into a habitat that has recently been made suitable for the species, they would probably use soft-catch leghold traps to capture the needed breeding stock to be translocated. Research workers also commonly use these traps, where they are still legal, in capture-mark-release studies. Many species, including dogs and cats, if captured with the newer leghold padded soft-catch, offset-jaws and tension-trigger traps, receive little injury. Much research continues in an effort to further enhance their humaneness and effectiveness.

Fur is a renewable natural resource and has been used traditionally by humans for clothing throughout time. Killing by trappers and hunters is not immoral, as any experienced naturalist understands. A trapper's relationship with animals is one of respect and conservation, as pointed out in a book by Herscovici (1985) on fur trapping and related animal rights activities. We need to build a better relationship with nature, similar to native peoples and those who trap for a livelihood.

Traps and snares help maintain healthy and productive wildlife populations by reducing competition for food and cover among the trapped species and by protecting desirable habitats from destruction and deterioration. Other benefits of trapping include damage control, removal of nuisance animals, economic and lifestyle benefits to rural people, controlling unwanted predation, protecting endangered species, providing subsistence and cultural use of wildlife by indigenous people and for research and disease mitigation to prevent outbreaks of serious animal and human diseases. Plague, for example, is usually a consequence of an unnaturally high population of key rodent species. Similarly, rabies is associated with excessive populations of skunks, foxes or raccoons.

Management agencies are sometimes criticized for insufficient knowledge of furbearers to ensure maintenance of healthy populations. Any wildlife species that has economic value in the United States will reap the benefits of money from license fees and taxes on equipment to hire biologists for research and wardens to police game laws.

Modern wildlife management strives to achieve a healthy balance between prey and predators—whether human or animal. If the breeding potential of a species declines due to fewer females, a reduced take is employed to reestablish maximum productivity. Overharvesting of furbearers is seldom a serious problem that cannot be easily corrected. In modified environments overharvesting is more common because there is no longer a predator-prey balance. As a consequence of careful wildlife management practices since the 1930s, the number of furbearers trapped in North America remains high yet sustainable. Indeed, there are so few people in most of Canada and the price of fur is so low that many furbearer populations go underharvested.

Traps and snares are essential to help landowners protect livestock, poultry and pets from carnivores, to prevent floods when beaver dams threaten a waterway and for other public health and safety reasons, whether or not removal of these animals provides only temporary relief. With some species, live-catch cage traps can be used. Reinvasion by pests into favorable habitats is a recurring problem.

Ranched fur-animals do not die just for vanity nor fur alone. For example, from mink an oil is obtained that is an ingredient used in hypoallergenic soaps, hair products and cosmetics. At the same time, fur fashion is the only guarantee that many furbearers will be born to live a quality life and eventually have the luxury to die humanely. Without fur markets there would be far fewer ranched furbearers.

On fur farms the animals are born only because their fur is wanted, not to eventually serve as food for other wild animals as in nature. About 60 to 80 percent of fur garments come from ranched furbearers raised for this purpose, while the remaining furbearers are trapped in the wild. Many wild furbearer populations, such as muskrats and mink, would not fare nearly as well in modified environments if they were not being harvested. If their fur had not been wanted, some species of furbearers would probably be extinct or nearly so. There is no moral difference between fur, leather, down or wool, all from animals, but some people object to using any part of animals.

Most species of furbearers, such as sable, mink, fur seal and otter, are appreciated for their luxurious fur, the dense understory of silky fur fiber, which is truly exquisite in some species. Everyone loves its feel and likes to rub such fur against their face and to stroke a fur piece. Synthetic fur is not the same. Not only is fur an excellent insulator, but also in some climates it is a necessary garment for people to survive harsh climates.

Trapping may be considered cruel by some, but rearing genetic strains of domesticated furbearers on fur ranches is no different than raising livestock or pets. Farm fur animals die humanely without prolonged distress, something their wild counterparts never experience naturally. Furbearers on fur farms are killed by methods approved by the American Veterinary Association—lethal injection, carbon monoxide or dioxide bottled gas. These are the same methods used by animal shelters.

The animal rights movement has had a positive effect by making people more conscious of the welfare of animals, but on the negative side they have moved quite successfully toward their goal of eliminating trapping altogether and making fur seem vulgar and symbols of someone who is tasteless and uneducated. In addition to trying to make wearing fur unfashionable, they are striving for legislative mandates against trapping. The public should realize that these same people also object to any use of fur no matter how humanely the animals are handled. Many bills have been introduced and passed in different states banning the use of leghold traps. Animal rights activists also seek "conscience" donations for their cause that rarely help animals. In reality most farmed furbearers live a good life, even though they may eventually become a fur coat.

The counter argument that supports the wearing of fur is that furs are natural products and such recycling is what nature is all about. It is really wonderful for the welfare of people that mink, foxes, beaver and other furbearers produce such a valuable and useful product. We can't shear furbearers as we do sheep, for fur needs to be attached to a skin, but even sheep must also eventually be killed. Some substitutes for real fur have the undesirable trade-off of exploiting the earth's finite supply of petroleum.

Fur protests have a long history. Current protests can be traced to a 1965 film, *Les Phoques de la Banquise*, by the Artek Film Company that showed men clubbing harp seal pups and reflexive postmortem spasms. Organizations saw a chance to create a lucrative movement if fur animals were made socially unacceptable. Attacks on the consumer market are still occurring in 2004, but on a much-reduced scale.

A similar objection to wearing fur has been claimed regarding animals raised on fur farms. With rare exceptions, such animals live a quality life and die "relatively" humanely. If set free, fur-ranched animals attempt to return to their origins, as happened in England when animal rightists commandos "liberated" 1,200 mink from what they called a "concentration camp" and again in the state of Oregon in 1997 when about 9,000 ranch mink were cruelly released illegally. These incidents show that some people who claim to have animals' best interests at heart do not necessarily understand nature sufficiently to see the big picture.

Ecologists know that natural predation is necessary to maintain healthy population densities of the prey species. Regulated predation by human hunters and trappers can be an essential tool in maintaining healthy populations of predators, game and fur animals in modified environments. Any student of nature is surely aware of just how violent nature really is.

Wildlife conservation is being hurt by extreme environmental and animal rights groups to the detriment of wildlife. Those who claim killing animals is morally wrong ignore the biological principles involved and usually won't detail how they want animals to die. These groups have effectively propagandized the public into believing hunters, fur trappers and fishermen are driving some wildlife resources to extinction. Nothing could be further from the truth.

Nature is composed of populations. The single animal, which often needs to be controlled, is biologically unimportant. The loss of a few individuals is insignificant. It is therefore morally correct to be inhumane to some individual animals if such action saves entire populations of that species. In modified environments it is primarily through man's consumptive acts of hunting and trapping that healthy reproducing populations and more desirable animal and plant communities can be preserved—which are the objectives of various government game departments. The regulation of population densities by hunting, trapping and fishing requires biologically sound discretion.

Humans have a near phobia of death, treating voluntary human deaths as obscene and illegal. This attitude has been applied to wild animals as well. What is needed is a healthy life-death ethic, with a deep ecological and moral conscience that appreciates the glory of death in nature. The death of some individual animals means an increased likelihood of an improved quality life for others within that species. Nature demands a death ethic. Biotic pyramids consist of food chains in which all animals feed on other organisms and, in turn, are usually eaten. People can humanize this recycling in modified environments and help nature by removing some of the surplus individuals.

My goal has not been to convince you that you should wear fur. That is your choice. Instead, my goal is to defend the right of others to do so and to show how using fur actually benefits furbearers. Wearing fur has been emotionalized intentionally by the animal rights movement to discourage use of animals no matter how humanely they are treated and how beneficial it may be to the species of furbearer.

This chapter has shown how there are no biological bases for opposing regulated hunting and trapping, only personal ones. It explains how hunters and trappers can humanize nature in modified environments by managing the density of game and furbearers, not to increase beyond the habitat's carrying capacity for the species. Philosophically, trapping has much in common with the principles of hunting. Critics of trapping are not after humaneness. They simply do not want any animal to be captured. Both hunting and trapping are legitimate activities that help preserve game species while at the same time benefiting humankind.

# CHAPTER 5

# Agriculture and Domestic Animals

The United States has changed from a system employing 10 million farmers and farm workers, with each farmer feeding 5 people, to a system in which only 2.1 million farmers each feed more than 100 people and also support exports of more than $35 billion annually (Weber et al. 1995). Human starvation and malnutrition are not widespread in the United States and other developed countries, in contrast to developing countries. A major explanation for this nutritional disparity is that food production is greatest where it is done to make money, not just to feed empty stomachs. Rice, wheat and corn provide about half of the calories people consume.

Domestic animals are bred, raised and managed for many purposes. Fortunately, in this country domestic livestock are generally used "responsibly." Today farmers do not mistreat livestock as much as some parents mistreat their children or their pets. In contrast to wild animals, domestic animals are not permitted to fight voluntarily, which in breeding rituals or in defense of their territory may even lead to the death of wild animals.

Farmers recognize that it would help if the raising of chickens, cattle and pigs could be freed to some extent from the economic restrictions of confined factory farming. But the public does not want the marked increases in food prices that would be required to satisfy animal welfare requirements. Also, such price increases would impose an unfair financial burden on the poor. Some form of factory farming seems to be a must, primarily because of the high human population.

In modern civilizations people no longer think of animals as being property, to be used or abused as they see fit. Formerly, it was true that how animals were treated was sometimes just an afterthought. Not too long ago, to survive economically, farmers were compelled to develop husbandry systems of extreme confinement in response to the public's desire for farmers to produce food as cheaply as possible. Only recently has it been fully recognized by most livestock operators that husbandry practices should not come at the expense of the animal's quality of life. Consequently, responsible stockmanship is now the order of the day. Farmers recognize that intensive management strategies are often still required to keep the cost of animal-based food and products at an acceptable level.

Operators of husbandry systems for poultry and livestock are now trying to come to grips with the need to embrace wider aspects of animal welfare, especially the prevention of behavioral problems of confined domestic animals. Consequently, today about the only animals which live a healthy, humane life and have a long life are the ones society exploits. Is it wrong for lambs, calves, piglets and chicks—for that matter, also horses, dogs, cats, furbearers and laboratory animals—to be born and have a protected healthy life with humane care and treatment, just because most of them may die prematurely and none of them are ever allowed to run free? Actually, a higher percentage of young animals die in nature than occur with domestic livestock.

Domesticated species are genetically programmed to depend upon humans for their existence. They have no conscious idea how their wild counterparts live or ever lived. As a result of animals' association with man, they are freed of many of the brutal and cruel constraints that otherwise keep the density of animal populations in check. They are largely protected from hunger, exposure to unfavorable weather, disease, enemies, cannibalism and intraspecific strife (of the animals). Compare the life of most domesticated species and of animals born in a zoo with those living in the wild, where daily they face many natural hazards, hence usually have a short life.

Domestic animals generally will not survive if set free. If people no longer exploited domestic animals, not counting about 10 billion chickens, perhaps 7 billion or so of others would not be born each year in America, to have a fairly good, even if short, life. Even in a modern chicken factory, chickens usually live longer than many of their wild ancestors, where natural mortality shortly following birth, or while still immature, is high. It may come as a surprise, but if the welfare of an animal is measured by whether or not it can breed, have a healthy, relatively long life with a low disease incidence, have a nutritious diet and be protected from the problems of living free, then surely most domestic animals enjoy a fairly high standard of welfare. Such animals are treated well, even if eventually sacrificed for human consumption or for other uses, instead of being eaten by a predator or dying of disease or starvation.

Farm animals should always be assured the freedom to stand and lie down, to extend their wings or legs and to make other normal posture adjustments. This has not always been possible. Where this does not now occur, changes must be made to insure that proper methods of confinement are used. Also, domestic animals should be assured an adequate supply of nutritious food, proper veterinary care and an environment that suits their physical and behavioral requirements. Thanks in part to the animal rights movement, this is now the usual treatment. However, we must remember, we cannot compare these animals with wild animals when considering their behavior or space requirements. Domestic animals are genetically and behaviorally different.

Ranchers know that if they take good care of their livestock and provide their basic behavioral and physical needs, that the animals will take care of their owners. A livestock producer serves many of the functions of a natural predator, only better, because he or she can regulate the number of individuals taken, depending upon many factors, and can also control the age and sex ratio of the "prey." In contrast to natural predators, livestock owners must operate under many humane regulations. They also show compassion toward their prey, unlike predators in nature.

Compared to the natural world, practically all domestic animals now live a fairly good life, free of nature's survival-of-the-fittest struggle that wild animals constantly face. Most domestic animals— being behaviorally and genetically different from their wild ancestors—could not survive in the wild. How far genetic engineering will proceed in the future with livestock is unknown, but it is rapidly following plant-breeding programs that are designed to improve crops.

Examples of poor livestock management, that may sometimes still exist, include rough handling, abuse of nonambulatory (downer) animals, transport of day-old Holstein calves and overloading of trucks (Grandin 1994). A few livestock auction yards may still need to improve their handling of sick animals, especially calves. Overgrazing by livestock is no longer the problem it once was.

Both America's culture and economy need livestock grazing, but the question is: How do we protect livestock grazing and at the same time also protect native ecosystems and the native fauna and flora?

More importantly, the fight is over grazing on public land, not private land. Obviously, something has to give, as grazing public lands is not compatible without compromises. But such compromising does not have to be as severe as accommodating for homes, cities, agriculture, timber production, fish, marine food, highways or converting it all into parks and refuges. However, it is näive to think that grazing public lands can leave them as they would have been without grazing. And it is not easy to identify which land is "suitable" for compromised grazing and which is not. The decision is difficult, as cities and agriculture for the most part have already claimed all the best land, richest in soil structure and plant production.

The guiding principle for administering public grazing lands should include conservation, restoration and maintenance of as much of the natural biological diversity as is feasible. Because of the established grazing leases and permits, pressure is being exerted to get the cattlemen to voluntarily relinquish their permits for just compensation. But this is difficult for those ranchers who for several generations have been operating under these leases. Understandably, they don't want to sell.

Livestock producers usually maintain their animals within a range of conditions that emphasize efficient performance and good health (Hahn and Morrow-Tesch 1993). Producers welcome new information that helps define how animals respond to environmental conditions and also improve proactive decision-making for managing their animals. However, they naturally follow the essential elements that ensure economic viability of their livestock enterprise.

Current research focuses on obtaining information about animals concerning which sort of environment best suits their well-being, considering such factors as space, noise, light, heat and odors. Livestock are now being trained to control certain aspects of their environment by being rewarded for the behavioral choice they select (operant conditioning techniques) regarding how they are handled, so as to indicate which procedure provides the least stress for them. Much progress is being made toward improving the welfare of animals and much credit for awareness of these needs goes to the animal rights movement, which has caused the process to speed up.

An important question for some, concerning livestock, is this: Should any animal be humanely slaughtered if it is no longer usable for other purposes or when it reaches the right age to be eaten? Or should such animals be left to die naturally from starvation and/or disease as some animal rightists insist? Let's look more closely at the livestock industry.

The instant unconsciousness resulting from a blow to the head of livestock is now often replaced by a gun that delivers the deathblow to the forehead or above the ear. (USDA banned the use of air guns in 2004 because of the medical concerns of blood from the brain traveling to muscle tissue.) The cylinder that is shot retracts back into the .22-powered pistol. In domestic stock-slaughtering operations, the brain-dead, unconscious animals are quickly suspended head-down and both arteries and veins in neck are severed. This is the most humane method of slaughtering domestic animals according to the American Veterinary Medical

Association, which based acceptability of methods of euthanizing animals with drugs and mechanical devices after considering pain, animal reflexes, human safety and vocalization that may cause distress to observers.

Please note that in the above paragraph I use the term euthanizing instead of killing. As stated earlier, people are more comfortable in "killing" pests and game, but prefer to "euthanize" their pet dog or livestock.

The National Cattlemen's Association considers the cow as Mother Nature's recycling machineSince 25 percent of food processing byproducts—such as sugar beet pulp, potato skins, almond hulls, fruit pits, cottonseed and grape skins from juice and wine production—are fed to cattle, they certainly ease landfill problems. Actually, 85 percent of what cattle eat is material that people cannot digest, such as range plants, corn stalks and wheat straw. Industrialized agriculture nearly always consumes more energy than it produces, thus surviving at the expense of capital in the form of fossil fuels. But for range plants, the sun provides the energy for those plants consumed by livestock.

Cattle provide us with protein; chemicals such as calcium, iron and zinc; vitamin A and the important vitamin B-12, which is not found in fruit or vegetables. It has been medically shown that a vitamin B-12 deficiency can impair one's ability to reason and can even cause irritability. Women, children, the aged and some ill persons are at greater risk if placed on restrictive "vegan" diets. Only in recent historical times have people had the opportunity to become vegetarians, if they wanted to. Most former societies had to rely on fish and/or red meat being available.

Many people are not aware that nowhere in the world can the food, that even vegetarians require, be grown without also controlling most of the native mammals and many species of birds to protect the crops. Also, are we supposed to make our cats and dogs become vegetarians and how do we justify killing animals to make pet food? If you accept "veganism," which is the complete avoidance of any use of animal products, billions of domestic animals would not be born each year to live a good life.

From cattle in addition to beef, people utilize the liver, brains, tripe, milk, hides and, to name some other benefits derived from cattle, they make sausage, butter, cheese, yogurt and ice cream. The nasal septum of slaughtered cows is processed to make chondritin sulfate, which I take along with glucosomine, because I lost meniscus cartilage in both knees due to mountain climbing for a year in New Zealand. Many important animal foods used by Americans come from cows, pigs, sheep, chickens, turkeys, tuna, salmon, flounder, cod, shrimp and oysters, to name some species. Even most vegetarians, to keep healthy, eat fish, poultry, eggs and dairy products.

Veal has received even harsher criticism, some justified, than other meat products. Examples of nonreputable veal production have occurred, but often they have been exaggerated to include the entire veal industry. However, the use of the illegal drug clenbuterol was used in veal-calf premises by some in the industry.

If you oppose eating veal, you must want practically all the male dairy calves killed at birth, since very few bulls are needed in breeding dairy cattle. A report conducted at University of California-Davis, School of Veterinary Medicine Cooperative Extension, for the California Legislature examined the treatment of 550 bull calves at 10 commercial special-fed veal facilities (Stull and McMartin 1992). The six principal issues categorized in this research were environment, housing, diet, health, stress and behavior. Nine of the ten facilities used indoor individual stalls, from 19-22 inches wide. Three of these did not tether calves for the first fifteen days, while six tethered the calves upon arrival. The tenth facility utilized indoor group pens, each housing 30 calves, which were previously housed in outdoor individual hutches until 8 weeks of age.

All facilities had functional supplemental lighting, with 6 of the 10 having natural light available. None attempted to incorporate darkness. The 19 to 22-inch width of stalls was found to be adequate for turning around and lying down for calves between 350-400 pounds. Nine facilities utilized diets consisting of liquid milk replacer throughout the complete production cycle. One facility provided a diet of grain along with milk replacer; this facility had a lower average daily gain as compared to those using only milk replacer diets. No medical evidence was detected of increased respiration rate, decreased rate of gain in growth or enlarged heart chamber size due to marginal anemia that was found in 10 percent of the calves. Data obtained from stress parameters (including serum cortisol levels, neutrophil: lymphocyte ratio and abomasal pathological changes) indicated the practice of housing and tethering calves in individual stalls was not stressful.

Data collected from 24 hours of videotaping demonstrated that calves in both individual stalls and group pens spent approximately 25 and 75 percent of total time standing or lying, respectively. The tether did not appear to be a significant stressor and it was concluded that the management practices of tethering calves in individual stalls are not stressful or harmful to calves.

With industrial pig farming there are real problems with getting rid of their wastes. Concerning modern pig farms: Is a domestic sow better off if she can build her own nest for her piglets outdoors, but then lose many of them to weather or to a predator, than if she is confined in an enclosure where she is warm, dry, healthy and loses very few of her piglets? Branding and dehorning of cattle is like the vaccination of children: Both cause some brief discomfort but are compensated by long-term benefits.

If you want caged poultry to be able to dust themselves, you will have to first infect them with parasites so they will want to dust. Sanitation, at most poultry farms, exceeds that found at many of the world's hospital communicable-disease wards. What about debeaking chickens? Sure, they don't like it, but it causes only brief discomfort. Even free-range (barnyard) chickens also often have to be debeaked for humane reasons to prevent cannibalism and fighting. It has been shown that if laying hens are provided with perches, there is a slight beneficial increase in bone volume (Hughes et al. 1993). Caged chickens are much healthier than barnyard birds, which have a higher mortality rate due to predators, fighting, ectoparasites and diseases. Also, there is not enough open space available to satisfy the current demand for eggs and chickens, if all commercial eggs had to be produced by free-ranging chickens.

Force-feeding ducks, as done in the Orient, has been mentioned frequently as an inhumane practice. I am sure the ducks don't like it, but some people forget that these animals gorge themselves in the wild to prepare for their long migration flights. If food is available, they may gorge themselves quickly before a predator appears. Physiologically, these birds have an expandable esophagus, which allows them to store food for later digestion and they also have the ability to store fat in the liver.

In terms of the available space and treatment of farm animals, farmers generally are strongly concerned about the health and well-being of their animals, contrary to what many urbanites think. Instead of the public being given the facts about how most livestock and poultry are kept and handled, too many of their impressions result from false allegations; but, fortunately, if there are real cases of abuse, they generally get reported by the press. All farmers are not perfect, but the worst abuses of livestock usually are from the part-time farmers, often farming for tax purposes.

It is very difficult to determine the degree of suffering or pain experienced by confined animals. It is easier to identify the hazards of running free. Sometimes, what causes stress for a wild animal may not harm the well-being of an inbred domestic animal. Stress even varies among individuals, depending on their sex, age and other factors. Also, freeing chickens, cattle and pigs from being under confinement complicates the economics of intensive farming, which requires a balance of ethical as well as scientific judgments. To abandon intensive farming, farmers will need economic help to remain solvent. This is the consequence of frugal shoppers and the desire of agribusiness for profits. When the agricultural industry is depressed, farmers cannot readily change practices. Fortunately, much research is underway to determine the most humane way to factory-farm by studying such factors as size of cages and stalls, light, air conditioning and bedding.

More *economical* ways of "enriching" the environment for caged and penned animals are needed, as well as a better understanding and alleviation of pain and distress and there may still be room for improvement in transport of animals, their slaughtering and design and management of husbandry systems. The basic problem is economics, for a farmer can scarcely adopt some proposed new animal management method if it will prevent him from competing at the marketplace. If certain changes in farming practices were temporarily subsidized, farmers might then be able to raise farm animals in a more natural environment. Such changes would then come about more rapidly.

In 1988 Sweden passed a stringent animal welfare program for chickens, cattle and pigs. In 1994 they banned use of confined cages for poultry. The woman who led this crusade also wanted to stop artificial insemination of livestock because she claimed it was unfair to their sex lives. Only time will reveal how successful or really necessary some of these restrictions were.

"Fundamental changes in the way societies produce and consume are indispensable for achieving global sustainable development" (Plan of Implementation, World Summit on Sustainable Development in Johannesburg, South Africa, 2002). Yes, we are in the age of consumerism, with many resources being consumed far beyond sustainable levels and it is obvious that this cannot continue indefinitely.

Agriculture should operate on a sustainable basis, but agriculture's problem of achieving long-term sustainability, with reduced fuel input, presents an unprecedented challenge. "Environmental sustainability" includes, but is not limited to, "sustained yield." Agriculture and environmental sustainability is applied at the aggregate level to all the values of an ecosystem, not just to certain species of plants or animals (Goodland 1995).

In many parts of the world, agroforestry—the growing of trees and shrubs together with cash or food crops in a sustainable manner—is also needed due to the expanding human population. Conversion of forest to pasture seems to be a logical process for both large and small-scale owners in Latin America's lowland tropics because forestry, agriculture and agroforestry lack the mechanisms through which value can be captured (Hecht 1993). Patch clearcutting as a forest regeneration method sometimes has drawbacks, even though it does increase biological diversity and helps species like Douglas fir that do not regenerate well in the shade of other trees.

To feed the world's population, agriculture is forced to rely on genetically modified organisms (GMO plant genomics, pest control, inorganic fertilizers, agricultural chemicals and finite energy resources, such as fossil fuel. Due to modern agriculture's dependency on chemicals, there is concern that we really don't know what will happen to these substances and their possible long-term effect on people and the environment. Many synthetic pollutant chemicals have the propensity to leapfrog around the world, as has happened with DDT.

Nitrogen-based fertilizers have turned the threat of human starvation into a plentiful supply of food. But this help to feed billions of people has also poisoned ecosystems, destroyed fisheries and even killed children throughout the world. Thus, by ensuring our food supply we have wreaked havoc on our air and water. Soil scientists and agronomists are researching ways and improving the use of nitrogen in farming practices so as to increase the efficiency of nitrogen both for food production and environmental reasons. The principal causes of acid rain are the sulfur and nitrogen oxide emissions from fossil-fuel combustion by power plants and vehicles. It is livestock, more than fertilizers, that are responsible for ammonia emissions contributing to the high ratio of deposition of nitrogen in forests. Yes, agriculture needs to reduce application of excess synthetic nitrogen fertilizer.

To help feed the world and reduce the need for so many pesticides, transgenic crops (GMO, genetically modified organisms) have been developed. Lori Brown (2004) reports that the global acreage of genetically modified crops has reached 58.7 million hectares. Today, it is much more and I think that with time both Europe and Africa, for example, will be more acceptable of GMOs. However, the Royal Society in London warns that the DNA that is added to food crops could create dangerous viruses. Toxins normally found in plants at a harmless level might increase. There could be a loss of important nutrients in plants. It is also claimed that insect-resistant plants might be more likely to become invasive weeds than would the parental variety. In addition, hybridization between a transgenic crop and related noncrop plants might spread novel traits to additional species.

Long-range studies of transgenic crops are also needed, as this subject still has unknowns. The most successful transgenic gene used is from the soil organism, *Bacillus thuringiensis* (Bt), which produces a substance that is deadly to certain insects. But crops do not have to be treated with highly toxic synthetic pesticides. However, due to the added fitness, a transgenic crop variety conceivably might gain weedy characteristics, produce hybrid progeny of compatible wild or weedy related species or produce hybrid progeny that are more difficult to control. To prevent an energized crop from outcrossing, a terminator gene can be placed in plants, such as corn or soybean and if the plant sterilization trait is activated, for example in seed sold to farmers, the seed from these plants is sterile. To at least slow down development of resistance, areas (refugia) are planted as a crop variety that isn't armed with the Bt gene.

The forty-year-old Delaney Clause of the Food, Drug and Cosmetic Act was eliminated in 1996. It had banned any food that contained any trace of a carcinogen chemical compound that, when used in artificially high doses in rodents or other test animals, caused cancer. Today, since science can now detect such minute and harmless amounts, even as small as one part per billion or million (1 ppb = 1 sec. in 32 years; 1 ppm = 1 sec. in 12½ days), the law was out of date. *Properly* used chemical pesticides currently are not a serious threat to human heath and some claim they are less dangerous than many "natural" pesticides used by organic farmers.

It will be difficult to convert to sustainable agriculture without losing necessary productivity, although we must be willing to pay for it. Knowing that changes are inevitable, we must decide what kind of a planet we want to live on and how willing we are to make sacrifices to achieve our goals of sustainable development since, please note, *unfortunately today's economics are based on growth and an increased exploitation of resources.*

Sustainable agriculture is the ability to satisfy indefinitely the need for agricultural products at socially acceptable environmental and economic costs. This means living on the interest without depleting the principal. Even though people must modify ecosystems, they should strive to leave them better than they found them. The analyses of the global economy by economists often seem to ignore the critical relationships of the ecosystems that are needed to support the economy.

The main difficulty in developing sustainable agricultural practices stems from the high research and monitory costs and/or loss in comparable yields. The new push of current research into sustainable agriculture is needed because most modern agricultural practices are not sustainable indefinitely. They cannot continue in perpetuity as they exist in a state of severe disequilibrium supported by continuous input of fuel, water and chemicals.

Preserving natural biological diversity is difficult when the human population grows rapidly and modifies habitats. This is what happens when displaced small-scale farmers in developing countries try to eke out an existence. This type of struggle to survive actually accounts for more deforestation than the combination of both logging and cattle ranching in the developed countries (Myers 1993). However, efforts to slow deforestation must start with an understanding of the behavior of the millions of small farmers who now seem forced to deforest (Rock 1996). This deforestation is different than the tragic harvesting of hardwoods going on in the tropics that is being done on a nonsustainable basis. Rangeland livestock production, using ecologically sound management practices, is probably the only sustainable land-based food production scheme capable of supporting larger human populations, and it should be encouraged in sub-Sahara Africa (Dodd 1994

If the human race is to survive, people cannot stop modifying the environment, but with careful management they can reduce the long-term damage they create if they take into account the environmental dimensions involved. Humans, just as all animals do, out of necessity modify the environment to their advantage. Human values are highly personal and really beyond the scope of critical judgment, so we are faced with serious social problems. Two outstanding books on the status of the world are Lester Brown's books on *Economy* (2001) and *Rescuing a Planet under Stress and a Civilization in Trouble* (2003).

Most of the world, including the United States, has been *too successful* in subduing wild nature. Years ago it was advantageous to encourage settlement of the West and provide subsidized programs for the development of its logging, grazing and mineral resources. But federal lands and the resources they contain are now considered a public trust, to be carefully managed for future generations. For example, no longer is it considered wise for the U.S. Forest Service and Bureau of Land Management to operate at an annual loss of many millions of dollars.

Today, the government's archaic mining law of 1872 provides minerals and land virtually free of charge to miners. Government also provides timber to timber companies at less than what it costs the government to prepare the sales. Forage for livestock on government land is often provided to ranchers for less than it costs to manage the range. These examples show how an agency can become the captive of the users, as many conservationists claim.

Costs of water and power from water projects provided to industries, farmers and other users are far below the government's costs to divert, dam, clean and dredge (Losos et al. 1995). Also, off-road vehicle enthusiasts, hikers, boaters and other recreationists pay much less than the actual upkeep costs of public recreational areas.

Some claim that to completely ignore the value of preserving natural biological diversity is to run the cataclysmic danger of making the planet less habitable, even for people, by destroying the natural function of existing ecosystems. Maintaining biodiversity is the best way to preserve this ecosystem function. The high loss of many species, caused by tropical deforestation, is a concern of all conservationists.

Sometimes, well-directed human actions can provide means to conserve biodiversity and restore it in locations that were previously degraded. It is not necessary to have all the native biota present in order to structure new ecosystems and maintain their resilience; ecosystems can, and often do, function well after there have been some changes in their biological composition (biodiversity).

The public is growing skeptical and distrustful of "scientific" solutions to land management and environmental problems, partly because scientists fail to translate their findings into everyday language. It is important to recognize the social value of scientific discoveries and how they affect people. The Forest Service planning strategies of 1995, called New Forestry or New Perspectives, encompass silvicultural methods that should initiate patterns of natural disturbances of diversity more closely than traditional high-yield forestry, hence better meet the desire for scenic viewing.

The Forest Service, which owns roughly one-third of the forested land in the United States, now has goals that involve not only learning how to produce timber, but also how to provide for fish and wildlife, water, recreation and all the other things listed in the 1960 Multiple-Use Sustained-Yield Act. But have we heard such promises before? Resources are managed in response to social values. This needed change in direction of the Forest Service is a result of changes in social values. According to Farnham et al. (1995), the U.S. Forest Service has significantly increased its emphasis on noncommodity programs of recreation, wilderness, wild and scenic rivers and the management of fish and wildlife habitat.

In 1996 Jim Lyons, assistant U.S. Secretary of Agriculture for Natural Resources and Environment, provided some interesting figures concerning how much various natural resources of the Forest Service contributed to the U.S. economy. It was $12.9 billion from fish and wildlife, $10.1 billion from minerals and $3.5 billion from timber. Yet only 21 percent of the agency's budget is spent on outdoor recreation.

Many think the U.S. Forest Service should practice ecosystem management by focusing on forest condition as the dominant forest goal, rather than multiple-use management of those forest products to be consumed by humans. Logging is inappropriate, for example, in some natural areas, wilderness areas, sensitive habitats, streamside protection zones and special interest areas. In 2001 President Clinton designated vast National Forest areas to remain free of logging, mining and road building. Wildfires in 2000 burned over 6.5 million acres in the western United States, but current data in national forests cannot prove whether logging reduces or increases the chance of catastrophic fires. The Bush administration does not seem to be as concerned with preserving biodiversity.

The unnatural build up of debris in unmanaged forests, i.e., when not thinned, does increase the fire hazard, including lightning-caused fires. Livestock grazing in upland forests of the interior West has reduced the understory grasses and sedges, which normally outcompete conifer seedlings. As a consequence, livestock grazing has reduced the abundance of fire fuels that formerly carried low-intensity fires through forests, increased the density of trees in Western forests, changed the species composition and further altered the ecosystem processes (Belsky and Blumenthal 1997). Browsing by native ungulates can reduce or eliminate seed production of shrubs, rendering long-term shrub restoration ineffective (Kay 1995).

We will be poorer in the future as a consequence of our current depletion of the earth's natural capital stocks. Somehow, ways must be found to develop more self-interest desires when protecting the land, the environment. We all care about the air we breathe, the water we drink and the fate of the soil that provides our sustenance. Any long-term success requires a truly broad-based environmentalism that explicitly includes the presence of a dense population of people and human needs (including all major human occupations), along with environmental protection and economic concerns. How can we achieve maximum conservation of land use and still provide a sustainable economic use of the resources? It is too expensive to establish additional parks and refuges to take care of all these needs.

Proper stewardship of the global environment requires balancing environmental conservation with the ever-expanding demands being placed upon the earth's natural resources by the growing industrial society and the human population's growing need for more agricultural resources and other uses of land. The "environmental justice movement" is a powerful concept that brings everyone down to the same level, by spreading out the costs of environmental damage from land use more equitably and reducing the overall amount of environmental deterioration. Healthy ecosystems play a major, yes critical, role in sustaining goods and services so important to humanity.

Since the environment and the economy are interdependent, our goal must be to create environmental and economic harmony in the way we use land. No small task! As stated by the International Society for Ecological Economics, without an ecological foundation, economic policy is blind and unsustainable; without an economic foundation, ecological policy is impractical.

To obtain sustainable land use, while at the same time the human population continues to grow, requires much remodeling of our resource use so as to accommodate growing human needs. Remember, large numbers of people are here and they are not going to go away. Similarly, to obtain sustainable development for our way of life, we must present economic needs in an equitable fashion while, at the same time, safeguard the earth's natural heritage for future generations. Sustainability for today must embrace a concern for a dream of tomorrow. To have a satisfactory tomorrow, land exploiters must be able to make a good living without being guided primarily by short-term profits.

Economic and environmental issues are inextricably intertwined and the issues must be monetized before sustained environmental improvement can be achieved. The impetus for such agreements must come from coalitions between government and the private sector. The concept of "commons" is important. When a resource is commonly held in the public trust, government has a responsibility to allow a public decision regarding judicious use of the common resource.

The public must concern itself with the implications of human-caused climate and subsequent sea-level changes on habitats. Since the rise in global temperature has occurred in tandem with rising levels of greenhouse gases, it is unlikely to be entirely natural in origin. There seems to be general agreement that global warming, regardless of what is causing it, will alter the distribution and abundance of plants and animals, with a loss of many species. Even if you think the "greenhouse effect" is really not a serious problem, people are unquestionably wrong to pollute the air to the extent that is happening today. Also, for some reason or reasons, the earth is warming.

A United Nations' expert panel concluded that the 1990s were the warmest decade on record and that Earth heated up more in the 20th century than in any other century during the past millennium. In 2003, the heat wave in France killed thousands of people. The Intergovernmental Panel on Climate Change (IPCC), a group of about 1,500 of the world's leading scientists on climate change, project a rise of 2.5-10.4°F this century. To do our part, society should take the precautionary measures necessary to help clean up the environment and reduce pollution.

Concerned scientists believe that greenhouse gas emissions of $CO_2$ and other gases that accumulate in the atmosphere, which cause solar heat to be held closer to the earth, should be reduced. I signed the Ecological Society of America's "Scientists' Statement on Global Climatic Disruption" of 1997 along with over 6,000 Ph.D.s. It states in part: "We are scientists who are familiar with the causes and effects of climate change as summarized recently by the Intergovernmental Panel on Climate Change (IPCC)," which concluded that global mean air temperature has increased from 0.5 to 1.1°F during the last 100 years and is expected to rise 1.8 to 6.3°F over the next century. Sea level has risen an average of 4 to 10 inches during the past 100 years and is expected to rise another 6 inches to 3 feet by 2100. As scientists, we urged President Clinton's administration to reduce U.S. emissions by the most cost-effective means.

There are many unknowns about our climate. According to William Dillon of the U.S. Geological Survey, gas hydrates (a crystalline solid, usually methane, that looks like water ice) are trapped in marine sediments on the ocean floor. When climate warms, it causes the crystals on the sea floor to melt. The release of the trapped methane and other gases then causes the sea level to drop, offsetting any rise caused by the warming.

Based on 121 years of records of the Rothamsted Experimental Station in southern England, the bulk of current warming took place before 1950. Robert C. Balling, an Arizona State University climatologist, found, based on mean annual temperature and precipitation from 1895 to 1998 in Kansas, that the significant warming occurred from 1915 to 1935, before the dramatic increase in U.S. fossil fuel use. J. D. Mahlam (1997) discusses the uncertainties in trying to predict human-caused climate change which remains a complex and unresolved scientific issue. Some scientists think that the growing amount of cloud cover may be due to contrails of jets and that jet airplanes could be responsible for half of the regional warming in the Northern Hemisphere attributed to greenhouse gases. Who knows?

Of the eight billion tons of carbon people dump into the atmosphere each year, mostly from fossil fuel, where does it go? Oceans act as carbon sinks. The oceans absorb huge amounts of the carbon dioxide, some used by mollusks to build their shells. But about a third remains in the atmosphere and warms the planet. But many problems are ahead if the planet continues to warm. In the February 2004 issue of the *National Geographic* magazine, Tim Appenzeller presents an interesting article: "The Case of the Missing Carbon," that explains the carbon cycle and the greenhouse effect of the human emissions of carbon dioxide, methane and other gases that may lead to damaging climatic changes, more floods, drought and intense heat waves with more destructive storms and extensive forest fires. Deforestation has been responsible for about one-quarter of the world's carbon emissions. Much is yet to be learned.

Mark Jacobson, an atmospheric scientist at Stanford University, found soot to be the second leading cause of global warming behind carbon dioxide. To reduce nitrogen emissions, we need to convert agriculture's high-input paradigm to one that emphasizes organic production; convert fossil fuel-based energy economy to one based on solar, wind, geothermal and other forms of renewable energy and slow destruction of natural areas, especially forests. Forest ecologist Pertti Hari of the University of Helsinki and his colleagues found that northern pine forests exude nitrogen oxides in quantities comparable to those produced worldwide by industry and vehicles. It's clear that the future of the climate system and its interactions with global social and economic consequences are unpredictable.

The impact of increased carbon fixation with elevated $CO_2$ may even lead to dietary deficiencies of essential nutrients for herbivores (Owensby et al. 1996). USDA and other researchers, however, have shown that as far as plants, including crops, are concerned the effects of increased $CO_2$ are very positive. A carbon dioxide-enriched atmosphere would be beneficial to all carbon-based ecosystems and food production would go up according to John Christy, a member of the International Panel on Climate Change (IPCC) established by the United Nations. He has found that the lower troposphere—the bottom five miles of the atmosphere—is significantly cooler than climate models predict, suggesting the surface temperature may become cooler.

Much research is underway to determine methods of decarbonizing our environment. New energy systems must be developed, but our oil dependence is a major problem. The demand for oil must be cut. If—and it's a big if—we could provide America's energy needs with conservation, higher fuel efficiency standards and greater wind power, there wouldn't be the pressure to drill for oil in the Alaska National Wildlife Refuge. It has been estimated that to make a significant reduction in $CO_2$ would require a 10-fold increase in reactors if done by converting to more nuclear energy.

A way to engineer a large sustainable world fishery would be by the addition of nitrogen to oceans. This would increase production of phytoplankton (Jones and Young 1996). The resulting photosynthesis would draw down the inorganic carbon level in the upper ocean, which would be replaced by $CO_2$ from the atmosphere. Thus, through the phytoplankton, $CO_2$ could be converted to fish.

The Arctic is undergoing profound changes due to warming. These include shrinking glaciers, melting sea ice, increased freshwater runoff and trees and shrubs encroaching on the tundra. With the current rate aquifers are drying out and with the per capita use of water increasing, it should be obvious that soon water shortage will be a major crisis.

Little information is available to predict how a change in climate may disrupt relationships between different species and the current structure of communities, but a mountain of new scientific evidence is beginning to convince skeptics that global climate change, whether or not it's man-caused, may be upon us. As we modify environments to serve our needs, we must do our best not to destroy all the forests, erode the topsoils, poison the waters and seriously damage the life-support systems of the planet by altering the climate unfavorably.

Ozone is created from various gases by bright sunshine and high temperatures, hence public compliance is important on hot afternoons when people need to defer, for example, painting with oil-based paints, using gasoline motors and even using lighter fluid to start charcoal grills. Ozone comes from many sources and may be carried by wind from one city or state to another. Regulations of big companies like oil refineries, utilities, auto manufacturers, steel producers and others have provided most of the gains in ozone reduction. Now it is up to the public's use of automobiles, gasoline lawnmowers, leaf blowers and motorboats to decline.

The bromine in methyl bromide, an agricultural pesticide, is believed to be capable of destroying 50 times more ozone than the chlorine in chlorofluorocarbons (CFCs). Trifluoromethyl sulphur pentafluoride ($SF_3CF_3$) is one of the most powerful greenhouse gases, 18,000 times as effective as carbon dioxide in trapping the earth's heat. The source is still a mystery, but it may come from transformers and other electrical equipment. Fortunately, this pollutant is still relatively scarce.

The extravagant use of the finite supply of fossil-fuel energy derived from coal, oil and gas, with its carbon dioxide byproduct, is serious. One carbon-free source of energy is nuclear power, which is not popular. True, $CO_2$ increases the productivity of plants and even reduces the ratio of transpiration of leaves (and water conservation is critical). It has been shown that city trees in New York doubled in the amount of biomass as did those outside the city.

The potential greenhouse effect (earth-warming) appears real (Schneider 1994) and other related atmospheric unknowns are serious concerns. Sulfate aerosols emitted by fossil fuel-burning actually shields the earth briefly from the full effect of greenhouse gases, but such aerosols last only weeks in the stratosphere.

Methane is produced whenever bacteria break down organic matter in the absence of oxygen and methane is said to have 25 times the heat-trapping properties of carbon dioxide, hence our increased production of methane could be a significant greenhouse contributor. Even though our knowledge of the carbon cycle is not yet firm, it seems clear that the dramatic increase of carbon dioxide in the atmosphere compared to preindustrial levels should encourage the world to curb $CO_2$ emissions into the atmosphere. Researchers at Duke University found that excess $CO_2$ in the atmosphere may enter the soil within 15 days.

Another global heat-trapping pollutant, perhaps 20,000 times that of carbon dioxide on a per-molecule-basis, is chlorofluorocarbon (CFC), which is used as a refrigerant, as a propellant in alcohol sprays, as a solvent to keep computer chips clean and in air conditioners and plastic foam beads. Our concern with CFCs is in global warming. However, CFCs and nitrogen oxides, not $CO_2$, are probably the worst culprits of climate change. There is a long time lag with CFCs and other ozone-depleting compounds between their release and when they reach the stratosphere and once there, CFCs can persist for centuries.

Another concern, although still slightly questionable to some, is the depletion of the stratospheric ozone layer, which shields the earth from dangerous ultraviolet rays that promote skin cancer and cataracts, weaken immune systems in people and other mammals and can kill fish and plant life. Actually, CFCs are inert, nonreactive, nontoxic, nonflammable, heavier-than-air chemical compounds. So far, to my knowledge, no scientific paper presents any observations of CFC molecules breaking up in the atmosphere.

Substitutes for CFCs and hydrofluorocarbons (HFCs) used as coolants are hydrochlorofluorocarbons (HCFCs), an ozone-benign transitional substance and a mixture of propane and butane, a hydrocarbon (HC). The developers, Henry Rosin and Hans Preiendanz, point out that the amount of fuel used in a modern HC refrigerator equals the amount used in two-and-one-half cigarette lighters.

Nitrous oxide, another more potent greenhouse gas than carbon dioxide, is also increasing in the atmosphere. It comes from automobiles and coal-fired chimneys. Nitrogen oxide leads to acidification of streams and lakes by leaching nutrients out of soil, and trees begin to die when soil becomes saturated with nitrogen. Human activities during the past century have doubled the natural annual rate at which fixed nitrogen enters the land-based nitrogen cycle. The pace is likely to accelerate and serious environmental consequences are already apparent (Vitousek et al. 1997).

Fortunately, the more abundant carbon dioxide does not change the basic chemistry of the atmosphere, as do some polluting gases; it mainly changes the composition. Title IV of the 1990 amendments to the Clean Air Act of 1970 has markedly lowered air pollution for oxides of nitrogen, sulfur dioxide (by nearly 50 percent), carbon monoxide, lead and certain types of particulates—all at a considerable savings to American taxpayers.

Of paramount importance, because of its potentially dangerous implications, is the contrasting of "nature protection" and "nature utilization," for total protection of some species in modified environments may do more damage to other animals, cause unnecessary suffering of protected species and even degrade whole ecosystems. Furthermore, not only do most areas contain humans, but people-occupied regions are also increasing in magnitude. Unless people can be better integrated in the conservation effort, success is very unlikely. Also, the concept of total protection, such as occurs to a degree in national parks, may have the dangerous psychological effect of causing some of the public and politicians to justify the exploitation of the remaining areas.

Current protected areas must remain and more need to be promoted. President Clinton established many in 2000-01. The exploitation of other types of areas should be guided by the concept of nature protection through nature utilization. There is much concern about a current endeavor to bring all native species under the control of the federal government. The worry is about the resulting accumulation of dollars and powers that environmental groups would obtain and the infringement of private property rights, as happened with the Endangered Species Act of 1972.

Those who oppose the concept of sustained use of renewable resources and promote either no use or exploitation of land must recognize the associated long-term problems. The human population of the world is consuming excessive amounts of this earth's natural resources and has caused the collapse of the world's fisheries, aquifers and many forests. An agricultural product, such as grain, will decline with any increase in temperature. The 2003 heat wave in Europe was devastating to crops and human health.

The dangerous proposal by the Bush administration to privatize and localize federal funds concerning national wildlife refuges and some national parks should be of great concern to the public. The Confederated Salish and Kootenae (CSTA) tribal government has proposed to take over the professional wildlife and land management duties of the National Bison Range in Montana. However, the tribal management plans actually include a minimum of 41 national wildlife refuges, including all national refuges in Alaska, and a minimum of 334 national parks, including Glacier in Montana, Redwood in California and Olympic in Washington (Reneau 2003).

CHAPTER 6

# Human Population Explosion and Its Impact On Wildlife Habitat

Practically all of today's wildlife, land use and environmental problems are the indirect consequence of the magnitude and rapid human population growth. The population of both China and India today is greater and growing faster than what was the entire population of the world 200 years ago. Then the world's population was only 800 million, whereas in 2003 it exceeded 6 billion. The United Nations projects that by 2050 the world's population will be about 8.9 billion, down from its earlier forecasts of 9.3 billion. More than a quarter million people are born every day.

This growth of the human population is overriding nature's death ethic, which exists to control population density. Humans both survive a long life and breed to the extent that the number of births in the world exceeds the death rate.

About 90 percent of the human population growth is in developing countries. The average global total fertility rate (TFR) was six children per woman in the 1960s but, fortunately, has declined to about three. In developing countries, excluding China, four is the average, but it is six in sub-Sahara Africa. The world population has tripled since 1920 and is headed toward doubling in just 45 years. We know that there is no way this present growth rate can continue, for if it does there will be 600 to 700 billion people by the middle of the 22nd century, an impossible number for the earth to support.

According to anthropologists, during the first one to two million years of human existence, the growth rate of the human population averaged only one to two people a year, whereas the current human population will soon be increasing nearly 100 million per year and even more later on. That is a dramatic change of the population growth rate. According to the World Bank, the world population will not stabilize at less than 12.4 billion, whereas the United Nations concludes that the eventual total could reach 14 billion. Ecologists don't think the earth can support such numbers without drastic changes in lifestyles. I agree and instead of voluntarily reducing this growth, it will require unpleasant tragedies to do so. Ecologists think the current population is already too high to be sustained. The carrying capacity of the earth for people, of course, depends on lifestyle and our use of natural resources, but few would voluntarily make the needed significant sacrifices of comfort and way of life.

According to nature's life-death ethic, no population of any species—including humans—can continue to increase indefinitely regardless of how much food there is. If civilization is to remain viable, we must end the arrogant assumption that natural resources, clean air and water are unlimited and that we can somehow survive a steady, increasing pollution in the biosphere.

Humans are crippling the natural systems that support many of the earth's renewable resources and are depleting nonrenewable resources—the soil, our diverse fauna and flora and the supply of ground water and fresh air. We used to think our ground water supplies were invulnerable to pollution. Not so. Much of our water is contaminated with industrial wastes, fertilizer and pesticides, thus making clean water a scarce and expensive commodity, even for wildlife. Human population pressures force us to live in a "chemical" world, but somehow we must introduce greater precautions to protect wildlife, as well as ourselves, from pollutants.

Estimates range between 50,000 and 100,000 synthetic chemicals in commerce production according to Anne Platt McGinn (2000). What will these chemicals, many of them persistent, eventually do to the environment? No one really knows. The known dangerous synthetics are called persistent organic pollutants (POPs). McGinn's worry is that agencies such as the EPA, charged with regulating the use of these POP compounds, have no realistic hope of catching up. Also, modern agriculture has a serious chemical dependency, which she calls an addiction. This dependency has ramifications far beyond immediate use. "One of the most comprehensive records of this form of pollution is the bark of living trees, which scientists can test to map the extent of contamination. The testing of trees at more than 90 temperate and tropical sites worldwide turned up *no sites* that were free from DDT, chlordane and dieldrin."

Personal consumption of goods is embarrassingly excessive. Humans, as well as animals, are primarily concerned with themselves. We are rarely willing to make environmentally significant sacrifices. Industrial nations represent 22 percent of the world's population, but consume 75 percent of the world's energy, 75 percent of its metals, 85 percent of its wood and 60 percent of its food. People must develop greater voluntary restraints in reproduction, otherwise conception may have to come under some form of government control as in China and as was attempted in India. Such restraints to pregnancies tend to occur with advances in standards of living, increased education and women's rights. Some claim a trend toward a global decrease in living standards exists because of overcrowding. Housing needs are expected to double in the next 50 years, primarily in the developing countries. Because of this, Negative Population Growth, Inc., rightfully proposes that the United States and the other countries of the world need a declining population.

Measures are needed in the developing world to reduce high birth rates and to limit population momentum. Religion's impact on nature cannot be ignored. The western monotheistic traditions of Christianity, Islam and Judaism have influence over a range of resources, including worldviews, symbols, rituals, ethical norms, traditions and institutional structures. These characteristics give religion much influence over the environment (Gardner 2003).

We have bestowed upon us at birth a sacred trust to exercise dominion over creation in responsible manner—whether you believe in God or not. We are fulfilling our charge as the earth's caretaker when we heed this call. However, because of religion, neither the United States nor the United Nations has a no-growth population policy. This must change. The only encouraging sign is that the *rate* of growth of the world's population is at last actually declining, although total population is still growing.

A nation's economic development does not necessarily solve its population growth problem. Women must have better access to contraceptive services, as misinformation and cultural taboos are still common barriers to birth control. In many countries women are viewed as property and lack equal opportunity. Women of the world not only need family-planning programs but also improved education and equal employment opportunities to alleviate poverty, as well as having access to insurance, credit, savings opportunities and basic household needs such as fuel and potable water. Women's wages still do not equal men's in any part of the world.

People are part of nature. Dwell on that fact of life for a moment. *Homo sapiens* are not going away anytime soon. To survive, we tap into the abundance of substance and energy the environment provides, as all organisms do. Skins, furs and all wildlife are renewable natural resources and we should manage them accordingly. With proper management we assist nature in utilizing resources with sensitivity befitting a supposedly evolved species. But man's seemingly endless appetite for resources and material things is devouring the earth's ground water and leaving polluted air, water and soil in a plundered planet. Throughout the 1970s the environmental movement was largely directed toward keeping things pristine, whereas now much of the environmental focus is on public health issues such as chemicals, pollutants and pests.

The expanding human demands on the earth's natural resources are unprecedented, due to the growth of the world's human population, new technology, rapid economic growth and everyone's desire for a better lifestyle. In the United States the premise of growth without limits is unsupportable. Somehow, nontragic ways must be found to change the principle of growth measured by increase of production and sales to one of conservation. Growth is at the heart of the environmental problem, because humans depend on uses or functions of the environment for all their activities. The combination of growth and environmental conservation is only possible in the case of technologies that are sufficiently clean, do not deplete energy stocks and other natural resources, leave the soil intact, leave sufficient space for the survival of plant and animal species and are no more expensive than currently available technologies (Hueting 1996).

Once the earth's carrying capacity is clearly exceeded, sustainable development of resources will no longer be achievable. It is even questionable now, as many think the human population has already exceeded the earth's carrying capacity. We must therefore become better caretakers and improve our stewardship of the environment or face an inevitable catastrophic collapse of civilization. We desperately need a sensible environmental ethic in the national conscience that includes the laws of nature and that includes a healthier acceptance of the life-death ethic as it applies to the human species. If we are going to attack the impact of population growth and pressures on resources, we must provide people at the grassroots level with an opportunity to feel empowered to effect change in their communities rather than dealing with pollution and environmental issues from the top down. Models are needed that consider the interactions between ecological and social dynamics.

Eventually, involuntary self-limitation in the form of premature deaths from starvation, pestilence (most likely from viruses for humans) and wars will prevent further increases in density. In some parts of the world today, human life expectancy is less than 40 years. Since all finite space is limited, human birthrates and death rates must somehow come in balance. Without more effective control of the birthrate, we are only delaying the inevitable—a later date with starvation to an even larger population.

It is sad that only a meager surplus of grain exists in the world today. Many industrialized countries can no longer produce enough food for themselves and cannot afford to buy it from others. In contrast, the United States continues to produce more food than it can consume and does not have adequate markets. There probably is enough food for the world's population in the short run. The problem is that it cannot be produced economically and on a sustained basis. Since we live in an economic world, food is mainly produced to make money, not to feed hungry stomachs, hence the coexistence of surplus food and starvation.

Ironically, we face acute human overpopulation due to advances in agriculture, public health, taboos against birth control, science and technology. These are human choices. The book by S. D. Mumford (1996) on *The Life and Death of NSSM 200* (NSSM refers to "National Security Study Memorandum") clearly explains how the Vatican manipulated the American government to distance itself from the strong link between world overpopulation and U.S. national security. It was a definitive interagency study of world population growth and its implications for the United States and global security requested by President Nixon in 1974 and endorsed by President Ford in 1975. This book explains why U.S. policymakers will not go against the church to solve the problem of population growth.

As economists have pointed out, the important point is not how many people the earth can support, but whether or not people will have the stamina to make the right choices to support the earth. The human economy is operating as if it is independent of the real world. The human population in developing countries has been largely freed from nature's mortality factors of disease, starvation and territoriality, but is unable to feed the population. This burgeoning human population has resulted in critical environmental consequences.

Only a few centuries ago large families (averaging eight children in the United States in the 1800s) were necessary because of the high mortality rates and the need for more hands on the farm. Today, families actually have far fewer babies, but the population continues to grow because more now survive and the average life span has increased substantially.

While we all want sex to remain an individual and private matter, procreation must become a public concern. RU-486 has been a controversial legal alternative to surgical abortion during the first seven weeks of pregnancy. The drug blocks development of progesterone, a natural hormone essential for maintaining pregnancy.

Not only is it illegal for a human to die voluntarily (euthanasia), now many people want to interfere with nature's death ethic by doing what they can to prevent wildlife from dying. This attitude is seriously upsetting nature's death ethic, which is so important to the balance of nature. Death, even premature death, is an integral part of life.

For people to have an abundant life and freedom from want, it will require a low death rate. But to achieve these goals requires a low birthrate. Ample food, permanent peace, good health and a high-quality life are *unattainable for all* human beings now and in the foreseeable future because of economic, social and political realities and also because of the magnitude of the human population.

A soaring population causes a shrinking of man's individual space on this earth. Hunger and overpopulation will not go away if we do not discuss them. Also, too many births are not just someone else's problem; it's everyone's concern. The legacy of overpopulation is erosion of civilized life. This is being witnessed in many parts of the world today.

A point often overlooked is that people, a dominant part of nature, will not go away, thus we need to strive for maximum cohabitation with all forms of life. It is absolutely essential for us to manage plant and animal communities in environments we have altered rather than leaving these to the whims of nature. As far as our welfare or that of many species is concerned, nature alone cannot provide satisfactory management schemes in these disturbed settings. Hence, we must manage and not leave the outcomes to nature.

Man differs from other animals principally in his intellect; his ability to read, communicate and use tools and his capability to regulate reproduction and to overcome nature's death-ethic mortality factors. We also differ from wild species in that man attempts to protect the genetically or physically unfit and even unwanted human births, something nature does not do. Nature's evolution has seen to it that all organisms, including man, are equipped with a strong breeding urge. With this innate biological capacity to overproduce, nature ensures survival of the species and enough food (prey) to support the predators of the balance of nature.

But before surplus animals and people die, they consume resources and contribute in general to other population stresses, all of which makes the environment less suitable, thus lowering its carrying capacity for that species.

Man needs space as much as plants and animals do. Unfortunately, wilderness areas and national parks will not be secure if the human population continues to grow. Even now, the attempt to preserve natural areas while allowing hordes of people to enjoy them creates perplexing problems. Simple answers to environmental problems are hard to find because so many societal values conflict.

Animal population densities are governed principally by the suitability of the habitat, interactions with predators and species-specific self-limitation when predation fails all natural laws. To some extent, the members of each wildlife species involuntarily prevent any further increase in their kind. This self-limitation results from undesirable stresses that reduce the number of births or cause a compensating increase in death rates. When natural predation no longer regulates the density of populations, members of the population become their own worst enemy.

Nearly all organisms are well adapted to their environment and have some built-in mechanisms for checking the growth of their population. Nature's population control processes are unemotional and impartial, conditions that people will instinctively wish humans to avoid. As with wild animals, the innate desire for large families can be strong, making it difficult to create sensible population densities.

Nature demands high premature mortality of all species, as every creature overproduces. Capitalizing on modern public health, medicines and agriculture, humans have overcome nature's life-death ethic. Our overpopulation has seriously impacted the biosphere and the current densities of many plants and animal species. All nature's components are predisposed to overpopulate and, in fact, they attempt to do so, hence the high number of predators, scavengers and decomposers found in nature.

Whenever the human population density has been markedly reduced through some catastrophe or our technology has appreciably increased the carrying capacity of our surrounding environment, the growth rate of the population increases. With this accelerated growth, the population of people, as with wildlife, then tends to overcompensate, temporarily growing beyond the upper limits of the carrying capacity of the environment. One could say that the world's overpopulation of humans is the result of education, technology and public health, because these factors have destroyed nature's death ethic but left her birth ethic of surplus offspring intact. The excess growth of wildlife usually is eventually checked, however, by the interaction of a number of different self-limiting stress factors, none of which are pleasant. Do we want this fate for the human civilization?

Only self-limitation can stem the human population growth tide. And the only question is whether the needed control in births will eventually be accomplished. It will happen either involuntarily by nature's undesirable stresses—as witnessed by the history of civilization—or consciously by having the human population voluntarily and permanently decline to an optimum carrying capacity. Some organized religions hamper the latter option and oppose birth control, thereby contributing to overpopulation. It is hypothetical, at best, to preach compassion on the one hand and then condemn millions to disease and starvation.

Man has transferred himself from being a significant member of the ecosystem to a highly dominant position. We mistakenly assume that the ecosystem is ours to control at will. However, dominion compels us to act responsibly and responsibility entails honesty with the biological facts of life and death. Lest we forget, we are a part of nature. We must embrace a paradigm that accepts us as we are, that our true place in the world is not to transcend nature but to live within nature.

It is past time to look back in history and eliminate those human behaviors that allowed our ancestors to survive millennia without long-term deterioration of ecosystems. We don't need them now. Early humans survived history by using the interest and not the principal of natural resources; hence hunting is one of the oldest occupations. American Indians, for example, did not exceed the earth's carrying capacity. Their survival rate was so low that it resulted in the total population of people remaining at a sustainable level.

Economic growth, unfortunately, is indispensable to the world economy as it currently functions, but a growing number of scientists are warning that unfettered economic growth is incompatible with long-term environmental sustainability. The developing countries do little about stemming the growth of the human population, but the developed countries do little to abate consumption of resources. An irreconcilable conflict seems to exist between the virtual necessity of economic growth and the absolute necessity of environmental preservation, which leads to dangerous optimism that economic and environmental problems will take care of themselves, or at least may be alleviated with a minimum of effort. This attitude precludes the search for institutional alternatives to economic growth (Gowdy 1992).

The daily economic pressures of individuals attempting to provide a decent civilization, especially for themselves, have led to the destruction of too many original ecosystems, sometimes inadvertently creating unproductive deserts. As tragic as it may sound, when an underdeveloped country's population density is growing too rapidly, both health and agricultural aid from the United States may not only be wasted but may severely aggravate an already deplorable social and economic situation in that country. Such a surplus population of people cannot be indefinitely sustained, because it will continue to multiply. That is harsh reality. All species must either check their birthrates by various means or be prepared to accept an unwanted compensating mortality factor to regulate their numbers.

Insidious economic pressures seem to prevent any effective management of many resources in a manner that would provide for their use in perpetuity. Concrete and pavement surely are not the epitome of the human species' fulfillment, even if they do prevent erosion of the soil underneath. An ecological appreciation of resource management is needed and an ecological consciousness must replace ecological atrocities.

Inevitably our natural resources will yield in the face of the current world population explosion. As the population swells, open space is inundated by a flood of housing and resources shrink further. We have lost many wetlands and flood plains that used to absorb floods. And, of course, wildlife has suffered. The United States and other developed countries consume a disproportionately large share of the world's nonrenewable and other resources, such as oil and minerals, at an ever-accelerating rate and these finite resources are, of course, subject to eventual exhaustion. Fortunately, many environmental agencies have at least been successful in slowing the process. But how can society stop the spawning of cars and other polluters? Automotive innovation has been slow, still relying on the internal combustion engine-powered, gasoline-fueled, steel-bodied automobile, when what is needed are low-emission cars that run on methane, electricity, hydrogen or, best of all, solar energy.

The human population first passed through the agricultural revolution, then the industrial revolution. These were followed by the public health revolution, and today I think the whole world is suffering from a revolution of rising expectations. Due to the selling pressures of business and the advertisement of goods and lifestyles, even by space satellites and cyberspace, people all over the world now have rising expectations of a universally high standard of living. Nearly everyone wants more material things and new experiences. But it all requires the use of limited resources.

As individual aspirations rise and per capita resources fall, the widening gap between the "haves" and "have-nots" will generate even more serious social and political pressures than already exist, with little thought of wildlife's welfare. The opening up of markets in Eastern Europe, China, Russia and other parts of the world is accelerating the depletion of resources and will contribute considerably to existing pollution problems. This "progress" is difficult to prevent because resources must be exploited to raise people's living standards.

Technology and science can and do increase our progress, but the current rate they are advancing is frightening. Can social, political and religious views change rapidly enough to cope with this advancement, for example, in personal living standards? Our native intelligence is so innovative that it may destroy us. While we possess the wisdom and insight to recognize what we are doing to the planet, we lack the collective courage to take bold steps to protect and sustain wildlife and the environment for future generations.

We have become a complacent society, unwilling to take any of the many options available for preventing surplus births. One-third of the world's over 6 billion people is under 15 years of age. International Planned Parenthood Federation estimates that more than 15 million girls, one in ten aged 15-19, become pregnant each year. Our primitive reproduction instincts cannot be allowed to continue in the face of modern survival rates; the two are no longer in balance. *To increase the chance for future babies to live, fewer must be born.* In the United States there are about 6 million pregnancies annually and nearly 60 percent are unintended, according to a report from the Alan Guttmacher Institute, resulting in about 1.6 million abortions. As has been said by others, if men had the babies and women made the laws, we wouldn't be discussing the abortion issue.

Our social institutions find it difficult to slow and stabilize human population growth without conflict from religious and human-rights issues. To say that it is a basic human right to decide the number and spacing of one's children, as much of our society now believes, is to say that humans have the right to do whatever they want to the environment without thought of its inevitable consequences to future generations. If other organisms do have rights, then such human behavior surely infringes on those rights, but, in essence, we are actually undermining our own species. To achieve "quality living" with abundant wildlife, our ultimate goal must be a declining population growth rate and a reduction in the size of the world's current population.

Other environmental problems threatening humans and wildlife are chemical pollutants that cannot be recycled, the pumping of ground water faster than it is replaced, the overutilization of forests and other natural resources, acid rain, increase of $CO_2$ and other chemicals in the atmosphere and numerous other problems. Nature can no longer "repair" on her own many of our misuses of natural renewable and nonrenewable resources, because the pressures of the human population have become too great. Perhaps the most serious crime of herbicides, insecticides, fungicides, nematocides, rodenticides, avicides and predacides is that they have enabled the human population in the world to increase so dramatically. These chemical tools have been very successful in protecting our health, plants, property, pets and stored produce, thus encouraging us to produce more people.

As Lester Brown (1995) emphatically points out in *Who Will Feed China?* we must launch a worldwide effort to stabilize our life support systems—soils, fisheries, aquifers and forests—and the climate system. As China industrializes, just as Japan, Korea and Taiwan already have, the demand for grain products grows rapidly while the amount of land available to produce grain diminishes, forcing those countries to import grain. In 1996 the global amount of grain cropland was only 0.12 hectares per capita, which is about half what it was in 1950. As grain production area declines, grain imports increase (Gardner 1996). A host of industrializing nations—including China, India, Vietnam, Indonesia, Malaysia and Thailand—are following Japan, Korea and Taiwan in sacrificing cropland to industrial development. This is insane public policy. This could have devastating effects on each country's ability to feed its growing population.

Grain provides half of humanity's food energy. Yet there is an upper limit to how much of a plant's photosynthetic product (photosynthate) can be genetically transferred to seeds. Scientists have increased it from 20 to 50-55 percent, but the absolute physiological limit is around 60 percent. There is also an upper limit as to how much grain production can be increased by use of irrigation and fertilizer and by more effectively controlling insects, diseases, weeds and vertebrate pests. With the Third World's income rising at a record rate, the per capita consumption increases for grain-intensive products like poultry, beef, pork, milk, eggs and beer, yet there is little new land available to produce more wheat, barley, oats, rice and corn. Yields per hectare cannot continue to increase as has happened in the past. There is an ultimate upper plateau of yield potential and aquifers are declining with society's high demand for water (Brown 1996).

As the Worldwatch Institute of Washington, D.C., reports, grain prices have increased rapidly over the last few years averaging, in 1998, 12 percent a year for wheat, 16 percent for corn and 9 percent for rice. One-fifth of humanity does not have access to clean drinking water, and since 1950 close to a third of global forest cover has been lost. For an excellent Worldwatch Institute reference on progress toward a sustainable society, see Starke (1998); on environmental decline, social conflict and the struggle for survival, see Renner (1996); and on a review of the animal rights debate, see Guither (1989).

Will there be food for all in 2020? The International Food Policy Research Institute concluded that we have the knowledge and the capacity to meet the food needs of every person without damaging the environment, but that it will require the political will and commitment of all members of society to take the required action and that seems unlikely (Pinstrup-Anderson and Randya-Lorch 1996).

Agriculture might be accused of having been too successful in that it has greatly increased the carrying capacity of people. Today, if everyone in America tried to grow their own food and factory-farming of animals did not exist, there wouldn't be sufficient open space. All environmental issues and even those concerning animal welfare are exacerbated, if not precipitated by, the enormity of human population growth, which is our most urgent and real priority. We don't need to find better ways of accommodating more people; we need to find ways to stop the rate of growth.

Prior to people entering the equation, nature's life-death ethic functioned flawlessly in regulating the fauna and flora of the world. Nature doesn't allow every acorn or pine nut to survive and grow into a tree. The reason only a very few seeds survive is that the mature trees take the moisture and sunlight needed by seedlings and many of the seeds and immature plants are consumed by other organisms. Nature requires a high birth rate and a high death rate to preserve natural biological diversity.

# CHAPTER 7

# Animal Welfare Versus Animal Rights

Most human beings display a compassionate attitude toward the creatures with which we share this planet. However, this admirable concern for animal welfare has shifted toward a disturbing trend that suggests animals are born with "rights." One can easily trace the popularization of animal rights to the mass media. The most notable watershed event, which accelerated the modern animal rights movement like nothing else, was the Walt Disney film "Bambi" in 1942. The "Bambi Syndrome" caught fire with Peter Singer's 1975 book, *Animal Liberation*.

This chapter raises many points that animal rightists, especially the extreme supporters of the movement, will find challenging. Viewed with an open mind, however, it may prepare them for insight into the views of animal-user proponents. The chapter will also provide information for those who oppose the animal rights movement. Even though I question extreme views on animal rights, I acknowledge that the animal rights movement has had at least one positive effect. People are now more conscious of the welfare of pets, livestock, laboratory animals and other wildlife species and I hope people will read Young's (2003) book on *Environmental Enrichment for Captive Animals*. However, the animal rights view has been coupled with a misunderstanding of nature's death ethic and that can be counterproductive when it causes increased suffering of wild animals.

Outdoor writer Kerasote (1996) succinctly explains the issues:

> . . . Unfortunately for the neatness of the argument,
> vegetarians, like the rest of us, drive cars, fly hang gliders and

buy kayaks, skis and mountain bikes. We are part of a culture
that mindlessly kills animals in the produc- tion not only of
our sporting equipment and household goods, but also in the
production of the seemingly most benign of our foods.

The point, in respect to outdoor ethics, is that anyone who
eats on planet earth or lives in a home or goes from one place to
another, even on bike or foot, remains a greater or lesser participant
in these cycles of life and death. One can do some of the killing
that living entails oneself or one can have someone else do it. And
I believe that the option that one chooses, or even merely one's
acknowledgement or disavowal of our participation in these cycles,
does matter both pragmatically and spiritually. In fact, I don't believe
the two can be separated.

Animal welfare, which I endorse, is an expression of kindness
and concern for the well-being of animals that people use in the
field, at home or in the laboratory. It's wonderful and
understandable that today most people would like to see almost
every living thing live a long and full life. But at what cost? Do we
get into trouble when we go against Nature? After all, she has
created an environment that requires various ways of regulating
the density of populations. Most organisms that failed to evolve
with changing environmental conditions are now fossils (and
there are a lot of them).

Animal rightists I have come in contact with in a course I
taught on animal welfare at UC-Davis and in my many public
debates seemed to oppose any management of animals, their use
and actually any exploitation of animals. However, in discussion
periods they usually admitted being unable to defend their views.
Some people try to give legal status to those animals known to
feel pain and suffering that is equal to the legal rights given to
people. The animal rightists' philosophy seems to ignore that the
need for an animal to feel and experience some pain is absolutely
essential to its survival. The same is true with humans. Pain and
distress are required for certain segments of the natural biological
system to function.

Even though some of the higher vertebrate animals clearly demonstrate insight and reason—i.e., intelligence—these sentient beings seldom demonstrate conscious compassion for other species, as do humans. Of course most people are species-centric and consider our kind more important than other species on earth, even though a very persuasive argument can be made that many of our fellow vertebrates are more biologically advanced than we are in some areas. For example, a mouse has a highly complex and evolved digestive system compared to ours. A philosophy that emphasizes Albert Schweitzer's reverence for life of all species may, in part, be contradictory to the survival of other species, for it ignores nature's life-death ethic.

To many people the issue is not animal "rights" per se but involves ethics, for they question any distress man may cause animals over which he has direct control. This is animal welfare, not animal rights, for it exemplifies cultural ethics, not absolute ethics that follow nature's laws. Sentientism is concerned with the pain and suffering of individual sentient animals. As the British philosopher Jeremy Bentham stated way back in 1789, "The question is not, 'Can they *reason?*' nor, 'Can they *talk?*' but, 'Can they *suffer?*'" Analyses of the ethical problems of animal experiments abound, but most yield little practical advice. Arkow (1998) applies the role of ethics in his analysis of animal welfare.

Mistreatment of animals understandably motivates those in the animal rights movement, yet a number of hard questions should be asked of them in the interests of an honest exchange of ideas. Is rodent-proofing a house denying rodents their rights? Should we share our woolen clothing with clothes moths and tolerate rats, fleas and bedbugs in our houses? I imagine more than a few animal rightists have probably sanctioned the killing of termites in the walls and foundations of their houses and of ants that invade their kitchens. Are rats equal to people? What respect should we show a dead rat? Should a lame horse that can't walk be kept alive?

How can one compare the distress of animals used in farming and research, or with those shot, trapped or poisoned, with that derived from "natural" suffering? A slow death from starvation, disease, cannibalism, battles with members of the same species or being maimed, killed or eaten alive by a predator hardly seems less painful. Can you imagine the experience of a fish being torn apart while fed alive to young osprey or eagles or eaten by any carnivore, or a wildebeest being torn apart and slapped about by a huge crocodile weighing a ton? How would you like to be swallowed whole by a giant pelican or garden snake? How much do birds and small rodents suffer when cats injure them just enough so they cannot escape and then they or their kittens play with them? While in Argentina, I noted that a lioness (cougar) with cubs might venture out of the Andes and maul more than a dozen sheep a night while training her cubs how to kill, and then carry away only one for food.

One cannot dismiss all these by simply saying they are acceptable ways of nature if the factors causing the brutality are due, even in part, to our upsetting the balance of nature by our modifying the environment. We should assist nature with modern wildlife management techniques if people are responsible for the distress of the animals and it is preventable. In human-altered environments, the killing by sportspersons, subsistence hunters and animal control personnel may temporarily reduce animal numbers artificially, but assist in preserving a healthier balance between animal populations and their habitat resources. They can even provide protection and sustainability of threatened or endangered species and their habitat.

Civilization has given the human race more leisure time. There's an old saying that you can't philosophize on an empty stomach. We can afford to express mercy and compassion toward other species, hence the animal rights movement. Even though, as other animals do, we must kill animals to survive, it still may make us uncomfortable. Indeed, we live by the "golden" rule and resist causing sentient animals to suffer. Yet we don't expect animals to show compassion and pity toward other species, especially those they eat. Instead of compassion, animals follow their instincts. In contrast we feel we have a duty to treat animals humanely and to not inflict unnecessary pain and distress because we consider ourselves civilized.

Many of the higher animals are sentient; that is, they have the ability to experience fear, pleasure, boredom, pain and suffering, although not to the same degree as humans, who have a more developed nervous system. How you treat animals is thought to be revealing of your character and a reflection of how much you value nature. Before the animal rights movement, people were gradually learning how to co-exist with wildlife. As we untangle the mysteries of nature, we can see how the animal rights movement may have unwittingly led many astray by ignoring nature's death ethic.

The evolving consensus toward the ethical treatment of animals, due in part to the animal rights movement, now transcends the animal welfare issue of humaneness and incorporates the notion that animals deserve the same respect as humans. When carried to the extreme, this view is dangerous; for it ignores the balancing act that is nature. Look closely and you will see that the animal rights movement does little to improve the humane treatment of animals or to better the quality of life for wild animals. They recommend no life at all for billions of domesticated animals, which they claim should never have been domesticated. Most views expressed by animal rightists, *inter alia*, are a travesty of nature and, too often, acrimonious as well.

## Statements Supported by Many Animal Rightists

How many of the following animal rightists' views can you accept? Most of these appear in *Animal Scam: The Beastly Abuse of Human Rights* by Marquardt et al. (1998). It is a very informative book. Kathleen Marquardt is the founder and chair of Putting People First, an organization committed to promoting animal welfare and fighting for the animal rights movement. The other two authors are Mark LaRochelle, press secretary of Putting People First, and Herbert M. Levine, a political scientist and freelance writer.

1. It is wrong to kill native predators to save a species that has become endangered as a result of our modifying the environment.
2. Some animal rightists claim they are justified in disregarding public laws on behalf of animals, such as hunter harassment, trespassing, arson and even making death threats.
3. Animals should have legal rights akin to those of humans.
4. It is morally wrong to exploit animals for food, recreation, research, sports, hunting or fishing.
5. It is wrong to take honey from bees, milk from cows, eggs from chickens and silk from silkworms.
6. Killing an animal is nearly equivalent to killing a person.
7. People are morally obligated to take care of animals as if they were human and to let them die naturally.
8. It is wrong to euthanize unwanted, displaced problem animals. They should be left to die nature's way.
9. All people should be vegetarians.
10. It is wrong to use animals in research no matter how humanely they are treated or how beneficial it is to that species, other animals or people.
11. It is better to let livestock die naturally, even if it is from starvation or disease, rather than for the surplus to be humanely slaughtered.
12. It is wrong to kill a few deer or other individual animals in a modified environment, even when such action would save the lives of many more individuals in the long run.
13. A livestock-killing coyote should be allowed to continue disemboweling dozens of domestic sheep or turkeys rather than be restrained in a padded leghold trap overnight and then shot.
14. Commercial and sport fishing are wrong because millions of fish are killed.
15. It is better to let animals die "naturally" by predation, starvation; disease and cannibalism than for them to be shot, trapped, poisoned or euthanized.

16. It was wrong to use animals in the development of blood transfusions, anesthesia, painkillers, antibiotics, insulin, vaccines for polio and tetanus, chemotherapy, CPR, coronary bypass surgery, reconstruction surgery, orthopedic surgery and other areas that have benefited humans.
17. Animal rights and animal welfare are separated by irreconcilable philosophical differences and enactment of animal welfare measures actually impedes the achievement of animal rights according to some (T. Regan and G. Francione).
18. It is wrong to kill a skunk, fox or raccoon infected with rabies or other infectious diseases.
19. It is wrong for a farmer or rancher to control pest animals to protect crops or livestock.
20. It's wrong to kill a muskrat even if it is threatening a dam.

The following quotations were taken from Marquardt et al. (1997). Some animal rights leaders made them and these will help you better understand their beliefs about the intrinsic rights of animals that should be conferred upon all wild and domestic animals. For example, from Chris DeRose, "A life is a life, if the death of one rat cured all diseases it wouldn't make any difference to me. In the scheme of life we are all equal."

"We have no right not to be harmed by those natural diseases we're heir to" (Tom Regan).

"I don't believe human beings have the right to life. That is a supremists perversion, a rat is a pig, as a dog is a boy" (Ingrid Newkirk of PETA). She has also stated that "even if animal research resulted in a cure for AIDS, we would be against it."

Ronnie Lee founder of the British Animal Liberation Front (ALF), said that ALF's goal was "to inflict an economic loss on people who exploited animals . . . To escalate events . . . all their industries are under threat and can't operate."

"Animal experimentation is just plain wrong. Human beings have no right to the knowledge gained from experimentation on animals—even if it's done painlessly" (Priscilla Feral, Friends of Animals [FOA]).

These folks are not interested in compromise. They are strident and inflexible, espousing their views with fundamentalist fervor. Some are nothing short of contemporary eco-theologians with strong and extreme ideals and who ignore other people's views. Based on my personal contact in classes and radio talk shows, rarely are they willing to seriously discuss or debate the real issues. When debating with leaders of animal rights organizations on radio talk shows, I have repeatedly asked: "How does your organization want animals to die?" None has satisfactorily answered the question because they can't. They know that animals die a horrible death when it is by nature's way.

Some extreme animal rightists oppose the eating of meat, milk, eggs and honey and want to ban the use of wool, leather, fur and down. They are abolitionists, not reformists, and they do not understand nature's life-death ethic. In reality the goal of the extremists is not to provide larger cages and a better environment for confined animals but to empty the cages and pens altogether. To the movement's credit, however, moderate animal rightists have succeeded in advocating larger cages that are now required for confined animals.

Many animal rightists' statements, as listed above, are designed to make you intuitively believe them as key biological facts. According to the U.S. Congress Office of Technology Assessment (OTA) in its January 1992 publication, "Technology Against Terrorist: Structuring Security," terrorism by animal rights extremists is an example of "single-issue political extremism."

"Organizations such as People for the Ethical Treatment of Animals (PETA), the militant Animal Liberation Front (ALF), the Humane Society of the United States and other radical animal rights groups attempt to hold us hostage to the false sentiments that arise from our having been distanced from nature. These groups promote a view of biology and nonhuman animals that is unrealistic and naive and they attempt to force their views on educators, researchers, zoos, rodeos, even pet owners. The perspective of the animal rights movement is quite different from that of the animal welfare movement," according to McInerney (1993).

As stated by Marquardt et al. (1993), formerly of the Putting People First organization, "animal rights is a pack of lies, superstitions and perverted philosophy mixed with a tiny bit of truth. That tiny bit makes them appear wholesome and honest—two things they most definitely are not. Putting a stop to the distortions foisted by animal rightists will not be easy. They have millions of dollars, good organization, media savvy and influence in high places. Keeping them honest will require a concerted effort from everyone who cares about human rights, animal welfare, conservation and Western culture and values. B. D. Colen wrote in *New York Newsday* (June 23, 1992) that the animal rights movement is built as much on a disdain of human beings as it is on a love of animals. Maybe the real problem is one of self-esteem.

As Henke (1985) tells it in her exhaustive account of the "Seal Wars," the tactics of those who wanted to save harp seals from hunters were disgraceful. The media was manipulated the hunter unfairly colored and the economic blackmail foisted on Canada was unprecedented in the history of modern protests. The hunt was defined as bad with no qualifiers. Canada and the seal hunters were given no voice to counter the distortions.

Network news programs and documentaries reported that Greenpeace, The Fund for Animal Welfare, International Fund for Animal Welfare, the Humane Society of the United States, the Seal Rescue Fund and The Animal Protection Institute all protested the killing of harp seal pups on the nursery ice in Canadian waters. It was a great emotional money-raiser for these organizations. The perception of cruelty inherent in the humane butchering method (clubbing) and the false allegation that many animals were actually skinned while still alive added to the story. They didn't point out that clubbing was a humane way of achieving instant unconsciousness. Audience shock and horror was assured with blood on white pups. For their drive for donations, the Seal Rescue Fund claimed the seals were also about to lose critical genetic diversity, which was later proven not to be true because their numbers were never low.

Do animals have rights other than to be treated humanely? There are no morally compelling reasons why people should confer upon nonhuman animals the same regulated killing rights society now gives people. No natural or biological laws require "Thou shall not kill" behavior; on the contrary, nature needs animals to kill and humans to be surrogate predators. We do not convey legal rights to animals; our laws merely define human obligations regarding how we treat animals. Rights apply to law-governed situations, and there are laws that protect animals from mistreatment, as well there should be. Nonhuman animals do not have responsibilities and the term "right" is reserved for a legitimate claim to a particular treatment or resource, a claim that carries concomitant responsibilities.

In contrast to animal rightists, animal "welfarists permit the humane destruction of pests for the benefit of people and animal populations as a whole. As Broom (1993) describes it, animal welfare is not something given to an animal by somebody else; it is statement of commitment to the quality of life for an individual creature. Welfare depends on an animal's state in respect to its conscious attempts to cope with the environment, not necessarily to the degree of suffering being experienced. For example, the welfare of an injured animal under anesthetic actually may not be very good if it's about to die, even though the animal does not detect its condition.

Pain, suffering and distress in animals are not identical to that of people, because the nervous systems differ. However, we believe that domestic and certain other higher vertebrate animals are susceptible to discomfort. Animals cannot easily communicate their perceptions of pain to us or to other species, but we know that an injured dog whimpers. According to Broom (1993), evidence suggests that animals may use self-narcotization to cope with difficulties by secreting endogenous opioids. This may be a way that animals deal with various painful situations for they seem to voluntarily expose themselves to some obviously unpleasant conditions.

The amount of pain associated with different serious injuries varies considerably. The reason some injuries cause no pain is not understood and no general statement explains the relation between tissue damage and pain in conscious adult humans. I once fainted, unconscious of the pain, when a car door slammed on the tips of several fingers. Awareness of pain came later. No one approves of inflicting unnecessary or unjustified pain on animals, especially when the pain is intentional. No one, in fact, really knows how animals experience pain, but by anthropomorphizing, we tend to assume that higher animals do feel pain in situations that would be painful to us. Still, we legally define cruelty as any act or omission whereby unnecessary pain or suffering is caused or permitted.

Animal welfare concepts ensure that animals used for food, experiments, clothing and entertainment are handled in an acceptable manner that causes no unnecessary pain or distress. Whereas, it appears that animal rights organizations basically are not interested in improving the treatment of animals or improving their quality of life. A survey by Richards and Krannich (1991), Oregon State University sociologists, showed that, "Most animal rights activists are interested only in abolishing animal based activity, not in improving animal treatment." Strangely, the Animal Liberation Front (ALF) and other animal rights organizations can claim compassion for all creatures yet, paradoxically, react violently toward other humans. Worse, they do not believe in preventing deer, raccoons and other animals from overpopulating and then dying miserably from starvation and disease.

Only humans have a conscience and practice ethical behavior. There is no evidence that animals have any form of god to worship. It's survival-of-the-fittest—regardless of kinship. Many animals eat their own kind as a necessary factor for survival and for preserving nature. Mock et al. (1990) point out that killing a brother or sister (avian siblicide) may be common among some species of nestling birds. It may benefit both the surviving offspring and the parents, even though the sibling aggression may not be related to food supply. Because of our human dignity and ethics, people no longer eat each other. But everything, including the human body, is eventually eaten, alive or dead, by other organisms, except when cremated.

Much of the public has been blinded by the emotional animal rights propaganda, which of course has been highly visible in the media. Animal rights organizations do NOT fund research to find nonanimal alternatives for biomedical research, for animal testing or for the development of more humane ways of harvesting animals. Their goal, as stated before, is to allow no use of animals. Animal rightists surely do not approve of the Japanese practice of swallowing live fish, shrimp, small squid and lobster, young yellowtail, small flapping flounders and finger-length eels. Some animal rightists even oppose the use of seeing-eye dogs and Helping-Hands monkeys for paraplegics.

Without pet vaccination programs, which many animal rightists object to, we could not establish a significant protection barrier between the effect of wildlife disease outbreaks, e.g., plague, between humans and pets. As Midgley (1993) puts it, "we are forced, somehow, to reconcile complementary principles and duties" of animal rightists.

The animal rights movement has gained its success by cleverly manipulating the media and, unfortunately, successfully threatening others with terrorism and costly litigation. Usually the best way to diffuse conflicts with animal rightists is to keep the media away. The way activists survive is by the publicity they create. The all-too-willing television media serves activists well by providing them this sought-after publicity. They must have conflict to raise funds.

The emotional sensationalism of animal rightists, when unchallenged, sounds so convincing. It is easy to see how many, especially idealistic, impressionable young people, fall blindly into their trap because they think they are helping animals. They are usually told that the animals were here first, so we should back off. Furthermore, their standard line is that people do not have the right to dominate animals. This works well with adults as well as young people.

In interviews with representatives from 13 key animal rights organizations, Hooper (1992), a former colleague at UC-Davis, found that the most common bottom-line concern that interviewees had with respect to animal welfare and rights issues was the alleviation or elimination of unnecessary pain and suffering. Since everyone has an opinion about how animals should be treated, Hooper favors increasing dialogue to help different groups find common philosophical ground. In another article on "Interpreting the Animal Rights Controversy," Hooper (1994) raises tough questions that both wildlife managers and animal rightists need to answer.

Vivisection, dissecting a living animal, is a legitimate function in physiology or medical research, if you agree that it is our obligation to explore and increase knowledge in all spheres, even if it requires the deaths of some animals. As Adrian R. Morrison points out, we are the only species capable of undoing "harm" we have caused the planet.

Only in recent centuries in the long history of *Homo sapiens* have human populations been able to safely afford to show compassion and mercy for other species, including those they shoot, trap, domesticate and eat. Yet one leader of an animal rights organization, while we were being interviewed by the press, said it was immoral to utilize the skin and fur from an animal that died naturally in the wild. After she had expounded on the above philosophy, I pointed out that she was wearing leather boots.

Animal rightists get stuck on the word "natural." Humaneness becomes insignificant to them if an event is considered natural—especially if people caused the situation. They claim it is unnatural to control predators to protect endangered species and that livestock should die naturally of starvation or disease rather than be humanely harvested.

What do animal rights organizations do with their millions of dollars? According to Marquardt et al. (1993) and Swan (1994), generally the money is used to raise more money, bail their terrorists out of jail and finance litigation. Since the threat of lawsuits and terrorism is very intimidating to universities and other organizations, litigation becomes an effective tool of some environmental organizations and animal rightists.

If society is going to reverse this trend, organizations need to sue animal rightists more frequently when they are dishonest or break the law, as Alaska did in 1993 in response to false statements about wolf control made by The Friends of Animals. As a result, government was able to reduce an overpopulation of wolves threatening wildlife. The National Animal Interest Alliance in the state of Washington has offered to help ensure that no scientist will have to face unscrupulous attacks by animal rights activists alone. Divided, all animal users are vulnerable. Legal responses must be made, no matter how difficult it is, against dishonest activists.

In some areas humane society wardens have the power to arrest people for humane reasons. Due to the takeover of some humane societies by animal rightists, such powers are often dangerous. Leaders of the Progressive Animal Welfare Society (PAWS) of Washington State consider any use of animals as cruel. In 1993 they were caught exercising an unprecedented abuse of this humane society's power in order to achieve their political agenda. They tried to destroy basic animal industries by using their newly acquired animal cruelty statutes.

From 1901 to 1993, nearly 80 Nobel prizes for medicine and physiology were awarded for biomedical research that used animals. Practically all drugs require animal testing by someone, as did vaccines for smallpox, polio, rabies, distemper, whooping cough, tetanus, tuberculosis, cholera, mumps, chickenpox, measles and yellow fever. Yes, animal research has saved countless lives and lessened suffering of people, as well as both domestic and wild animals.

Many authors have pointed out how animal research has alleviated more pain and suffering among animals than has ever been inflicted upon research animals. Literally billions of animals undergo therapeutic surgery and are immunized against or treated for various diseases every year by veterinarians throughout the world; all this is based on research with animals. Animal research done to help people often helps animals even more, as Marquardt et al. (1993) point out, "Animals treated for hookworm, heartworm, Giardia, tuberculosis, rickets, white muscle disease, brain tumors, birth defects and cancer all benefit from animal research. It saves dogs from rabies, distemper, parvovirus, infectious hepatitis, parainfluenza and leptospirosis; and cats from rhinotracheitis, pneumonitis, feline leukemia, enteritis and dilated cardiomyopathy. It provides treatment for poultry with Newcastle disease, Marek's disease, fowl cholera, duck hepatitis, hemorrhagic enteritis, fowl typhoid and fowl pox; horses with strangles, tetanus and encephalomyelitis; sheep with anthrax and bluetongue; and pigs with influenza and swine erysipelas."

Medical advances derived from research with animals have contributed substantially to the quality and length of life for people, pets, farm animals, zoos, wildlife and endangered species. Today, perhaps 90 percent of Americans live past 50 years, thanks to animal research. Now we usually die from diseases of old age, such as cancer and heart disease. Of course, many causes of cancer and heart diseases can be avoided by diet, exercise and not smoking, but if you are unlucky and contract one of these illnesses, I am sure you would want the best medical help that is available. The battle against AIDS, too, requires research with animals.

Before the French chemist and bacteriologist Louis Pasteur developed a vaccine against rabies, thousands of dogs and other animals died annually from the disease. Animal research was essential in the development of a vaccine for tetanus and the Salk vaccine for poliomyelitis. Lithium, used to treat manic-depressive illness, has saved countless lives and billions of dollars, but its development depended on animal testing. Most people understand the urgent need to develop better contraceptives to help control the exploding human population, pet population and overpopulation of deer, skunks, raccoons, wild horses and pests such as rats, mice and coyotes. The paradox is that animals must be used in contraceptive tests.

As Marquardt et al. (1993) explains, some medical advances from research with animals include treatment for cancer, Hodgkin's disease, river blindness, jaundice, beriberi, pellagra, leprosy, hypertension, ulcers, asthma, arthritis, epilepsy and mental illness, not to mention such miracles as anesthesia, chemotherapy, tranquilizers, antibiotics, transplantation and monoclonal antibodies. And we mustn't forget that the scientific method requires research experiments to be replicated to ensure validity.

The purpose of the scientific approach is not just to prove something. It is to prove or disprove a hypothesis. Will a model reproduce earlier observations, thus enabling successful predictions of new findings? Concerning humane dissection of animals in education, McInerney (1993) points out that "molded plastic, cotton and video display terminals provide neither the sensory nor the informational content of actual tissues and organs and to argue otherwise is disingenuous at best, dishonest at worst."

Thanks in part to the animal rights movement, laboratory animals today are rarely mistreated, neglected or used frivolously by researchers. Actually, researchers are usually compassionate with their animals and have invested many hours and resources in their study. Ethical scientists, who fortunately include most scientists, agree that animals deserve to be treated kindly and with respect.

Researchers need healthy animals, hence they provide for an animal's physiological and psychological well-being. They take reasonable care to avoid undue suffering to ensure humane and responsible science. Nearly all test animals are first anaesthetized if there is to be pain and then euthanized when the tests are terminated. Cruel treatment of animals in laboratories is rare and is not even remotely akin to the suffering that occurs when laboratory animals are stolen and then released into nature, where they usually soon die.

The use of alternatives to animal research, when available, is ethically correct and usually much cheaper, but alternatives will never be able to completely replace the use of whole animals. Why? It's because there is no substitute for studying the psychology and behavior of live animals and of field studies. It is wishful thinking to believe we can find answers to many health and behavior questions without using animals in tests. Do you want a surgeon operating on you who was trained only with computer or plastic models instead of live, anesthetized animals? Are you willing to be the first live flesh the surgeon has cut? Medical students no longer receive surgical experience on live animals. The "dog labs" no longer exist, making it more difficult for surgeons to learn how to control bleeding—hemotosis—which can be life-threatening. It was the animal rights movement's lobbying efforts that resulted in these changes in the Federal Animal Welfare Act and its enforcement by the USDA.

When people who oppose research or testing on animals suffer from an accident or illness, it is doubtful that any of them would request that all medical treatments be withheld just because they had been developed or tested on animals. To do so would deny one treatment from anesthesia, painkillers, blood transfusions, insulin, antibiotics, vaccines, chemotherapy, CPR, coronary bypass surgery, orthopedic surgery and reconstructive surgery.

Animal testing has provided life-saving treatment for heart disease, AIDS, malaria, cancer, mental diseases and other illnesses. Indeed, practically all drugs require animal testing. Vaccines for smallpox, rabies, polio and distemper, among others, all required animal testing. Research by behaviorists aids in the care of pets, farm animals and the occupants of zoos. Most captive animals live much longer than their wild relatives do. To prohibit the use of unclaimed cats and dogs in pounds or animal shelters for research and teaching only shortens the life of these unwanted animals, while also necessitating the breeding of other animals for these purposes.

Since so much about the complex biology of humans and animals is still a mystery, it is, of course, impossible to simulate the unknown with computers. *In vitro* systems (cell and tissue culture) are desirable when they can be used, and they are much cheaper. However, *in vitro* systems can mimic only a small facet of the functions of a whole organism. Of interest, the alternatives we now have that no longer require animals could not have been developed without first using animals.

The need for whole-animal experimentation has been lessened to some extent by developments in the molecular and cellular fields, including the use of rats as a way of delivering proteinaceous drugs across the blood-brain barrier. Such discoveries provide many new possibilities for the treatment of pain and central nervous system disorders. An animal model for cystic fibrosis has also been developed in genetically altered mice. This will enhance our understanding of how the disease progresses and will hasten the development of new treatment. The loss of the hair-like cells of the inner ear has long been attributed to irreversible hearing loss and balance disorders. Research with birds and guinea pigs has shown that these cells can regenerate in adult humans, as well as during fetal development. There are many more examples.

As pointed out in Chapter 1, humans sometimes approve of going against nature's death ethic because they voluntarily control many of nature's mortality factors. And don't we look forward to eliminating leukemia, Alzheimer's disease, AIDS and diabetes? Likewise, our goal is to have better vaccines, more effective treatments and cures for high blood pressure, coronary-artery disease, stroke and a myriad of other ills. All of these developments and more are possible within the next couple of decades, some of them sooner, because of the research medical scientists are now doing with animals. To assert that most research goals could be obtained without using whole animals is simply not true. What is needed is assurance that test animals are used responsibly and as humanely as possible.

Complete replacement of research animals in the field of toxicology is also unlikely to happen any time soon. As with whole-animal tests, the alternatives, which are mainly cell and tissue cultures of various mammalian species, are meant to help scientists assess the potential biological risk of specific compounds. Even when *in vitro* tests indicate potential toxicity, they do not always indicate how whole-organism models might respond. As Gillis (1993) points out, "according to the researchers, who develop in vitro alternatives, there is one simple reason why animal testing cannot be completely eliminated—public safety. Manufacturers must convince regulatory agencies that any new headache concoction, anti-cancer drug, or pesticide that might be swallowed, injected or inhaled is acceptably safe for human use."

With man-animal relationships, there are no absolutes concerning use of animals. Even human rights to life and liberty are not absolute. It seems reasonable to require humans to treat animals as humanely as is possible. Even though we may claim to use animals for human benefit or as a moral duty to advance human welfare, we cannot excuse any infliction of unnecessary pain and distress caused in animals.

It is difficult to reconcile shortening the life of research animals even if the benefits derived are for man or animals. No two people will come up with the same formula, as each of us has a different ethic concerning this issue. Ideas that diverge from the dominant conventional models or paradigms of using such animals for our benefit face an uphill struggle for acceptance. Changing public viewpoints is difficult and slow.

The American Medical Association points out that it is not possible to protect all animals against pain and still conduct important biomedical research. Actually, no legislation or standard of humane care can eliminate this necessity. However, some extreme people urge that such research not be done, no matter how beneficial it may be either to animals or people. When planning a research experiment with animals, federal law requires that a veterinarian be consulted and that anesthetics, tranquilizers and analgesics be used—except when their use could interfere with the result of the experiment. Analgesia is the loss of sensibility to painful stimulation without the loss of consciousness.

It's wishful thinking to believe that we can find answers to many health and behavior questions without researching and testing with animals. For example, natural changes in viruses can unequivocally only be researched in animals. Surgeons cannot be trained as well with models as they can with live, anesthetized animals. Animal research has saved lives and lessened the suffering of both people and animals. Yet many in the animal-activist, anti-science movement are responsible for violent and illegal acts that have endangered both human and animal lives and destroyed property. They threaten our freedom of choice of health and lifestyle, whereas most people also want more research, especially if it will eliminate any disease or handicap they or their loved ones may have. Most people also want assurance that the things they eat or wear are safe. It is easy to justify the social benefits of animal experimentation to solve a problem afflicting you or a friend, and even easier to criticize if you are not personally affected.

The American people want assurance that the products they use when recovering from an illness or that they use in their daily living are safe. Congress has enacted laws that require product safety. Today, all projects involving animal testing supported by funds from the U.S. Public Health Service must comply with the regulations of the Animal Welfare Act, as amended, and the Health Research Extension Act. These laws were enacted to protect research animals and require any institution that uses laboratory animals to operate a sound animal welfare program. Researchers increasingly understand that finding alternatives to "painful" experiments on animals needs to become a high research objective.

Cosmetics and household goods must be tested on animals to ensure safety. For economic reasons, commercial products are not tested unless researchers are confident in the product's safety, then animals must be used to confirm that safety. Less than one percent of all animals used in testing are used for these purposes. Cosmetics produced without animal testing must rely on safety data derived from other related animal and human studies that involve the same ingredients or similar formulations that were done somewhere else.

American poison control centers rely upon information derived from animal studies. If Europeans had done more animal testing of thalidomide before prescribing it in the 1960s for pregnant women suffering morning sickness, they would have learned that thalidomide may cause tragic birth defects in babies. It was never approved in the United States because of insufficient testing with animals. Yet some U.S. women involved in tests and others who purchased the drug in Europe had deformed babies in the 1960s and 1970s.

Public health service agencies conduct and support toxicological testing to determine the harmful effects of commonly used products. It is essential for the public's safety to have toxicologists determine whether products are unhealthy or even deadly to humans and animals. As long as we value human and animal life, it is obvious that research with animals will be required.

To confirm the safety of a product, the toxicologist must know how the substance is absorbed, distributed, used, stored and released by a living body. This knowledge includes long-term and cumulative health effects that might lead to cancer, promote birth defects, modify reproduction or disrupt the nervous system. Compounds, moreover, can follow different pathways in the body. For example, it is possible for the liver to render an otherwise perfectly harmless substance harmful by producing toxic metabolites. No one wants to use an unsafe product.

To obtain answers to toxicology questions, progress may require the slow process of piecing together evidence laboriously collected by many people over long periods of time, but much has been accomplished. Just since 1900, research with animals has extended the human life span in the United States an average of about 25 years, according to the National Institute of Health.

Since we live in an economic world, much of the research on animals is obviously done primarily for economic reasons, but it is done only if the final product is popular and needed in the marketplace. To the benefit of society and the welfare of animals, universities and government perform much animal research. Fortunately, these researchers are usually conscientious in the manner and care in which they handle the experimental animals.

The morality of experimentation upon animals is hard to appraise and bioethical views are changing. No longer can one justify painful research with animals to advance knowledge just for the sake of knowledge. However, the practical benefits from research with animals can be difficult to predict. Major advances in research have come from basic, mission-oriented research as well as from applied research. Who is to decide whether sacrificing a few animals is justified to learn how to keep many others from suffering and dying prematurely?

The ethics of using animals in research is relevant and needs to be debated. But animal experimentation is not, as some claim, intellectual lethargy, scientific greed or ethical perversion of mandates. Still, it is good that research designs now come under closer scrutiny by committees and government. Rodents are used a lot because without short-lived animal subjects, entire fields of scientific research requiring multiple generations would be unattainable. Disease research involves entire organisms and thus requires animal models. Test-tube studies are not enough. With drugs and toxicants, only the whole animal can be truly fail-safe.

Furthermore, we trust tests on whole animals more than those using isolated cell cultures.

Before animals are used in research, all institutional animal care and use committees must extensively review any proposed protocol, a process that includes noninstitutional animal welfare representation. These reviewers may require changes in procedures and even suggest nonanimal alternatives. When government funds are used on a project, additional reviewers assure compliance to the National Institute of Health Guide. Furthermore, if questions concerning improper use of animals do arise, the researcher will be unable to publish the results.

Current laws administered by the Food and Drug Administration (FDA), including the Federal Food, Drug and Cosmetic (FD & C) Act, are designed to ensure product safety and effectiveness. These laws place responsibility on the FDA to ensure that human and animal drugs, biologics and medical devices are safe and effective and, along with USDA, also that food products are safe and wholesome. They point out that animal testing by manufacturers seeking to market new products is often necessary to establish product safety.

The Food and Drug Administration supports and adheres to the provisions of applicable laws, regulations and policies governing animal testing, including the Animal Welfare Act and the Public Health Service Policy called "Humane Care and Use of Laboratory Animals." Moreover, in all cases in which animal testing occurs, the FDA advocates that research and testing derive the maximum amount of useful scientific information from the minimum number of animals and employ the most humane methods available within the limits of scientific capability.

With reference to cosmetic products, the Federal Food, Drug and Cosmetic Act does not specifically require that cosmetic manufacturers test their products for safety in the context of premarket approval by the agency. However, if the safety of a cosmetic product—a lotion, deodorant or shampoo—is not adequately substantiated, the Act considers the product misbranded and the manufacturer may be subject to regulatory action unless the principal display panel bears the statement, "Warning—the safety of this product has not been determined."The eye and skin irritancy tests on rabbits are considered among the most reliable for evaluating the safety of a substance to be introduced into or around the eye or placed on the skin, but in recent years the number of rabbits used in these tests has been greatly reduced.

We constantly need to stress the importance of the "3 Rs" in animal research. They are (1) *Replacement*: Use alternatives to animals or substitute a species of lower intelligence (mice for chimpanzees); (2) *Reduction*: Minimize the number of subjects required; and (3) *Refinement*: Change procedures when possible to further minimize any stress on the animals.

For greater than four centuries in Europe and more than a century in the United States, movements have arisen to oppose the use of animals for the benefit of humans. This opposition has targeted scientific research that involves animals. The FBI has identified the more militant animal rights bands, such as the Animal Liberation Front (ALF), as terrorist groups.

It certainly is not cruel treatment when an animal is first anesthetized or put to sleep before it is used in biomedical research or in the training of medical, veterinary or other students. Effective and officially approved methods of quickly euthanizing different species of laboratory and food animals that are considered humane include use of carbon dioxide, barbiturates, halothane, stunning, cervical dislocation, decapitation, captive bolt gun shot, microwave irradiation and tricaine methanesulfate.

We all have our vested interests in the sense that we want to see our own objectives about humane treatment of animals achieved. There is great concern among many conservationists, professional wildlife managers, researchers, livestock operators and sportsmen about some extreme opposing measures pursued by some groups besides animal rightists. Their actions often increase the amount of distress animals experience, especially among wild animals in man-modified environments.

Animal rightists have misled a well-meaning, highly concerned portion of the public into thinking their donations will save animals and improve wildlife conservation. In 1997 *Newsweek* estimated that there were 7,000 or so animal rights groups in the United States with a combined annual budget of $300 million. The amount of money involved is much more today.

The animal rights movement spends vast sums in direct mail appeals, with the result, after paying the fund-raiser, that at best a small percentage of the contributions can be used for the advertised cause, with most of this going to overhead. Except for making the public more aware of the need for humane treatment of animals, which is important, such organizations do little to improve the welfare of animals.

Animal rightists sometimes resort to sensationalist propaganda to manipulate people's emotions about trapping and hunting. Animal rightists would have you believe that hunters, trappers and sport fishermen are driving some animals to extinction, when these groups have actually done more to protect wildlife than most others.

The public demands greater participation in decision-making, but every environmental solution has trade-offs, so the public should think hard about these issues before contributing money. Americans should also look closely before contributing to anti trapping, shooting and poisoning solicitations, as wildlife conservation still demands these tools to maintain healthy animal populations.

Much confusion exists today because scientists must be objective, whereas some animal rights advocates do not seem to be constrained by honesty. Many fund-raising statements should be viewed with a healthy dose of skepticism since no branch of government is required to monitor their accuracy. Litigation—a tool of some advocates—polarizes opinions. Fortunately, environmental mediation and mitigation of substitute habitat is being required when some habitat is going to be lost to development.

If you belong to an environmental organization, are you getting tired of the deluge of "alert" mail requesting donations for environmental emergencies? Groups using this strategy are losing credibility. The danger is that the public will no longer believe legitimate environmental and animal welfare alerts. The leaders of advocacy organizations chart policy set by their boards, but it is important to note that the donating members don't get to vote on these decisions; the board does it. Also, these organizations have to compete with each other for the diminishing public dollar.

The Nature Conservancy is one of the few environmental organizations that actually uses most of your donation to purchase habitats to preserve natural biological diversity. They are reported to have more money than the combined assets of the Sierra Club, Greenpeace, Friends of the Earth, National Audubon Society, Izaak Walton League, Wilderness Society and the National Wildlife Federation. The Nature Conservancy is a master at brokering deals to exchange certain kinds of natural resources for beneficial purposes.

One reason why many wildlife issues, such as managing the density of deer and their predators, are sometimes so difficult to resolve, occurs when environmental obstructionists polarize the issues, then lobby members of Congress and agency officials. Often when they don't get their way, they sue. Since it is difficult for them to raise funds with mediation and compromise, we are deluged instead with costly litigation. Lawyers strive to win, not compromise and lawyers have replaced biologists at the helm of many environmental organizations. Former Chief Justice Warren E. Burger (1983) pointed out how law schools have traditionally steeped students in the adversarial tradition, rather than teaching skills to resolve conflicts. Lawyers are natural competitors and once litigation begins, they use every tactic available to win. Unfortunately, environmental issues have become choice litigation subjects.

The public needs to feel empathy for a realistically managed nature, instead of simply seeking environments devoid of people. Hutchins et al. (1982) point out that by adhering to a philosophy that emphasizes a reverence for life, you may have to ignore the conditions necessary for life. Since people are needed as a surrogate predator, one may be unfaithful to his/her own philosophy about ecology. Because every environmental issue has trade-offs, too frequently some so-called "humane" donations can actually make matters worse.

Advocacy organizations thrive on controversy, so that they literally cannot "afford" to have their propaganda issues resolved.

Indignation is their bread and butter—hence the persistent efforts to emotionalize pet issues and keep them in litigation. Animal rights groups, with their millions of dollars, have gained control of many former legitimate animal welfare organizations, thereby confusing the public.

One aspect of the animal rights movement is that the leaders must constantly search for new issues in order to maintain their "watchdog" credibility. Biological principles and common sense unfetter their rhetoric. Some groups are highly skilled at arousing public emotions. As mentioned earlier, the showing of a young harp seal being clubbed to death on snow was very effective, even though this method is very humane as the seals are instantly stunned unconscious. It is probably the best procedure for harvesting surplus young of this species. For those opposed to harvesting any harp seals, it was a successful way of arousing the public.

If harp seals were being overexploited, then all that would be necessary is to reduce the quota harvested each year. The opposing groups never proposed this approach. The harp seal issue was a bonanza for Greenpeace, after it failed trying to create a nuclear issue in Canada. But once the Scandinavian countries, Canada and others proved harp seals were not being overexploited, Greenpeace abandoned the subject as it was no longer a lucrative issue.

For many good reasons biologists seldom try to challenge unsound lawsuits or tactics used by some environmental extremists. They can't afford to. It is therefore no wonder, as Feirabend (1984) points out, why we are forced to accept what public pressure then demands of the state legislatures and Congress and what the courts ultimately dictate. Unfortunately, it is essentially a tacit admission of guilt when scientists, professional wildlife managers, conservationists and others let these falsifications pass uncontested for fear of being attacked. Equally articulate rebuttals from scientists are sorely needed, for biologists are much more knowledgeable about these issues.

We can hope that the outrageous activities of the ALF (Animal Liberation Front, founded in 1973 as the Band of Mercy) will eventually prove counterproductive and die out. The sad part is that they, PETA, The Fund for Animals, The Humane Society of the United

States and others can attract so much media attention without fair representation from the other side of the issues. Without much trouble you can identify for yourself the organizations that use cheap shots and emotional dogma against hunting, trapping, research and agriculture. Or you can obtain details about them by reading *Animal Scam: The Beastly Abuse of Human Rights* by Marquardt et al. (1993), which I have quoted frequently in this chapter. These organizations clearly have too many deep-pocket leaders. Usually, the more emotional their solicitations for funds, the less likely it is that any of your donation will be used to help an animal.

Manipulating the public by creating fictitious balance-of-nature issues rarely helps the environment. In the long run, such action shakes public confidence in trained wildlife specialists and the environment suffers. This action also threatens the future of wildlife conservation by creating controversy between sportsmen and birdwatchers, hunters and anti-hunters, urbanites and agriculturists. Yet we all need to cooperate with each other to help nature in modified environments.

Environmental pollution is a public health concern that involves habitats, wildlife and land use. It is paramount that the health of our natural systems and the vitality of ecosystems be preserved by consensual agreement. Ownership of natural resources cannot carry with it inviolate, market-driven, private rights of the "I-can-do-whatever-the-heck-I-want-to-because-it's-mine" exploiter. Community interest in the management of resources cannot be ignored. When dealing with nature, the attitude that "I can do as I damn well please and to hell with everybody else because it is my land" is intolerable.

Good environmental organizations, such as The Wildlife Federation, Sierra Club, Audubon Society, et al., are needed to expose environmental insults by individuals, business enterprises and governments. These organizations have been very successful with this mission and their help is still needed. However, some organizations prefer litigation instead of mediation because it is difficult to raise funds by compromising. Court decisions rarely address the real issues, since it is difficult to develop environmental solutions in courts.

Some state wildlife agencies seem willing to yield decision-making to these groups to avoid harassment. Universities and other organizations also fear harassment. Individuals from some of these agencies, by contrast, are sometimes a little too cozy with the environmental groups. This becomes obvious when environmental groups hire key employees of state and federal agencies soon after they retire, in the same way generals in the military once were commonly employed by defense industries immediately after they retired.

For many reasons, wildlife managers find it difficult to obtain the public support they deserve. Wildlife managers cannot raise money, as they are not supposed to have "causes." They must think positively about wildlife and environmental issues. Yet objectivity sometimes necessitates a different politically unpopular point of view. However, if the wildlife profession doesn't use its knowledge and give Congress and other leaders a better understanding of the issues, extremist groups will control wildlife legislative decisions.

All environmental decisions must be based on reasonable compromises, but vested interest groups make this difficult. Serious debates and discussions are needed to help members of the public establish their own ethics about animal exploitation based on facts rather than only emotions. This is the objective of this book. Every solution to environmental issues has trade-offs and opposing sides need to hear each other.

A common fund-raising technique used by many organizations is to dramatize key issues by requesting the reader to complete a national or international survey, census or ballot concerning that organization's fund-raising issues. The questions are usually so mundane and simple that the recipient's answers are a foregone conclusion. The survey always ends with an appeal for emergency financial support so the agency can resolve these critical and vital issues. By then your emotions will be sufficiently aroused to make you feel benevolent and generous instead of alert.

Too many people leave scientific knowledge aside and allow their emotions to influence their decisions. This is what has happened with many environmentalists' activists. The public is trapped by vested interests. It is impossible to be elected to a public office without being indebted to key campaign contributors. Therefore, the best way for organizations to raise money is by polarizing issues and creating legal injunctions to get publicity. Contributors to animal rights and environmental organizations need to be cautious, especially if the solicitations appear highly emotional. Even though your financial support is badly needed, one must be selective.

In conclusion, to protect America's wildlife and other natural resources and to improve the quality of the human environment, we must understand nature better and work with it.

## A Summary of Issues Concerning Animal Rightists

The following list of issues is to serve as a review of this chapter and to provide the reader with a summary of key issues in need of consideration.

1.  Does nature give animals "rights" other than the right to try to survive and reproduce?
2.  Some claim it morally wrong to use animals in science, agriculture, hunting, fishing, any sport or as pets, no matter how humanely they are treated or how beneficial it may be to other animals or to people.
3.  Is it wrong to prevent our pets, farm and research animals from experiencing the distresses their wild counterparts encounter when they run free in the natural world?
4.  Should people help nature by being surrogate predators where natural predators no longer exist?
5.  Should we protect animals from nature's cruelty when man has altered the environment and upset the natural predator-prey relationship leading to the suffering?
6.  Is it okay to kill native predators to save a native species that has become endangered because we have modified its habitat?
7.  Since wild animals can overproduce just as cats and dogs do, but spaying and neutering are not realistic alternatives, is it

ever better for people to remove them by more humane methods?

8. Are we justified in killing a few individual animals if it is necessary to provide a quality life for the remaining population?

9. To prevent overpopulations, is it necessary for a large number of the offspring of all species to die before they reproduce?

10. Since the density of many animal populations will be inevitably modified if people alter the suitability of their habitats, is it appropriate to help regulate any resulting undesirable and unnatural population densities instead of leaving the outcome to nature?

11. Do you agree that no agricultural crop, reforestation or home landscaping could survive either economically or aesthetically if all native animals, especially mammals, were given full protection and allowed to graze and browse where they pleased?

12. Do we have a moral responsibility to temper nature's brutality, when we can, if the suffering is the consequence of our modification of the environment?

13. How do you want surplus animals (any animal) to die?

14. In California, epidemics of plague seem to occur only when ground squirrels and some other native rodents have become excessively abundant due to man's modification of the environment. When this happens, is it okay to poison the infected fleas in rodent burrows and to use poison or traps to prevent such unnatural high densities of rodents from occurring?

15. Are there positive points of the animal rights (not animal welfare) movement?

16. In what way does the animal rights movement benefit the conservation of wildlife resources or preserve biological diversity?

17. Are game species better off because people want to exploit them?

18. Do regulated hunting, fishing and trapping usually result in the improvement of the quality of life for game species?

19. When a population of deer is undergoing suffering and mortality from starvation or diseases, would you condone deer hunting, where either firearms or bow and arrows can be safely used, to lower the population to the carrying capacity of that habitat?

20. Should it be illegal to use the modern, padded, offset-jaw traps and leg snare to capture troublesome predators or furbearers?

21. Can't some animal damage control practices improve the welfare of other animals?

22. Do current laws and regulations of institutions adequately prevent unnecessary pain and distress of research animals and require that nonanimal alternatives be used when feasible?

23. In order to support animal rights principles, are you willing to forgo all medical treatments developed or tested on animals, such as blood transfusions, anesthesia, painkillers, antibiotics, insulin, vaccines, chemotherapy, CPR, coronary bypass surgery, reconstructive surgery, orthopedic surgery and others?

24. Should misplaced or surplus mammals be translocated if it will give them another chance for life, even though translocated mammals suffer much distress and probably will die while looking for their former home?

25. Is the animal rights philosophy based on any biological principle?

CHAPTER 8

# Conclusion

One must understand nature's life-death ethic in order to be objective about society's need to manage nature. This is necessary so that wild animals and people can cohabit better in a world that is composed of human-modified environments. Nature also needs to be better understood, so we can appreciate how and why wild and domestic animals need to be used responsibly for food, game, pets or for research and materials. The ecology and management of the agriculture-urban interface has room for improvement to ensure the future health of wildland ecosystems.

Since humans have radically modified most environments and the original predator-prey balance no longer exists, it is essential that people assist nature's survival-of-the-fittest regime by being a "responsible" surrogate predator. All animals exploit other animals, but humans are the only ones who do it under many regulations designed to ensure the welfare of the species and to minimize unnecessary pain and distress, and who also show compassion and pity toward their prey. Nature doesn't do this.

For the welfare of future generations, we want to be sure that this planet is still worth inhabiting, even though it is bound to be quite different from what it is today. It is essential that we recognize the catastrophic consequences that will result when an abundant species like *Homo sapiens* exceeds its carrying capacity and can no longer be governed by natural forces. As a consequence of people counteracting nature's death ethic, the excessive human population has had undesirable effects on the environment. For us to maintain healthy ecosystems, we need to extend an ethic of stewardship and responsibility toward the resources of the land and oceans and a strong policy of sustainable use of the environment.

Nature's life-death ethic is what maintains the balance of nature. Human social ethics need to be shaped around nature's birth-and-death ethic and also other laws of nature, rather than emotional propaganda. Our quest should be for environmental excellence. The whole world must recognize that continued growth—whether economic or demographic—is unsustainable.

All species produce a surplus of offspring. This is necessary to provide food for other animals and is the source of the energy required to maintain the balance of nature. Therefore, the life of all species requires an effective mortality factor by predation or by some form of self-limitation (disease, starvation, competition, territoriality or cannibalism). To not allow nature's death ethic to play its role can be a death trap to entire populations of animals. We must also recognize that some pain and distress are natural phenomena that also have survival benefit.

Once people modify the environment and top carnivores like grizzly bears, lions and wolves are reduced or eliminated for safety reasons, as has happened in most of the world, people must step in and help nature reestablish a new balance. Why? Nature demands meat-eaters, though they do not necessarily have to complete the cycles that return energy and nutrients to the beginning. The excessive growth in the human population forces undesirable environmental modifications. This rapid growth and resulting unsustainable resource use have finite limits.

This book is intended to stimulate readers to rethink their relationships with animals, with the environment and, perhaps most importantly, with themselves. The sustainability of a viable and diverse natural resource base and good public health depend on our capacity to better manage these critical resources in an economical, social and environmentally acceptable way.

People work diligently to ensure a better quality of life—free of starvation, diseases and, arguably, fighting between individuals and populations. Why shouldn't we afford similar opportunities to the animals we share this planet with?

Human interaction with the environment always alters the composition of habitats and the native fauna and flora. In these modified environments, meeting the habitat requirements of people, animals, plants and other organisms becomes profoundly complicated. That's why it is essential to manage species composition and diversity. This process cannot be left to nature alone. We must intervene to prevent extinctions. Furthermore, our active involvement is necessary to maintain a more desirable near-natural balance. Healthy animals are productive animals.

In modified environments the choice is ours: Should we let a new survival-of-the-fittest balance evolve, at the cost of extinctions? Or should we help nature by correcting both the species and the habitats? The choice is clear. We have a moral obligation to help nature regulate the balance of nature.

When it comes to people's emotions about nature's death ethic, too many seem to lack the critical-thinking, reflective judgment and, most significantly, evidence-based reasoning. Is that why they are unable to use their thinking skills to defend their views? Students at the end of my animal welfare class volunteered the mystery they experienced: "They didn't know why, but they could not change their philosophy about animals dying, even though they said they realized that their views were emotional and contrary to nature's death ethic, which they believed." We need to understand nature. Our understanding of ecosystem function is more primitive than one might think. We don't eliminate habitats; we only alter them.

Our hope is to capitalize on what we have learned about the ecological consequences of pollution, pesticides, heavy metals and other environmental insults so we can maintain the earth as a habitable planet. We are not just concerned with the richness or abundance of different entities, such as the number of species and variety of habitats. Exotic fauna and flora, even though usually undesirable, actually increase biological diversity, but not natural diversity. This is a crucial distinction. Natural biological diversity refers to the original distribution of species.

Saving endangered species is an important building block of environmental consciousness. Our desire to save a displaced animal from death is usually prompted by conscience, not true compassion for that animal. We instinctively want to give all animals another chance when possible. What we must do is properly manage and control wildlife in today's human-modified ecosystems. Management is the humane course of action. Overabundant populations destroy our wildlife heritage. The rhythms of nature beget an ethic of life and death. Chosen or not, it is our responsibility—indeed, our inheritance—to be responsible stewards and regulate the density of animals. Many animal-borne diseases, such as plague and rabies, are a consequence of humans modifying habitats and undesirable species becoming overabundant.

We must search for more environmentally acceptable alternatives to help people and animals coexist. This has been my lifetime goal. Sometimes it is only a single member of a species that needs to be controlled. Usually animal control is of little biological significance as nature sustains itself through populations, not by a few individuals. Unfortunately, some people prefer to let animals suffer and die by nature's edicts of self-limitation. The archer, hunter or trapper unquestionably provides a more humane alternative.

There is no biological basis for opposing regulated hunting, trapping and fishing—only an emotional one. Licensed hunters, fishermen and trappers have done more to protect wildlife and their habitats, thus also preserving biological diversity, than any other group. In California, where mountain lions are now a completely protected species, more of the surplus lions are being killed annually under depredation permits than were ever taken by hunters when lions were managed as a hunted game animal.

Americans enjoy the cheapest and most bountiful food in the world. Unfortunately, we don't have scientific knowledge on how to bring ecological and economic health into harmony. In 1900 about one-half of our human population lived on farms; now it's only about one out of 50. When I asked my ecology students what would happen if everyone now tried to grow their own food, they discovered, much to their surprise, that the natural environment would be largely destroyed. They found that homeowners simply couldn't do it as efficiently as farmers could. It would require much more land, water, animal damage control and pesticides.

Animals of economic value usually have a high quality of life. Financial support from hunting, fishing, trapping and excise taxes on equipment used makes it possible to employ wildlife biologists and wardens to ensure the well-being of animals. Very importantly, funds from sportsmen also help preserve the game's habitats. These wildlife habitats are one of the nation's most important assurances of natural biological diversity. The greatest threats to biodiversity are habitat destruction, invasive species, pollution and overharvesting. Margolis (2004) explains how invasive species spread by landscape disturbances, roads, railways, canals, clinging to hulls or hiding in bilge water or packing material. One reason such invasive species are hard to prevent is every trade barrier created to do so harms both buyers and sellers.

It is imperative that society incorporates nature's life-death ethic to create biologically sound wildlife management. This book has attempted to raise pertinent facts about nature, as well as issues that the hunter, trapper, agriculturist and animal rightist need to address. In a broad sense, nature's life-death ethic seems to involve our culture; that is, all human value-bearing social, economic and political aspects as well as the arts, sciences, humanities and religion.

Many legitimate questions can and should be asked about the morality of using animals. You must decide for yourself. This book makes the case that society needs to support the ethical and moral responsibility implicit in the use of animals in research, for food, as game and for recreation, and that unnecessary pain and distress not be inflicted. Managing nature's life-death ethic enables more animals to live a good life in today's world.

A middle ground exists between man's unabashed exploitation of natural resources and the total exclusion of human use of the resources. This book has tried to reach those with a sufficiently open mind to look objectively at the facts and desire to clarify their own ethics about nature.

Legal rights are not ascribed to animals, yet animals have value and they deserve respect and humane treatment. In fact, unnecessary pain and distress should be prohibited. But who defines "unnecessary"? Deciding when pain and trauma are justified is more an issue of personal ethics than a set of unchanging moral principles or values, hence the conflict in viewpoints. Young wild animals must experience some pain and distress or they will never be able to survive in nature's survival-of-the-fittest regime. The availability of suitable habitats is the key to the welfare of wild animals and it is primarily the hunters, fisherpersons, trappers and organizations like The Nature Conservancy who pay for habitat preservation.

We must recognize that for humans, an abundant life and freedom from want requires a low birth rate and a low death rate, whereas with wildlife just the opposite occurs, as nature's life-death ethic requires a high birth rate and a high premature death rate. Without doubt the human population explosion must be checked. If babies of the future are to live as they do now, fewer must be born or, as with wildlife, a higher premature death rate will inevitably eventually occur.

We are morally obliged to manage nature as best we can since we have disrupted it. We must learn to be fair, humane and even loving toward animals. When used properly for our welfare, domestic animals benefit. Remember, we are dealing with human-modified environments in which the original predator-prey balance no longer exists. This is why people must help nature's life-death ethic by functioning as nature's surrogate predator. People are the only predators that kill under regulations designed to benefit the prey. They are also the only predators that show compassion toward the prey they take. To help nature in modified environments we must understand nature's life-and-death ethic and live in accordance with its mortality factors.

Nature's high birth rate serves the twofold purpose of providing prey for predators in nature's complex chain of sustenance and ensuring that enough individuals survive and procreate to sustain the species. When this balance is disturbed by humans, as it is in today's world, it becomes the responsibility of people to fulfill nature's promise by culling or controlling animal populations through various means. These include regulated sport hunting and trapping to keep animal populations from exceeding the carrying capacity of their habitats.

People are unwittingly killing wild animals with kindness, by causing overpopulations. If you really love wild animals, don't feed them and do not let them overpopulate in modified environments; this condemns them to nature's harsh self-limiting mortality factors. We must abide by the laws of nature.

The world's human population provides a good example of what happens when many of nature's mortality factors are not allowed to function. To provide for the growing human population, look what is happening to the world's renewable and nonrenewable resources, the availability of water for domestic and agricultural use, erosion, environmental pollution and, presumably, our effects on global warming. Human cultures are dangerously out of sustainable relationship to the natural environments. It is time to embrace a new environmental awareness grounded in the biological facts of life and guided by a truly compassionate ethic of sustainable stewardship. The public needs to recognize that nature needs us. We need to alert the next generation. They are the losers if we don't. I do hope this book has helped you clarify and strengthen your own ethics about nature and the environment.

# Glossary of Terms

Acclimation—Process of adaptation by an individual organism to a new situation.

Acclimatization—An adaptive change in the heredity of a population or portion of a species tending to fit it for a particular set of environmental conditions.

Active ingredient—The chemical in a pesticide product responsible for the pesticidal effect.

Acute toxicity—The capacity of a chemical to cause death or injury from a single exposure. $LD_{50}$ is a common indicator of the acute toxicity.

Adaptation—The fitness of an organism within its genetic structure for its environment or the process (acclimation) by which it becomes fit.

Aggressive Behavior—Includes both combat and aggressive display to drive the stimulus object away or otherwise modify it by intimidating, injuring or even killing it.

Agonistic Behavior—Aggressive behavior associated with conflict or fighting between two individuals.

Alarm Call—Some animals, especially many birds, produce alarm calls, while themselves free, when they sight a predator or other alarming circumstance.

Analgesia—Loss of sensibility to pain of a fully conscious person or animal.

Analgesic—A drug causing freedom from pain (analgesia).

Anesthesia—Loss of sensation, produced by anesthetics.

Animal Month—A month's tenure upon rangeland by one domestic animal.

Animal Rights—A view that it is never justified to sacrifice the interests of one individual to benefit another individual.

Animal Unit Month (AUM)—The estimated number of acres necessary to provide forage for one horse, one cow-and-calf, five sheep or their equivalent, for one month under proper use.

Animal Welfare—Ensuring that all exploited animals are handled in an acceptable, responsible manner that does not cause unnecessary pain and distress.

Anthropomorphism—To attribute a characteristic that belongs only to humans to things not human.

Antifertility Agent—A substance that prevents effective reproduction.

Autecology—Individual ecology.

Avicide—Toxicant used against birds.

Avoidance Behavior—Behavior that postpones an aversive event and thus provides escape from conditioned aversive stimuli.

Balance of Nature—The relationship of the population densities of the diverse species of organisms that make up an ecologic community.

Behaviorist—A scientist who studies learning and related phenomena, most commonly in domestic or laboratory animals.

Bioaccumulation—The process by which chemicals accumulate in the body tissues of animals. Chemicals with high bioaccumulative potential are passed up the food chain when predators consume prey that contain the residue of that chemical.

Biodiversity—The variety and variability among living organisms at all levels and the process that links the ecological system complexes in which they occur. The richness and complexity of the natural life of an area. Usually implies the "natural or original" diversity that existed in an area.

Biogas—Chemical energy, mainly methane, that has been extracted from organic materials in sealed containers.

Biogeography—The geographic distribution of organisms.

Biological Conservation—Conservation of fauna and flora.

Biological Control of Vertebrates—An attempt to reduce the population density of a pest species (i.e., increase mortality, reduce natality or cause a significant emigration) either by increasing predation, manipulating the conditions of the habitat, introducing or stimulating epizootics or by the application of antifertility or immunocontraception agents.

Biological Diversity—A measure of the variety and variability among living organisms and the ecological complexes in which they occur. It usually refers to the original natural diversity of species that existed in an area before being disturbed by people.

Biological Integrity—Refers to a system's wholeness, including presence of all appropriate elements and occurrence of all processes at appropriate rates and under little or no influence from human actions.

Biomass—The total quantity of living material present at a given moment in a particular situation (wt/unit surface area of habitat).

Biome—Regional climates interacting with biota and substrate to produce large, easily recognizable community units called biomes.

Bioregions—Natural assemblages of plants and animals, defined by physiographic and climatic limits, with discernible but dynamic boundaries existing simultaneously along both spatial and temporal trajectories.

Biosphere—The portion of the earth in which all ecosystems and life operate.

Biotic Province—A major ecological division of a continent that covers a continuous geographic area.

Brownlash—A label to describe the backlash against "green" environmental policies of anti-science propagandists.

Brush Control—Reduction of brush by fire, chemical or physical means to reduce its competition with more desirable species of forage for space, moisture, light and nutrients.

Carrying Capacity—The maximum density of a particular species of animal that can be maintained in a given ecosystem on a sustained basis without deteriorating the habitat, i.e., the number of individuals that a habitat can perpetuate in a healthy condition.

Chaparral—A brush community composed of evergreen sclerophyllous (stiff, leathery leaves) species.

Chemosterilant—A chemical substance which causes sterilization or prevents effective reproduction.

Circadian Rhythms—Activity cycles approximating 24 hours under constant conditions (*circa*—about, *diem*—day).

Climax—A biological community in a state of relative ecologic equilibrium with its habitat because it is no longer experiencing further successional changes.

Communication Signals—A chemical or physical production by an individual that influences the behavior of recipient individuals of the same species.

Community—An assemblage of ecologically related organisms composed of two or more species.

Conservation—The perpetuation (not preservation per se) and wise use of natural, faunal and floral resources, including air, water and soil, as well as conservative use of nonrenewable resources such as natural gas, oil and minerals.

Consumers (Macroconsumers)—Heterotrophic organisms, chiefly animals, which ingest other organisms or particulate organic matter.

Cruelty—Willful infliction of pain or distress upon an animal.

Cyclic—A population with great annual variation between high and low densities (excluding seasonal fluctuations) which occur with cyclic regularity.

Decomposers (Microconsumers, Saprobes or Saprophytes)— Heterotrophic organisms, chiefly bacteria and fungi, which break down the complex compounds of dead protoplasms, absorb some of the decomposition products and release simple substances usable by the producers.

Demography—A study of populations, especially births, deaths and related statistics.

Density-Dependent and Density-Independent—Factors that control a population's density may or may not depend upon the population's density, e.g., density-dependent factors are believed to be important in determining the "equilibrium" density of each species.

Desertification—A reduction of the biological potential of the land, its biological diversity, that leads to desert-like conditions.

Dispersal—1. Abandonment of a former home range. 2. "Innate dispersal"—predisposed at birth with a dispersal instinct usually activated at puberty. 3. "Environmental dispersal"—result of intraspecific pressures; the selection of a new home range, part of which is usually within the confines of the parental home range.

Distress—Suffering from pain, discomfort or trauma. Usually a state that can be relieved if the animal devotes substantial effort or resources in its response.

Distress Call—A desperation signal emitted by animals, especially birds, when variously restrained and handled.

Diversity—See *Biological Diversity*.

Dominance—An individual is said to be dominant over another when it has priority in feeding, sexual and locomotor behavior and when it is superior to another or other individuals in aggressiveness and in group control.

Ecological Equivalents—Organisms that occupy the same niche in similar communities of different biogeographic regions.

Ecological Pyramid—A method of illustrating trophic structure and/or function in which the producer level makes up the base, with successive levels of organisms leading to top carnivores at the apex.

Ecology—Derived from the Greek *oikos*, meaning house or place to live. A branch of biology concerned with organisms in relation to each other and their environment.

Economic Control—The reduction or maintenance of a pest density below the economic-injury level to a crop.

Economic-injury Level—The lowest population density (usually of insects) that will cause economic damage.

Economic Threshold—The density at which control measures should be determined to provide the necessary time to initiate control in order to prevent an increasing pest population (usually of insects) from reaching the economic-injury level.

Ecosystem—An ecological community (of organisms) together with its habitat (climate and physical features of the environment).

Ecosystem Management—The integration of ecological, economic and social principles so as to protect ecological integrity, sustainability, natural biological diversity and productivity of biological and physical environmental systems.

Ecotone—A narrow or broad intermediate transitional strip between adjacent communities.

Emigration—An individual or species leaving a community more or less permanently (geographic migration).

Endangered Species—A species whose prospects for survival and reproduction are in immediate jeopardy due to loss of habitat, change in habitat, overexploitation, predation, competition or disease. See *Threatened, Peripheral* and *Rare species.*

Endemic—Area over which animals or other organisms occur naturally or where a breeding population has become established.

Energy Flow—The total assimilation at a given trophic level equal to the production of biomass and respiration.

Environment—All the organic and inorganic features that surround and affect a particular organism or group of organisms, i.e., both the biotic and physical factors of the habitat.

Environmentalism—A movement supported by people concerned about the quality of the environment.

Environmentalist—In a broad sense, someone who is concerned about the welfare of the environment.

Epidemiology—A study of the various factors that determine the frequency and distribution of diseases within populations of animals.

Equilibrium Position—The average density of a population over a period of time in the absence of permanent environmental change.

Eradicate—Often used to imply the local extermination of a species. Best stated as local eradication.

Ethics—Philosophical moral standards or values of conduct and judgment.

Ethologist—A behaviorist typically trained in zoology, who studies behavior of all kinds of animals.

Euthanasia—Act or method of causing death painlessly.

Eurythermal—Often used to imply the complete extinction of a species over a large continuous area such as an island or a continent. Not a good term for animal damage control because it also denotes making a species extinct.

Exotic—An alien or introduced organism that is not native to the region in which it is found.

Extermination—Often used to imply the complete extinction of a species over a large continuous area such as an island or a continent unless stated as local extermination. Not a good term for animal damage control because it also denotes making a species extinct.

Extinction—The complete disappearance of a species. Behaviorally, the resulting reduction in the magnitude or other dimension of a response that has been elicited by a conditioned stimulus.

Food Chain—A sequence of species within a community, within which each member serves as food for the species next higher in the chain.

General Adjustment Syndrome—Response of an organism to nonspecific stress in its attempt to maintain homeostasis.

Governing Mechanism—The actions of environmental factors, collectively or singly, which so intensify as the population density increases that they prevent any increase beyond a characteristic high level and which relaxes as the density falls so that extinction is made unlikely.

Habitat—The environmental situation (usually only climate and physical features of the environment) in which or on which any community, species or individual lives. Habitat suitability is the key to survival of a species.

Habitat Stability—Natural biomes have a well-established, relatively stable, animal-soil-vegetation complex, which is not delicately balanced due to self-limitation of species when natural predation is not operating.

Homeostasis—The ability of an individual, society or community to regulate itself so that it is able to exist in a frequently changing environment.

Home Range—The area over which an individual animal habitually travels while engaged in its daily activities. It can be a daily, seasonal or lifetime home range.

Humane—Responsible treatment of animals that is kind, merciful, tender and considerate.

Immigrant—An individual or species entering a community where previously it was not present.

Immunity—Following repeated exposures to pesticides, drugs or pathogens, the organism acquires the ability to resist harm from the agent or infection.

Immunocontraception—Genetic engineering to produce microorganisms that express species-specific gamete antigens to be spread through the target animals by sexual transmission, contagion or arthropod vector.

Imprinting—The recognition of parental characters through learning in a brief, usually very early, stage in animals' lives. May apply to learning about food and habitat characteristics of the environment.

Indicators—Indicator species of plants or animals often recur again and again in widely separated ecosystems of similar types and serve as an indicator of certain general characteristics, health or status of that part of the environment.

Indigenous—A naturally occurring species.

Innate—Inborn. In behavior, it refers to genetic differences between responses of individuals or species. The terms *innate* and *learned* are sometimes difficult to differentiate concisely in animal behavior.

Integrated Control—A management system that, within the area of associated environment and population dynamics of the pest species, uses all suitable techniques and methods as compatibly as possible to maintain pest populations at levels below those causing economic injury.

Integrated Pest Management (IPM)—Effort to bring together a set of nonlethal control strategies and a minimum of lethal methods to achieve efficient control of a pest.

Interspecific—Interrelationships between members of different species.

Intraspecific—Interrelationships between members of the same species.

Introduction—The release of a free-ranging animal or species into a location where the species does not occur naturally. See Reintroduction.

Invasions—Spread of a species into a community where it was not formerly represented.

Invasion Biology—The study of the reproduction, dispersal and ecological impact of organisms that occur outside their native range, including exotic pests and biological control agents.

Irruption—An unusually high population density of either a cyclic or noncyclic species.

Latency of Response—The measure of time elapsing between onset of stimulus and the beginning of the response to it.

$LC_{50}$—The dose of a chemical that can kill 50 percent of the test animals. $LC_{50}$ is expressed in milligrams of a chemical per liter of water.

$LD_{50}$—The dose of a chemical that can kill 50 percent of the test animals. $LD_{50}$ is expressed as milligrams of a chemical per kilogram of body weight.

Learning—The process that produces adaptive change in individual behavior as the result of experience.

Liebig's "Law" of the Minimum—The basic requirement of essential materials which an organism must have to exist and thrive in a given situation.

Life-Zone—Area over which climatic factors control the distribution of certain major vegetation types and also are accompanied by characteristic subordinate plants and associated animals.

Limits of Tolerance—Organisms have an ecological minimum and maximum requirement and the range in between represents the limits of tolerance.

Limiting Factors—Any environmental factor that limits the distribution and/or the size of a population.

Marginal Habitat—Where individuals or populations live a tenuous existence and may not successfully reproduce.

Memory—Modification of behavior by experience.

Migrations—Seasonal migrations, e.g., the regular annual geographic or change-in-elevation round trips made by many birds and game mammals; "geographic" migration implies a more or less permanent movement of a species into a new geographic area (emigration).

Mitigation—Replacement elsewhere of the form and function of a natural habitat or renewable resource that is to be adversely affected.

Monoculture—Growing one kind of crop over a sizable area.

Multiple Use—Harmonious use of land for more than one of the following purposes: grazing of livestock, wildlife production, recreation, watershed, mining and timber production, but not necessarily the combination of uses that will yield the highest economic return or unit output.

Natality—Birth rate.

Natural—A process that is the consequence of nonhuman-caused events.

Natural Control—The maintenance of a more or less fluctuating population density with certain definable upper and lower limits over a period of time by the combined actions of abiotic and biotic elements of the environment.

Natural History—A term that has come to imply the study of the animal, vegetable and mineral world in a popular, nontechnical manner with emphasis being on the species or subject rather than environmental relationships (ecology).

Natural Selection—Differential survival with the elimination of the less-fit individuals in competition for existence.

Nature Reserve—An area that has been set aside from development for the purpose of perpetuating natural conditions.

Neutered—An animal sterilized by removal of sufficient sexual organs.

Niche—That portion of a habitat a species occupies for shelter, for breeding sites and for other activities including the food that it eats and all the other features of the ecosystem that it regularly utilizes.

Nonrenewable Resources—Minerals, fossil fuels and other materials which are not replenishable.

Olfaction—Smell is characterized by a sensitivity to volatile substances in extreme dilution, whereas the gustatory or tasted receptors require more gross contact with a chemical stimulant.

Ontogeny—The life cycle of biological development of a single organism.

Outdoors—It requires both space and biological diversity.

Overabundant animals—Successful species that have increased in abundance, usually due to human-induced changes in communities or ecosystems, to the point that they outcompete other species and degrade the habitats and their own welfare.

Overpopulation—A population level that the habitat and species present cannot sustain indefinitely without being debilitated.

Pain—An unpleasant sensory and emotional experience that may be associated with actual or potential damage to the individual.

Peck Order—Social dominance by which individuals are able to dominate individuals lower in the peck order, but in their turn may be pecked or dominated by those individuals that rank higher. pH—The measure of the concentration of hydrogen ions in a solution. As the number of hydrogen ions increase, the solution becomes more acid.

Peripheral Species—A species or subspecies whose occurrence in the United States or in a state is at the edge of its natural range, and which is rare or endangered within the United States or state, although not in its range as a whole. (See *Endangered, Threatened* and *Rare* species.)

Pesticide—A substance or mixture of substances intended for destroying, repelling or mitigating any vertebrate or invertebrate pest or preventing the species from becoming a pest.

Pheromones—Intraspecific chemical stimuli (e.g., sex odors) perceived by members of the same species from the external environment that induce selective species-specific responses that do not have to be learned (*pherein*—to carry and *hormon*—to excite).

Phylogeny—The racial history or evolutionary development of a species.

Physiognomy—Apparent characteristics; outward features or appearance of habitat, community, etc.

Physiological Adaptation—Genotypically controlled process of an organism, whereby it adjusts internally to environmental influences.

Physiologic Homeostasis—The maintenance of the internal environment (both intra—and extracellular) within limits conducive to the survival of the organism. (See *Homeostasis*.)

Placebo—An inactive harmless substance that contains all of the same ingredients except the toxic or test material.

Pollution—Environmental (e.g., air, water, land, cities) contamination.

Population—A group of individuals of the same species.

Population Density—The primary factors determining the density of a vertebrate species are the suitability of the habitat conditions, natural predation and species self-limitation.

Population—Environmental pollution resulting from too many people.

Predator—An animal that kills and feeds on other organisms.

Primary Productivity—Gross primary productivity is total rate of photosynthesis including the organic matter used up in respiration. The net primary productivity is the rate of storage of organic matter in plant tissues in excess of the respiratory utilization by plants.

Producers—Autotrophic organisms, largely green plants, which are able to manufacture food from simple inorganic substances and sunlight.

Quality Life—When a reasonable proportion of the young of a species' population are able to live long enough to reproduce and are not seriously distressed from human-caused factors.

Range Management—The art and science of planning and directing range use to obtain sustained maximum animal production, consistent with perpetuation of the natural resources involved.

Rare Species—A rare or threatened species or subspecies is one that, although not presently threatened with extinction, exists in such small numbers throughout its range that it may be endangered if its environment worsens. A Status Undetermined species or subspecies is one that has been suggested as being rare or endangered, but more information is needed. (See Endangered, Threatened and Peripheral species.)

Recreation—A constructive use of leisure time, the value of which must be measured in terms of its contribution to a healthy society. It can no longer be considered a secondary use of natural resources.

Reintroduction—The release of an animal or species into an area where that species formerly lived.

Renewable Natural Resources—Those parts of man's environment which have utility for him and which, even though used, may by his actions be maintained or increased in quantity and/or quality. It excludes nonrenewable natural resources such as minerals, but includes air and water with all of their components.

Repelling or Attractive Biosounds—Sounds produced by any animal that influence the behavior of a pest species.

Resistance—The natural or genetically acquired ability of an organism to ward off the deleterious effects of such noxious agents as poisons, toxins, irritants or pathogenic microorganisms.

Riparian—The area or vegetation along a stream or river that is influenced by the waterway.

Rodenticide—A pesticide applied as a bait, dust or fumigant to destroy or repel rodents and other types of nonrodent mammals, such as moles (insectivores), and rabbits and hares (lagomorphes).

Rope Firecracker—Slow-burning rope fuse in which firecracker fuses can be inserted at irregular intervals to frighten birds.

Sanitation—The establishment of environmental conditions favorable to health or to reduce pest problems.

Sentient—Having conscious feelings.

Selective Pesticides—A pesticide which, while killing the target pest individuals, spares much or most of the other fauna, including beneficial species, either through differential toxic action or through the manner in which the pesticide is utilized (including formulation, dosage and timing for use).

Self-Limitation—In the absence of adequate predation, species involuntarily have their population densities prevented from exceeding certain levels by the interaction of intraspecific stress factors (e.g., psychological, competition for food or mates, territoriality, disease or other vicissitudes of life) which cause various increases in mortality, reductions in natality or emigrations due to territoriality from the overpopulated areas.

Sere—Any sequence of successional stages leading from a definite pioneer stage to a climax of any kind.

Social Behavior—Activities elicited by other members of the same species but, in some cases of another species, that have some effect on other individuals.

Social Dominance or Rank—Conditions under which certain individuals dominate the others in the group by their strength or aggressiveness.

Society—An assemblage of individuals all of the same species.

Sound Frequencies—Cycles per second, now often referred to as Hertz or Kilohertz (Hz or kHz) instead of cycles or kilocycles.

Spayed—A female animal sterilized by having its ovaries removed.

Species—A group of interbreeding populations (actually or potentially) reproductively isolated from other similar groups.

Species-Integrity—A view that promotes the value of species as well as individual animals and humans.

Speciesism—The assumption that one species has the right to exploit other species. Humans and animals share one principle of classification, i.e., being of different species, and there is no argument in principle for preferring experiments on animals to those on man.

Stability Principle—Any natural enclosed system, with energy flowing through it, tends to change until a stable adjustment with self-regulating mechanisms is developed (e.g., mortality rate correlated with increase in density).

Stupefacients—Drugs used as a pesticide to cause birds to go into a state of stupor to facilitate their being captured and removed, or so that their erratic behavior will frighten other birds away from that area.

Subclimax—Any important successional stage below the climatic climax.

Succession—The natural replacement of one community by another.

Suffering—A more general term than pain, including anything from distress to death, and might be a consequence of pain or distress. It is a specific state of mind.

Survival-of-the-fittest—Nature's life-death ethic permitting those animals to survive that are best adapted.

Sustainable Development—The development of resources that meet the environmental and economic needs of the present without undue degradation or compromising the ability of future generations to meet their needs.

Sustainability—A state of development in which we equitably meet the resource needs of current and future generations without causing a net loss of environmental integrity.

Synecology—Population or community ecology.

Synergistic Effects—Where the degree of control achieved by a combination of methods exceeds the sum of the independent effects of each method.

Territory—That portion of a home range that is defended against trespass by other members of the same species.

Threatened Species—A rare species or subspecies that is likely to become endangered unless current trends are reviewed.

Tolerance—An organism's ability to endure a pesticide or drug without ill effect due to its state of innate resistance or acquired immunity.

Translocation—The transport and release of a captured animal (or one rehabilitated) from one location to another away from its former home range.

Trap Night—A term used to express the ratio of individuals captured depending upon the number of traps and the number of nights they were set. Six trap-nights equal two traps set for three nights.

Trophic Levels—A term used to distinguish the more important levels of food production and utilization, e.g., starting with primary producers (usually green plants), then primary consumers (herbivores) and followed by secondary consumers (predators), each being a trophic level.

Ungulate—Mammals that have hoofs.

Veganism—The complete avoidance of any use of animal products.

Vegans—Those who practice strict vegetarianism, i.e., avoiding not just meat but all products from animals.

Vegetarian—One who avoids eating meat. *Semi-vegetarian*—One who does not eat red meat. *Pesco-vegetarian*—Eats fish, dairy products and eggs. *Ovo-vegetarian*—Eats eggs. *Lacto-ovovegetarian*—Eats dairy products and eggs.

Vertebrate Control Objectives—To accomplish the desired effect with a maximum of safety to man and other forms of life, a series of measures that can be carried out as humanely as possible with a minimum of disturbance to the biotic community. It is the alleviation of the *problem* to a tolerable level, not necessarily the destruction of vertebrate animals.

Vertebrate Pest—Any native or introduced, wild or feral species of vertebrate animal that is currently troublesome locally or over a wide area, to one or more persons, either by being a health hazard or a general nuisance or by destroying food, fiber or natural resources. A pest to one person may at the same time have esthetic or recreational value to another.

Virtue Ethics—A moral stance that requires us to live or act in accordance with virtues, such as justly, generously, kindly and so on.

Watershed—The land area where surface water is drained by a river, stream or creek through one outlet or river mouth.

Wetlands—An area too aqueous to walk on and too solid for boats.

Whorls—Ring of branches around the main stem.

Wilderness—In contrast to those areas where man dominates the landscape, a wilderness is a relatively unaltered ecosystem of any size where man is a visitor who does not remain.

Wildlife Control—Reduction of animal numbers for the well-being of other organisms, resources or for public health reasons.

Wildlife Management—The art of making land produce either a sustained optimum density or a restricted density of a wildlife species, for its own well-being and/or to accommodate humans.

Zoonoses—An animal disease that can be transmitted to man.

# References

The following references provide useful information about the issues discussed in this book, but some are not cited in text. No attempt has been made to review the extensive literature on the subjects covered in this book. The author's personal library contains about 24,000 catalogued reprints.

Allison, Rachel. 1993. Administration policies and old-growth: An interview with Assistant Secretary of Agriculture James R. Lyons. *J. Forestry* 91 (12): 2-23.

Angermeier, P. L., and J. R. Karr. 1994. Biological integrity versus biological diversity as policy directives. *BioScience* 44: 690-97.

Greening Earth Soc. 1998. In *Defense of carbon dioxide: A comprehensive review of carbon dioxide's effects on human health, welfare, and the environment*. Spec. Publ., Greening Earth Soc., Arlington, VA.

Appenzeller, Tim. 2004. The case of the missing carbon. *National Geographic* 208 (2): 88-117.

Arkow, P. 1998. Application of ethics to animal welfare. *Applied Anim. Behavior Soc.* 59: 193-200.

Arrow K., B. Bolin, R. Costanza, P. Dasgupta, C. Folke, C. S. Holling, B.-O. Jansson, S. Levin, K.-G. Mäler, C. Perrings, and D. Pimentel. 1995. Economic growth, carrying capacity, and the environment. *Ecological Economics* 15: 91-95. Reprinted from *Science*, 268 (1995): 520-21.

Asner, G. P., T. R. Seastedt, and A. R. Townsend. 1997. The decoupling of terrestrial carbon and nitrogen cycles. *BioScience* 47: 226-34.

Atkinson, I. A. E., and E. K. Cameron. 1993. Human influence on the terrestrial biota and biotic communities of New Zealand. *Tree* (Elsevier Science Pub.) 8 (12): 447-51.

Ballard, W. B., L. A. Ayres, P. R. Krausman, D. J. Reed, and S. G. Fancy. 1997. Ecology of wolves in relation to a migratory caribou herd in northwest Alaska. *Wildl. Monogr.* 135: 1-50.

Barbier, E. B., ed. 1993. *Economics and ecology: New frontiers and sustainable agriculture.* London: Chapman & Hall.

Barnes, J. I. 1996. Changes in the economic use value of elephant in Botswana: The effect of international trade prohibition. *Ecological Economics* 18: 215-30.

Barnes, R. F. W. 1985. Woodland changes in Rhuaha N. P. (Tanzania) between 1976 and 1982. *African Journal of Ecology* 23: 215-21.

Barnes, R. F. W., and E. B. Kapela. 1991. Changes in the Ruaha elephant population caused by poaching. *African J. Ecol.* 29: 289-94.

Baskin, Yvonne. 1994. Ecosystem function of biodiversity. *BioScience* 44: 657-60.

Bason, M., and J. R. Beddington. 1991. An assessment of the maximum sustainable yield of ivory from African elephant populations. *Math. BioSc.* 104: 73-95.

Beauchamp, W. D., R. R. Koford, T. D. Nudds, R. G. Clark, and D. H. Johnson. 1996. Long-term declines in nest success of prairie ducks. *J. Wildl. Manage.* 60: 247-59.

Beier, P., and R. F. Noss. 1998. Do habitat corridors provide connectivity? *Conservation Biol.* 12: 1241-52.

Bekoff, M., and D. Jamieson. 1991. Reflective ethology, applied philosophy, and the moral status of animals. In *Perspectives in ethology,* Vol. 9, edited by P. P. G. Bateson and P. H. Klopfer, pp. 1-47. New York: Plenum Publ. Corp.

Belsky, A. J., and D. M. Blumenthal. 1997. Effects of livestock grazing on stand dynamics and soils in upland forests of the interior West. *Conservation Biol.* 11: 315-27.

Bendel, P. R., and G. D. Therres. 1994. Movements, site fidelity and survival of Delmarva fox squirrels following translocation. *Am. Midl. Nat.* 132: 227-33.

Berryman, J. H. 1994. Blurred images: And the future of wildlife damage management. *16th Vertebrate Pest Conf.* Edited by W. S. Halverson and A. C. Crabb, pp. 2-4. Davis: University of California.

Bicak, C. J. 1997. The application of ecological principles in establishing an environmental ethic. *Amer. Biol. Teacher* 59: 200-06.

Boertje, R. D., P. Valkenburg, and M. E. McNay. 1996. Increases in moose, caribou, and wolves following wolf control in Alaska. *J. Wildl. Manage.* 60: 474-89.

Bongaarts, John. 1994. Population policy options in the developing world. *Science* 263: 771-76.

Bonner, R. 1993. *At the hand of man: Peril and hope for Africa's wildlife.* New York: Alfred A. Knopf.

Boonstra, R., C. J. Krebs, and N. C. Stenseth. 1998. Population cycles in small mammals: The problem of explaining the low phase. *Ecol.* 79: 1479-88.

Bradley, M. P., L. A. Hinds, and P. H. Bird. 1997. A bait-delivered immunocontraceptive vaccine for the European red fox (*Vulpes vulpes*) by the year 2002? *Reprod. Fertil. Dev.* 9: 111-16.

Brass, D. A. 1994. *Rabies in bats: Natural history and public health implications.* Ridgefield, CT: Livia Press.

Bright, Cris. 1998. *Life out of bounds: Bioinvasion in a borderless world.* New York: W. W. Norton.

Broom, D. M. 1993. Welfare and conservation. In *Animal welfare and the environment*, edited by R. D. Ryder, pp. 90-101. United Kingdom: Duckworth/RSPCA.

Brown, Lester R. 1995. *Who will feed China.* New York: W. W. Norton.

————. 2001. *Economy.* New York: Earth Policy Institute, W. W. Norton & Co.

————. 2003. *Rescuing a planet under stress and a civilization in trouble.* New York: Earth Policy Institute, W. W. Norton.

Brown, Lester R., C. Flavin, and H. French. 1998. *State of the world 1998.* Washington, DC: Worldwatch Inst.

Brown, Lester R., G. Gardner, and B. Halweil. 1998. Beyond Malthus: Sixteen dimensions of the population problem. *Worldwatch Paper 143.* Washington, DC: Worldwatch Inst.

Brown, Lester R., M. Renner, and B. Halweil. 1999. *Vital signs 1998*. Washington, DC: Worldwatch Inst.

Brown, Lori. 2004. State of the world: A year in review. In *State of the World 2004*, pp. xxi-xxv. Washington, DC: Worldwatch Inst.

Buckle, A. P., and R. H. Smith, eds. 1994. *Rodenticide pests and their control*. Wallingford, England: CAB International.

Burger, W. E. 1983. Conflict resolution. Isn't there a better way? *National Forum* (Phi Kappa Phi Journal) 63 (4): 3-5.

Cairncross, F. 2004. What makes environmental treaties work? *Conservation in Practice* 5 (2): 12-16, 18-19.

Campbell, B. M., J. R. A. Butler, I. Mapaure, S. J. Vermeulen, and T. Mashove. 1996. Elephant damage and safari hunting in *Pterocarpus angolensis* woodland in northwestern Matabelel and Zimbabwe. *Afr. J. Ecol*. 34: 380-88.

Cape, J. N. 1993. Direct damage to vegetation caused by acid rain and polluted cloud: Definition of critical levels for forest trees. *Environmental Pollution* 82: 167-80.

Carbyn, L. N. 1989. Coyote attacks on children in western North America. *Wildl. Soc. Bull*. 17: 444-46.

Caro, T. M., N. Pelkey, M. Borner, K. L. I. Campbell, B. L. Woodworth, B. P. Farm, J. Ole Kawai, S. A. Huish, and E. L. M. Sererre. 1998. Consequences of different forms of conservation for large mammals in Tanzania: Preliminary analysis. *Afr. J. Ecol*. 36: 303-20.

Chasey, D. 1996. Rabbit haemorrhagic disease: The new scourge of *Oryctolagus cuniculus. Lab. Animals* 31: 33-44.

Cheek, R. 1997. *Learning to talk bear*. Columbia Falls, MT: Skyline Publ.

Childs, J. E., J. N. Mills, and G. E. Glass. 1995. Rodent-borne hemorrhagic fever viruses: A special risk for mammalogists. *J. Mammalogy* 76: 664-80.

Christenson, N. L. 1996. The report of the Ecological Society of American Committee on the scientific basis for ecosystem management. *Ecol. Applications* 6: 665-91.

Coffman, M. S. 1994. *Saviors of the earth? The politics and religion of the environmental movement*. Chicago: Northfield Publ.

Cohen, A. N. 1992. Weeding the garden. *Atlantic Monthly*, November: 76-78.

Cohen, J. E. 1995. *How many people can the earth support?* New York: W. W. Norton.

Conover, M. 2001. *Resolving human-wildlife problems.* Boca Raton, FL: CRC Press.

Conover, M. R., W. C. Pitt, K. K. Kessler, T. J. DuBow, and W. A. Sandborn. 1985. Review of human injuries, illnesses, and economic losses caused by wildlife in the United States. *Wildl. Soc. Bull.* 23: 407-14.

Cooper, J. E. 1995. Wildlife species for sustainable food production. *Biodiversity and Conservation* 4: 215-19.

Costanza, R., R. d'Arge, R. deGroot, S. Farber, M. Grasso, B. Hannon, K. Limburg, S. Naeem, R. V. O'Neill, J. Paruelo, R. G. Raskin, P. Sutton, and M. van den Belt. 1997. The value of the world's ecosystem services and natural capital. *Nature* 387: 253-60.

Crowder, A. A., E. A. Ripley, and R. E. Redmann. 1995. *Environmental effects of mining.* Delray Beach, FL: St. Lucie Press.

Cumming, D. H. M., M. B. Taylor, G. S. Cumming, M. S. Cummomg, J. M. Dunlap, A. G. Ford, M. D. Hovorka, D. S. Johnston, M. Kalcounis, Z. Mahlanyu, and C. V. R. Portfors. 1997. Elephants, woodlands, and biodiversity in southern Africa. *S. Afr. J. Sci.* 93: 231-36.

Curtin, C. G. 1993. The evolution of the U.S. National Wildlife Refuge System and the doctrine of compatibility. *Conservation Biol.* 7: 29-38.

DellaSala, D. A., D. M. Olson, S. E. Barth, S. L. Crane, and S. A. Primm. 1995. Forest health: Moving beyond rhetoric to restore healthy landscapes in the inland Northwest. *Wildl. Soc. Bull.* 23 (3): 346-56.

Decker, D. J., T. L. Brown, and W. F. Siemer, eds. 2001. *Human dimensions of wildlife management in North America.* Bethesda, MD: The Wildlife Society.

Dekker-Robertson, D. L., and W. J. Libby. 1998. American foreign policy—Global ethical trade-offs. *BioScience* 48: 471-77.

DeLong, D. C., Jr. 1996. Defining biodiversity. *Wildl. Soc. Bull.* 24: 738-49.

DeSabata, Giacomo. 1995. The false myth of unlimited economic growth. *Environ. Conserv.* 22: 199-200.

Dodd, J. L. 1994. Desertification and degradation in sub-Saharan Africa. *BioScience* 44: 28-34.

Dolins, F. L., ed. 1998. *Attitudes to animals.* New York: Cambridge University Press.

————. 1999. *Views in animal welfare.* New York: Cambridge University Press.

Dubos, R. 1973. Humanizing the earth. *The Rotarian* 122 (6): 15-18.

Dunn, Seth2001. Hydrogen futures toward a sustainable energy system. *Worldwatch Paper 157.* Washington, DC: Worldwatch Inst.

————. 2002. Reading the weather vane: Climate policy from Rio to Johannesburg. *Worldwatch Paper 160.* Washington, DC: Worldwatch Inst.

Dwyer, J., and F. M. Loew. 1994. Nutritional risks of vegan diets to women and children: Are they preventable? *J. Agric. And Environ. Ethics* 7: 87-109.

Eaton, R. L. 1998. *The sacred hunt: Hunting as a sacred path.* Ashland, OR: Sacred Press.

Edwards, C. A., R. Lal, P. Madden, R. Miller, and G. House, eds. 1993. *Sustainable agricultural systems.* Delray Beach, FL: St. Lucie Press.

Ehrlich, P. R., and G. C. Daily. 1993. Population extinction and saving biodiversity. *AMBIO* 22: 64-68.

Ehrlich, P. R., and A. H. Ehrlich. 1990. The population explosion. *Amicus J.* 12 (1) 22-29.

Eisler, R. 1995. Sodium monofluoroacetate (1080) hazards to fish, wildlife, and invertebrates: A synoptic review. *Biol. Rept. 27*, National Biological Survey, USDI.

Elphick, C. S., and L. W. Oring. 1998. Winter management of California rice fields for waterbirds. *J. Applied Ecol.* 35: 95-108.

Estes, J. A. 1996. Predators and ecosystem management. *Wildl. Soc. Bull.* 24: 390-96.

Fagre, D. B. 1981. Inhibition of predatory attacks by captive coyotes: Conditioned avoidance for a repellent prey and its mimics. Ph.D. thesis. University of California, Davis.

Farnham, T. J., C. P. Taylor, and W. Callaway. 1995. A shift in values: Non-commodity resource management and the Forest Service. *Policy Studies J.* 23: 281-95.

Fayrev-Hosken, R. A., P. Brooks, H. J. Bertschinger, J. F. Kirkpatrick, J. W. Turner, and I. W. M. Liu. 1997. Management of African elephant populations by immunocontraception. *Wildl. Soc. Bull.* 25: 18-21.

Feirabend, J. S. 1984. The black duck: An international resource on trial in the U.S. *Wildl. Soc. Bull.* 12: 128-34.

Festing, M. F. W. 1994. Reduction of animal use: Experimental design and quality of experiments. *Lab. Animals* 28: 212-21.

Flecknell, P. A. 1994. Refinement of animal use—Assessment and alleviation of pain and distress. *Lab. Animals* 28: 222-31.

Fox, M. A. 1986. *The case for animal experimentation: An evolutionary and ethical perspective*. Berkeley: University of California Press.

Fritts, T. H. 1988. The brown tree snake, *Bioga irregularis*, a threat to Pacific Islands. U.S. Fish and Wildlife Serv., *Biol. Rept.* 88 (31).

Galindo-Leal, C., and M. Weber. 1994. Translocation of deer subspecies: Reproductive implications. *Wildl. Soc. Bull.* 22: 117-20.

Gardner, Gary. 1996. Asia is losing ground. *World Watch* 8 (6): 18-27.

Gardner, Gary. 2003. Engaging religion in the quest for a sustainable world. In *State of the World*, pp. 152-175. Washington, DC: Worldwatch Inst.

Garnett, G. P., and E. C. Holmes. 1996. The ecology of emergent infectious disease. *BioScience* 46: 127-35.

Garrettson, P. R., and F. C. Rohwer. 2001. Effects of mammalian predator removal on production of upland-nesting ducks of North Dakota. *J. Wildl. Manage.* 65: 398-405.

Garrettson, P. R., F. C. Rohwer, and J. M. Zimmer. 1996. Effects of mammalian predator removal on waterfowl and non-game birds in North Dakota. *Trans. 61 No. Am. Wildl. and Natur. Resource Conf.*, 94-101.

Garrot, R. A., P. J. White, and C. A. V. White. 1993. Overabundance: An issue for conservation biologists? *Conservation Biol.* 7: 946-49.

Geist, V. 1988. How markets in wildlife meats and parts, and the sale of hunting privileges, jeopardize wildlife conservation. *Conservation Biol.* 2: 15-26.

Gentile, J. R. 1987. The evolution of antitrapping sentiment in the U.S.: A review and commentary. *Wildl. Soc. Bull.* 15: 490-503.

George, K. P. 1994. Discrimination and bias in the vegan ideal. *J. Agricultural and Environmental Ethics* 7: 19-28.

Gianpietro, Mario. 1994. Sustainability and technological development in agriculture. *BioScience* 44: 677-89.

Gillis, A. M. 1993. Toxicity tests minus animals? *BioScience* 43: 137-40.

Ginnett, T. F., and S. E. Henky, eds. 2001. The role of predator control as a tool in game management. *Proc. of a Symposium*, Texas Agric. Res. & Exten. Center, San Angelo, TX.

Goodland, Robert. 1995. The concept of environmental sustainability. *Annu. Rev. Ecol. Syst.* 26: 1-24.

Gowdy, J. M. 1992. Economic growth *versus* the environment. *Environ. Conserv.* 19: 102-04.

Gowdy, J. M., and S. O'Hara. 1995. *Economic theory for environmentalists*. Delray Beach, FL: St. Lucie Press.

Grandin, Temple. 1994. Farm animal welfare during handling, transport, and slaughter. *JAVMA* 204: 372-77.

Grant, Lindsey. 1996. *Juggernaut: Growth on a finite planet*. Santa Ana, CA: Seven Locks Press.

Gregory, N. G. 1994. Preslaughter handling, stunning, and slaughter. *Meat Science* 36: 45-56.

Grizzle, R. E. 1994. Environmentalism should include human ecological needs. *BioScience* 44: 263-68.

Gross, Bob, and R. J. Laacke. 1984. Pocket gophers girdle large true firs in northeastern California. *Tree Planters' Notes* 35 (2): 28-30.

Grumbine, R. E. 1994. What is ecosystem management? *Conserv. Biol.* 8: 27-38.

Guither, H. G. 1998. *Animal rights: History and scope*. Southern Illinois University Press.

Haber, G. C. 1996. Biological, conservation, and ethical implications of exploiting and controlling wolves. *Conserv. Biol.* 10: 1668-81.

Hahn, G. L., and J. L. Morrow-Tesch. 1993. Improving livestock care and well-being. *Agric. Engineering*, May: 14-17.

Hall, P., J. Hall, and L. Amkrant. 1992. Fur trapping: Forget Bambi, face reality. *Triology* 4: 88-90.

Hall, T. R., W. E. Howard, and R. E. Marsh. 1981. Raptor use of artificial perches. *Wildl. Soc. Bull.* 9: 296-98.

Hamilton, D. 1992. Animals and ethics. *Missouri Conservationist*, October: 15-18.

Hamilton, D. A., B. Roberts, G. Linscombe, N. J. Jotham, H. Noseworthy, and J. L. Stone. 1998. The European Union's wild fur regulation: A battle of politics, cultures, animal rights, international trade, and North America's wildlife policy. *Trans. 63rd No. Am. Wildl. and Natur. Resour. Conf.*, 572-88.

Hardy, D. T. 1990. *America's new extremists: What you need to know about the animal rights movement.* Washington, DC: Washington Legal Foundation.

Hecht, S. B. 1993. The logic of livestock and deforestation in Amazonia. *BioScience* 43: 687-95.

Heinen, J. T. 1995. Thoughts and theory on incentive-based endangered species conservation in the United States. *Wildl. Soc. Bull.* 23 (3): 338-45.

Henke, J. S. 1985. *Seal wars: An American viewpoint.* Newfoundland: Breakwater Books.

Herenda, D., and O. Jakel. 1994. Poultry abattoir survey of carcass condemnation for standard, vegetarian, and free range chickens. *Can. Vet. J.* 35: 293-96.

Herscovici, A. 1985. *Second nature: The animal-rights controversy.* Toronto: CBC Enterprises.

Hoagland, J. L. 1985. Infanticide in prairie dogs: Lactating female kill offspring of close kin. *Science* 230: 1037-40.

Hobbs, N.T. 1996. Modification of ecosystems by ungulates. *J. Wildl. Manage.* 60: 695-713.

Höft, Robert, and Martina Höft. 1995. The differential effects of elephants on rain forest communities in the Shimba Hills, Kenya. *Biol. Conservation* 73: 67-79.

Hollingsworth, William. 1996. *Ending the explosion: Population policies and ethics for a humane future.* Santa Ana, CA: Seven Locks Press.

Hooper, J. K. 1992. Animal welfarists and rightists: Insights into an expanding constituency for wildlife interpreters. *Legacy,* November-December: 21-25.

————. 1994. Interpreting the animal rights controversy: Are you ready for the tough questions? *Legacy,* January-February: 20-21.

Howard, W. E. 1949. Dispersal, amount of inbreeding, and longevity in a local population of prairie deermice on the George Reserve, southern Michigan. Contrib. Lab. Vert. Biol., University of Michigan, Ann Arbor.

————. 1965. Control of introduced mammals in New Zealand. N.Z. Dept. of Sci. and Industrial Research, Information Series, no. 45.

————. 1982. A tiger problem in India. *10ᵗʰ Vertebrate Pest Conf.* Edited by R. E. Marsh. University of California, Davis.

————. 1983. Viewpoint: The coyote-1080 conspiracy—An aborted attempt to drive livestock off federal lands. *Rangelands* 5: 134-35.

————. 1989. Nature's role in animal welfare. Eighth Hume Memorial lecture, UFAW, Potters Bar, England

————. 1990 (rev. 1991). *Animal rights vs. nature.* Davis, CA: Howard Press.

————. 1996. Damage to rangeland resources. In Chap. 23, *Rangeland Wildlife.* Edited by P. K. Krausman, pp. 383-94. Denver, CO: Society of Range Management.

————. 2004. *Saved by bed bugs.* Bend, OR: Global Publishing Services.

Howard, W. E., and R. E. Marsh. 1984. Ecological implications and management of feral mammals in California. Presented at 3ʳᵈ Intern. Theriological Conf., 1982, Helsinki, Finland. In *Mammals—Problems and potential,* pp. 31-41. IUCN.

Howard, W. E., R. E. Marsh, and C. W. Corbett. 1985. Raptor perches: Their influence on crop protection. *Acta Zool. Fennica* 173: 191-92.

Howard, W. E., and R. H. Schmidt. 1984. Biological rationale for 1080 as a predacide. *Proc. 11th Vertebrate Pest Conf.* Edited by D. O. Clark, pp. 138-45. University of California, Davis.

Hubert, G. F., Jr., L. L. Hungerford, and R. D. Bluett. 1997. Injuries to coyotes captured in modified foothold traps. *Wildl. Soc. Bull.* 25: 858-63.

Hueting, Rorefie. 1996. Three persistent myths in the environmental debate. *Ecological Economics* 18: 81-88.

Hughes, B. O., and M. J. Gentle. 1995. Beak trimming of poultry: Its implications for welfare. *World's Poultry Sci. J.* 51: 51-61.

Hughes, B. O., S. Wilson, M. C. Appleby, and S. F. Smith. 1993. Comparison of bone volume and strength as measures of skeletal integrity in caged laying hens with access to perches. *Veterinary Science* 54: 202-06.

Hutchins, M., V. Stevens, and N. Atkins. 1982. Introduced species and the issue of animal welfare. *Intern. J. Studies of Animal Problems* 3 (4): 318-36.

Jacobson, J. J. 1994. Population mythology: Gender, social justice, and politics. *Amicus J.* 16 (1): 9-10.

Jedrzejewska, B., and W. Jedrzejewska. 1998. Predation in vertebrate communities. *Ecological Studies* 135, Springer, Verlag Berlin, Germany.

Jones, I. S. F., and H. E. Young. 1996. Engineering a large sustainable world fishery. *Environ. Conserv.* 224: 99-104.

Jones, M. J. 1993. Sustainable agriculture: An explanation of a concept. Crop Protection and Sustainable Agriculture, Wiley, Chichester (Ciba Foundation Symposium 177), pp. 30-47.

Kapis, M. B., and S. C. Gad, eds. 1993. *Non-animal techniques in biomedical and behavioral research and testing.* Boca Raton, FL: Lewis Publ.

Kasworm, W. F., and T. J. Thier. 1995. Transplanting grizzly bears *Ursus arctos horribilis* as a management tool—Results from the Cabinet Mountains, Montana, USA. *Biol. Conservation* 71: 261-68.

Kay, C. E. 1995. Browsing by native ungulates: Effects on shrub and seed production in the greater Yellowstone ecosystem. In *Proc. Wildland Shrub and Arid Land Symposium.* Compiled by B. A.

Roundy, E. D. McArthur, J. S. Haley, and D. K. Mann. U.S.F.S., Intermountain Res. Sta., Ogden, Utah.

Kellert, S. R. 1982. Striving for common ground: Humane and scientific considerations in contemporary wildlife management. *Intern. J. Studies Animal Problems* 3 (2): 137-40.

Kerasote, T. 1996. Outdoor ethics—Asking the hard questions. Keynote address. Izaak Walton League of America, *Outdoor Ethics* 15 (1-3).

Kettlewell, P. J., and M. A. Mitchell. 1994. Catching, handling, and loading of poultry for road transportation. *World's Poultry Sci. J.* 50: 54-56.

Kirkpatrick, J. F., J. W. Turner, Jr., I. K. M. Liu, R. Fayrev-Hosken, and A. T. Rutberg. 1997. Case studies in wildlife immunocontraception: Wild and feral equids and white-tailed deer. *Reprod. Fertil. Dev.* 9: 105-10.

Kline, A. D. 1995. We should allow dissection of animals. *J. Agric. and Environ. Ethics* 8 (2): 190-97.

Korpimäki, E., and C. J. Krebs. 1996. Predation and population cycles of small mammals. *BioScience* 46: 754-64.

Krebs, J. W., J. S. Smith, C. E. Rupprecht, and J. E. Childs. 1998. Rabies surveillance in the United States during 1997. *JAVMA* 213: 1713-28.

Kreeger, T. J. 1997. Contraception in wildlife management. *A.P.H.I.S., USDA Tech. Bull.* 1853.

Krohn, C. C., and L. Munksgaard. 1993. Behavior of dairy cows kept in extensive (loose housing/pasture) or intensive (stall) environment. *Appl. Anim. Behav.* 37: 1-16.

Kyrklund, B. 1992. The potential of forests and forest industry in reducing excess atmospheric carbon dioxide. *Nature et Faune, FAO Regional Office So. Africa* 8 (1): 16-19.

LaFrance, J. T., and M. J. Watts. 1995. Public grazing in the west and "rangeland reform '94." *Amer. J. Agr. Econ.* 77: 447-61.

Leuthold, W. 1996. Recovery of woody vegetation in Tsavo National Park, Kenya, 1970-1994. *Afr. J. Ecol.* 34: 101-12.

Levin, P. S., and D. A. Levin. 2001. The real biodiversity crisis. *American Scientist* 90: 6-8.

Lewis, D. M., and P. Alpert. 1997. Trophy hunting and wildlife conservation in Zambia. *Conservation Biol.* 11: 59-68.

Linnell, J. D. C., R. Anes, J. E. Swenson, J. Odden, and M. E. Smith. 1997. Translocation of carnivores as a method for managing problem animals: A review. *Biodiversity and Conservation* 6: 1245-57.

Loeb, J. M., W. R. Hendee, S. J. Smith, and M. R. Scharz. 1989. Humanism vs. animal rights: In defense of animal research. *JAMA* 262: 2716-20.

Losos, E., J. Hayes, A. Phillips, D. Wilcove, and C. Alkire. 1995. Taxpayer-subsidized resource extraction harms species. *BioScience* 45: 446-55.

Lutts, R. H. 1990. *The nature fakers.* Golden, CO: Fulcrum Publ.

McAdoo, J. K., L. T. Vermeire, and W. Gilgert. 2004. The other grazers. *Rangelands* 26 (3): 30-37.

MacIntyre, A. A. 1982. The politics of nonincremental domestic change: Major reform in federal pesticides and predator control policy. Ph.D. thesis. University of California, Davis.

Mahlman, J. D. 1997. Uncertainties in projections of human-caused climate warming. *Science* 278: 1416-17.

Mahoney, S. P. 1999. Wildlife conservation in the 21st century: Can hunters and anglers continue to lead? *78th Annual Conf.*, pp. 4-11, Western Assoc. of Fish and Wildlife Agencies, Cheyenne, WY.

Manahan, S. E. 1997. *Environmental science and technology.* Boca Raton, FL: Lewis Publ.

Mansfield, T. M., and S. G. Torres. 1994. Trends in mountain lion depredation and public safety threats in California. *16th Vertebrate Pest Conf.* Edited by W. S. Halverson and A. C. Crabb, pp. 12-14. University of California, Davis.

Margolis, M. 2004. Fending off invasive species: Can we draw the line without turning to trade barriers? *Resources* (spring), no. 153: 18-22.

Marquardt, K., H. M. Levine, and M. LaRochelle. 1993. *Animal scam: The beastly abuse of human rights.* Washington, DC: Regnery Gateway.

McGinn, A. P. 1999. Safeguarding the health of oceans. *Worldwatch Paper 145*. Washington, DC: Worldwatch Inst.

McInerney, J. D. 1993. Animals in education: Are we prisoners of false sentiment? *Amer. Biol. Teacher* 55: 276-80.

McKibben, B. 1989. Reflections: The end of nature. *The New Yorker*, 11 September, 47-105.

Meek, P. D., D. J. Jenkins, B. Morris, A. J. Ardler, and R. J. Hawksby. 1995. Use of two humane leg-hold traps for catching pest species. *Wildl. Res.* 22: 733-39.

Melton, D. A. 1985. The status of elephants in northern Botswana. *Biol. Conserv.* 31: 317-33.

Midgley, M. 1993. A problem of concern. In *Animal welfare and the environment*, edited by R. D. Ryder, pp. 62-67. United Kingdom: Duckworth/RSPCA.

Miller, L. A. 1997. Delivery of immunocontraceptive vaccines for wildlife management. Contraception in Wildlife Management. *USDA Tech. Bull.* 1853: 49-58. Washington, DC: GPO.

Mills, E. L., L. H. Leach, J. T. Carlton, and C. L. Secor. 1995. Exotic species and the integrity of the Great Lakes. *BioScience* 44: 666-76.

Mladenoff, D. J., R. G. Haight, T. A. Sickley, and A. P. Wydeven. 1997. Causes and implications of species restoration in altered ecosystems. *BioScience* 47: 21-31.

Mock, D. W., H. Drummond, and C. H. Stinson. 1990. Avian siblicide. *American Scientist* 78 (5): 438-49.

Monamy, Vaughn. 2000. *Animal experimentation: A guide to the issues*. England: Cambridge University Press.

Morris, P. A. 1997. Released, rehabilitated hedgehogs: A follow-up study in Jersey. *Animal Welfare* 6: 317-27.

Moulton, M. P., and J. Sanderson. 1998. 2d ed. *Wildlife issues in a changing world*. Boca Raton, FL: Lewis Publ.

Mowat, G., B. G. Slough, and R. Rivard. 1994. A comparison of three live capturing devices for lynx: Capture efficiency and injuries. *Wildl. Soc. Bull.* 22: 644-50.

Moyle, P. B. 1994. The decline of anadromous fishes in California. *Conservation Biol.* 8: 869-70.

Moyle, P. B., and T. Light. 1996. Fish invasion into California: Implications for invasion biology. *Ecology* 77: 1666-70.

Muller, L. I., R. J. Warren, and D. L. Evans. 1997. Theory and practice of immunocontraception in wild mammals. *Wildl. Soc. Bull.* 25: 504-14.

Mumford, S. D. 1996. *The life and death of NSSM 200.* Research Triangle Park, NC: Center for Population and Security.

Musiari, M., and P. C. Paquit. 2004. The practice of wolf persecution, protection, and restoration in Canada and the United States. *BioScience* 54: 50-60.

Myers, N. 1993. Environmental refugees in a globally warmed world. *BioScience* 43: 752-61.

Nettles, V. F. 1997. Potential consequences and problems with wildlife contraceptives. *Reprod. Fertil. Dev.* 9: 137-43.

Newman, S. 1994. Quantitative and molecular-genetic effects on animal well-being: Adaptive mechanisms: *J. Anim. Sci.* 72: 1641-53.

Nicoll, C. S., and S. M. Russell. 1994. The unnatural nature of animal rights/liberation philosophy. *P.S.E.B.M.* 205: 269-73. Revised from *Ohio J. Science* 93 (1993): 118-21.

Niemeyer, C. C., E. E. Bangs, S. H. Fritts, J. A. Fontaine, M. D. Jimenez, and W. G. Brewster. 1994. Wolf depredation management in relation to wolf recovery. *16th Vertebrate Pest Conf.* Edited by W. S. Halverson and A. C. Crabb, pp. 57-60. University of California, Davis.

Noss, R. F., and A. Y. Cooperrider. 1994. *Saving nature's legacy: Protecting and restoring biodiversity.* Covelo, CA: Island Press.

Noss, R. F., E. T. LaRoe III, and J. M. Scott. 1995. Endangered ecosystems of the United States: A preliminary assessment of loss and degradation. USDI, *Natl. Biol. Survey Biol. Rept.* 28.

Novak, M.A., and S. J. Suomi. 1989. Psychological well-being of captive primates. In *Science and animals: Addressing contemporary issues.* Edited by H. N. Guttman, J. A. Mench, and R. C. Simmonds, pp. 5-12. Bethesda, MD: Scientists Center for Anim. Welfare.

O'Bryan, M. K., and D. R. McCullough. 1985. Survival of black-tailed deer following relocation in California. *J. Wildl. Manage.* 49 (1): 115-19.

Obrycki, J. J., J. Losey, O. R. Taylor, and L. C. H. Jessie. 2001. Transgenic insecticidal corn: Beyond insecticidal toxicity to ecological complexity. *BioScience* 51: 353-61.

Ostfeld, R. S. 1997. The ecology of Lyme-disease risk. *American Scientist* 85: 338-46.

Otzen, U. 1993. Reflections on the principles of sustainable agricultural development. *Environ. Conserv.* 20: 310-16.

Owensby, C. E., R. C. Cochran, and L. M. Auen. 1996. Effects of elevated carbon dioxide on forage quality for ruminants. In Chap. 24, *Carbon dioxide, populations, and communities*, pp. 363-71 San Diego: Academic Press.

Paoletti, M. G., and D. Pimentel. 1996. Genetic engineering in agriculture and the environment. *BioScience* 47: 665-73.

Parker, J. 1993. With new eyes: The animal rights movement and religion. *Perspectives in Biol. and Medicine* 36: 338-46.

Paton, W. 1993. *Man and mouse: Animals in medical research.* 2d ed. England: Oxford University Press.

Pedersen, V. 1991. Early experience with the farm environment and effects on later behavior in silver foxes (*Vulpes vulpes*) and blue foxes (*Alopex lagopus*). *Behavioral Processes* 25: 163-69.

Peter, Thomas. 1994. The stratospheric ozone layer—An overview. *Environmental Pollution* 83: 69-79.

Phetteplace, Ed. 1997. The natural world vs. animal rights, pp. 113-115. Norwich, NY.

Phillips, R. L. 1996. Evaluation of 3 types of snares for capturing coyotes. *Wildl. Soc. Bull.* 24: 107-10.

Phillips, R. L., K. S. Gruver, and E. S. Williams. 1996. Leg injuries to coyotes captured in three types of foothold traps. *Wildl. Soc. Bull.* 24: 260-63.

Phillips, R. L., and C. Mullis. 1996. Expanded field testing of the No. 3 Victor Soft Catch® trap. *Wildl. Soc. Bull.* 24: 128-31.

Pimentel, D., C. Harvey, P. Resosudarmo, K. Sinclair, D. Kurz, M. McNair, S. Crist, L. Shpritz, L. Fitton, R. Salfouri, and R. Blair. 1995. Environmental and economic costs of soil erosion and conservation benefits. *Science* 267: 1117-23.

Pimm, S. L. 1991. *The balance of nature*. Chicago: University of Chicago Press.

————. 2001. *How we know what we say we know*. New York: McGraw Hill.

Pinstrup-Andersen, P., and R. Pandya-Lurch. 1996. Food for all in 2020: Can the world be fed without damaging the environment? *Environ. Conserv.* 23: 226-34.

Proulx, G., ed. 1999. *Mammal trapping*. Sherwood Park, AB, Canada: Alpha Wildlife Research & Management Ltd.

Proulx, G., and M. W. Barrett. 1994. Field testing the C120 magnum trap for mink. *Wildl. Soc. Bull.* 21: 421-26.

Proulx, G., A. J. Kolenosky, P. J. Cole, and R. K. Drescher. 1995. A humane killing trap for lynx (*Felis lynx*): The Conibear 330™ with clamping bars. *J. Wildl. Diseases* 33: 57-61.

Raloff, Janet. 1995. When nitrate reigns: Air pollution can damage forests more than trees reveal. *Science News* 147: 90-91.

Raj, A. B. M. 1994. An investigation into the batch killing of turkeys in their transport containers using mixtures of gasses. *Research in Veterinary Sci.* 56: 325-31.

Reading, R. P., and S. R. Kellert. 1993. Attitudes toward a proposed reintroduction of black-footed ferrets (*Mustela nigripes*). *Conservation Biol.* 7: 569-79.

Reaka-Kudla, M. L., D. E. Wilson, and E. O. Wilson, eds. 1997. *Biodiversity II: Understanding and protecting our biological resources*. Washington, DC: Joseph Henry Press, National Academy Press.

Regan, T. 1983. *The case for animal rights*. Berkeley: University of California Press.

————. 1986. *Animal sacrifices: Religious perspectives on the use of animals in science*. Philadelphia: Temple University Press.

Regan, T., and P. Singer. 1989. *Animal rights and human obligations*. Englewood Cliffs, NJ: Prentice Hall.

Reneau, S. C. 2003. Should we privatize our national treasures? *Outdoors Unlimited* 64 (9): 12.

Renner, M. 1996. *Fighting for survival*. New York: W. W. Norton.

Rhodes, R. 1997. *Deadly feasts*. New York: Touchstone, Simon & Schuster.

Richards, R. J. 1988. *The evolution of morality*. Chicago: University of Chicago Press.

Richards, R. T., and R. S. Krannich. 1991. The ideology of the animal rights movement and activists' attitudes toward wildlife. *Trans. N. A. Wild. and Nat. Res. Conf.* 56: 363-71.

Robinson, A. J., R. Jackson, P. Kerr, J. Merchant, I. Parer, and R. Peck. 1997. Progress towards using recombinant myxoma virus as a vector for fertility control in rabbits. *Reprod. Fertil. Dev.* 9: 77-83.

Rock, M.T. 1996. The stork, the plow, rural social structure and tropical deforestation in poor countries? *Ecological Economics* 18: 113-31.

Rollin, B. E. 1989. *The unheeded cry: Animal consciousness, animal pain, and scientific change*. New York: Oxford University Press.

Rolston, H., III. 1992. Ethical responsibilities toward wildlife. *J. Amer. Veterinary Med. Assoc.* 200 (5): 618-22.

Sageoff, Mark. 1996. On the value of endangered and other species. *Environmental Mgt.* 20: 897-911.

Salwasser, Hal. 1994. Ecosystem management: Can it sustain diversity and productivity? *J. Forestry* 92 (8): 6-10.

Sampat, Payal. 2000. Deep trouble: The hidden threat of groundwater pollution. *Worldwatch Paper 154*. Washington, DC: Worldwatch Inst.

Sandoe, P., R. Crisp, and N. Holtug. 1996. *Animal ethics*. Dept. Ed., Philosophy and Rhetorics, University of Copenhagen. To appear in *Animal welfare*, edited by M. Appleby and B. Hughes. Wallingford, England: CAB International.

Sapontziz, S. F. 1995. We should not allow dissection of animals. *J. Agric. and Environ. Ethics* 8: 181-89.

Sawwin, J. L. 2004. Mainstreaming renewable energy in the 21st century. *Worldwatch Paper 169*. Washington, DC: Worldwatch Inst.

Schaller, N. 1993. The concept of agricultural sustainability. *Agriculture, Ecosystems and Environment* 46: 89-97.

Schmidt, R. H. 1994. What is wildlife damage management. *Wildl. Control Tech.* 1 (1): 4, 5.

Schneider, S. H. 1994. Detecting climatic change signals: Are there any "fingerprints"? *Science* 263: 341-47.

Schubert, C. A., I. K. Barher, R. C. Rosatte, C. D. MacInnes, and T. D. Nudds. 1998. Effect of canine distemper on an urban raccoon population: An experiment. *Ecological Applications* 8: 379-87.

Schubert, C. A., R. C. Rosatte, C. D. MacInnes, and T. D. Nudds. 1998. Rabies control, and adaptive management approach. *J. Wildl. Manage.* 62: 622-29.

Schulz, C. E., and A. Skonhoft. 1996. Wildlife management, land-use and conflicts. *S. Afr. J. Wildl. Res.* 26: 151-59.

Shelton, J. 1994. *Bear encounters survival guide.* Hagensborg, BC, Canada: Pogamy Productions.

Sibanda, B. M. C., and A. K. Omwega. 1996. Some reflections on conservation, sustainable development, and equitable sharing of benefits from wildlife in Africa: The case of Kenya and Zimbabwe. *S. Afr. J. Wildl. Res.* 26: 175-81.

Sigma Xi. 1992. Sigma Xi statement on the use of animals in research. *American Scientist* 80: 73-76.

Singer, P. 1993. Foreword to *Animal welfare and the environment*, edited by R. D. Ryder, pp. vii-x. United Kingdom: Duckworth/RSPCA.

Sinyak, Y. 1994. Global climate and energy systems. *The Science of the Total Environment* 143: 31-56.

Skare, Mari. 1994. Whaling: A sustainable use of natural resources or a violation of animal rights? *Environment* 36 (7): 12-36.

Skonhoft, A. 1995. On the conflicts of wildlife management in Africa. *Int. J. Sustain. Devel. World Ecol.* 2: 267-77.

Smith, J. A., and K. M. Boyd, eds. 1991. *Lives in the balance: The ethics of using animals in biomedical research.* England: Oxford University Press.

Solbrig, O. T. 1991. The origin and function of biodiversity. *Environment*, June, 17-38.

Sorabji, R. 1993. *Animal minds and human morals.* Ithaca, NY: Cornell University Press.

Soule, M. E., and G. H. Orians, eds. 2001. *Conservation biology: Research priorities for the next decade.* Covelo, CA: Island Press.

Stapp, F., M. F. A. Antolin, and M. Ball. 2004. Patterns of extinction in prairie dog metapopulations: Plague outbreaks follow El Nino events. *Front. Ecol. Environ.* 2 (5): 235-40.

Starke, Linda, ed. 1998. *State of the world 1998*. Washington, DC: Worldwatch Inst.

Starke, Linda, ed. 2000, 2001, 2002, 2003, 2004. State of the world. *A Worldwatch Inst. Report on progress toward a sustainable society.* Washington, DC: Worldwatch Inst.

Stork, N. E. 1993. How many species are there? *Biodiversity and Conservation* 2: 215-32.

Strand, R., and P. Strand. 1993. The hijacking of the humane movement. Wilsonville, OR: Doral Publ.

Stull, C. L., and S. P. McDonough. 1994. Multi-disciplinary approach to evaluating welfare of veal calves in commercial facilities. *J. Anim. Sci.* 72: 2518-24.

Stull, C. L., and D. A. McMartin. 1992. Welfare parameters in veal calf production facilities. Vet. Med. Coop. Exten., University of California, Davis.

Sugal, C. 1997. The price of habitat. *World Watch*, May-June, 18-27.

Swan, J. A. 1994. *In defense of hunting*. San Francisco: Harper Collins.

Thrash, I., P. J. Nel, G. E. Theron, and J. du P. Bothma. 1991. The impact of the provision of water for game on the woody vegetation around a dam in the Krueger National Park. *KOEDOE* 34: 131-48.

Tickell, C. 1996. Economical with the environment: A question of values. *Applied Ecol.* 33: 657-61.

Torres, S. 1996. Mountain lions—California's largest carnivore. *Outdoor Calif.* 57 (33): 8-9.

Tuxill, John. 1998. Losing strands in the web of life: Vertebrate declines and the conservation of biological diversity. *Worldwatch Paper 141*. Washington, DC: Worldwatch Inst.

Tyndale-Biscoe, C. H. 1994a. The CRC for biological control of vertebrate pest populations: Fertility control of wildlife for conservation. *Pacific Conservation Biol.* 1: 163-68.

———. 1994b. Virus-vectored immunocontraception of feral mammals. *Reprod. Fertil. Dev.* 6: 281-87.

Varner, G. E. 1994. What's wrong with animal byproducts? *J. Agric.*

*and Environmental Ethics* 7 (1): 7-17.

VanVuren, D. A. J. Kuenzi, I. Loredo, A. L. Leider, and M. L. Morrison. 1997. Translocation as a nonlethal alternative for managing California ground squirrels. *J. Wildl. Manage.* 61: 351-59.

Venette, R. C., and J. R. Carey. 1998. Invasion biology, rethinking our response to alien species. *Calif. Agriculture* 52 (2): 13-17.

Viljoen, P. J., and J. du P. Bothma. 1990. The influence of desert-dwelling elephants on vegetation in the northern Namib Desert, South West Africa/Namibia. *J. Arid. Environ.* 18: 85-96.

Vitousek, P. M., J. Aber, R. W. Howarth, G. E. Likens, P. A. Matson, D. W. Schindler, W. H. Schlesinger, and G. D. Tilman. 1997. Human alteration of the global nitrogen cycle: Causes and consequences. *Issues in Ecology*, no. 1 (spring).

Warburton, B., and I. Orchard. 1996. Evaluation of five kill traps for effective captures and killing of Australian brushtail possums (*Trichosurus vulpecula*). *New Zealand J. Zool.* 23: 307-14.

Warren, L. S. 1996. *The hunter's game.* New Haven, CT: Yale University Press.

Warren, R. J., ed. 1997. Deer overabundance. *Special Issue Wildl. Soc. Bull.* 25: 213-586.

Watts, R. G., ed. 1997. *Engineering response to global climate change.* Boca Raton, FL: Lewis Publ.

Weber, G. M., T. J. Hoban, P. A. Kendall, and L. S. Bull. 1995. Consumer concerns about modern technology in agriculture: Considerations for undergraduate and graduate teaching. *J. Anim. Sci.* 73: 2727-32.

Webster, John. 1995. Animal welfare: A cool eye towards Eden. UFAW, Potters Bar, England.

Wilcove, D. S., M. McMillan, and K. C. Winston. 1993. What exactly is an endangered species? An analysis of the U.S. endangered species list: 1985-1991. *Conservation Biol.* 7: 87-93.

Wilson, E. O. 1992. *The diversity of life.* Cambridge: Harvard University Press.

Winston, M. L. 1997. *Nature wars: People vs. pests.* Cambridge: Harvard University Press.

Yaffee, S. L. 1994. *The wisdom of the spotted owl.* Covelo, CA: Inland

Press.

Zaidle, D. L. 1997. *American man-killers*. Huntington Beach, CA: Safari Press.

Zaunbrecher, K. I., and R. E. Smith. 1993. Neutering of feral cats as an alternative to eradication programs. *JAVMA* 203: 449-52.

# Questions

*Chapter 1: Nature's Death Ethic*

1. Since the balance of nature requires a fairly high premature death rate, how does any artificial life-support system we might provide for animals destined to die upset the natural balance?

2. Since people exist and are very much a part of nature, what environmental role and rights do you think people have in the natural scheme of things?

3. Even though we all oppose converting forests or grasslands to deserts, discuss whether conversion of vegetated areas to deserts benefits desert-adapted species. Give other examples.

4. Give examples of natural deaths of species that can be considered humane.

5. What role should humans play in nature's survival-of-the-fittest scheme where people have modified the environment and upset the original predator-prey balance?

6. How good or how bad is it that all land masses, except the two poles, have a richer, that is, more diverse, fauna than would be present naturally because of the many introduced exotic and domesticated species?

7. Because the population densities of lemmings, arctic hares and their predators naturally fluctuate a great deal, even where man has not altered the environment, is nature in balance in these regions? Can you define "balance"?

8. Is it all right for animals to suffer when their distress can be classified as "natural"? Are all activities by humans that affect wildlife "unnatural" and thus undesirable?

251

9. When it can be done easily, do you think it is ethical to offer assistance to animals that are suffering "natural" brutality? How about if the suffering is a consequence of our altering the environment, for example, a house cat with a live bird? Give other examples.

10. In disturbed ecosystems where natural predators have been permanently reduced or where a prey species can now multiply beyond any possible control by natural predators, discuss whether it is better to let all animals regulate (self limit) their own numbers, even though it usually will be with much suffering or whether people should help control or harvest the unnatural surplus animals so there will be much less overall suffering.

11. Because tornadoes and hurricanes are "natural," why isn't it wrong for meteorologists to try to find ways of deactivating them?

12. Are people justified in converting native vegetation (weeds) into a more attractive garden or park composed of exotic plants? Give examples of nonnative fish, birds or mammals that you think can be considered desirable introductions and why.

13. Why do animals voluntarily seek out what are very hurtful, distressful and sometimes lethal situations as part of their normal territorial and sexual behavior?

14. How distressful is it for sentient animals to eat their offspring or to observe them being eaten by other offspring or predators or be cannibalized by their mate or die of starvation?

15. Since I am sure you agree that people should not treat animals callously and cruelly, explain whether you think it is okay to let animals suffer in modified environments when we could alleviate much of the distress by culling or other action?

16. Using examples of several species, how do you want the surplus animals to die in modified environments?

17. Do you favor nature's tooth-and-claw predation bloodbath, starvation, diseases and cannibalism, especially if it is the consequence of our modifying the environment? How do you want animals to die, naturally or as humanely as is reasonably feasible? Give examples of several species.

18. Define biological diversity. Do we usually mean the degree of diversity that existed before humans modified the environment, that is, "natural" biological diversity?
19. What effect does successful establishment of introduced exotic fauna and flora have on biological diversity?
20. How critical are individual species of wildlife to the welfare of humans and the health of communities? Give examples.
21. What happens biologically and ecologically when a species of plant or animal becomes extinct? Give examples.
22. Discuss whether or not the Endangered Species Act should be restricted to vertebrate animals, plants and significant invertebrates like crabs, shrimp and clams.
23. Is preventing the normal natural rate of premature deaths of a species in modified environments usually undesirable?
24. List some introduced exotic species that you think have been desirable and explain how they have affected the habitat they occupy.

## Chapter 3. Managing Wildlife and Pests

25. Since we can largely dominate all species and have considerable control over nature, what do you think is our moral/ethical responsibility to wildlife populations that have been adversely affected by building our home or other actions that take over their habitats?
26. Should we let animals be governed as much as possible by natural forces, even if they inflict greater suffering and even local elimination of some species? Or should we manage/control the populations as best we can to preserve biological diversity and to keep them as much as possible in a managed healthy, balanced state with a better quality life?
27. In modified environments, can man respond to wildlife's needs more rationally and ethically than nature since nature seldom emulates good wildlife husbandry practices and does not operate under humane regulations? Give examples.
28. Once people have disrupted the natural balance, do we have a moral obligation to correct problems as best we can by using the most humane wildlife management procedures available?

29. Discuss whether people have a moral obligation to protect from cruel predation animals they have domesticated.

30. For humane reasons, if you think it is wrong to prevent coyotes from killing lambs, cats and dogs, do you think people should stop raising sheep or having pets in such localities or should we control the coyotes? How do you suggest children should be protected from urban coyotes?

31. Give examples to support your opinion whether to control a species that has become so abundant in a human-modified environment that it threatens other native species. Or should we let nature take its course even though we know it is impossible to reestablish the original habitat and fauna?

32. What liberties will you grant those who must manage and control competing or predatory species, especially when such action is needed to save an endangered species?

33. Do you think it is all right to control introduced predators, such as cats, if they are about to eliminate a native species? Give other examples.

34. Explain why we should or shouldn't control native predators when they are about to eliminate a "desirable," but introduced, species.

35. Epidemics of plague, at least in California, seem to occur only when certain native rodents become abnormally abundant due to man's modification of the environment. If you oppose the poisoning of their fleas or using control methods to prevent such high densities of these rodent species from occurring, suggest alternate solutions.

36. How do you propose to control rabies or Lyme (tick) disease?

37. What should be done when the burrows of muskrats or beaver are threatening the safety of dams or levees or beaver dams are causing flooding?

38. Explain your views on whether a surplus livestock-killing coyote should be allowed to continue disemboweling dozens of sheep or turkeys rather than be restrained for a day in a padded, offset-jaw, leg-hold trap and then shot.

39. Does a coyote suffer more when it is trapped and then shot than does a fully conscious live sheep while having its small

intestines eaten by a coyote? Discuss the morality of this subject.

40. Discuss whether animals usually suffer more when they die naturally than when they are shot, trapped or poisoned.

41. Discuss whether you think people should become a humane predator to help nature and to preserve biological diversity where people have altered the natural environment.

42. What do you think about killing native predators to save a species that has become endangered because we modified its habitat?

43. What options do homeowners have when an animal is destroying their lawn or garden?

44. What is your ethic concerning making an inevitable death of a dying or doomed animal more humane?

45. Think about it. This is a tough question. How do you want different species of surplus wild animals and excess domestic animals to die? Give examples and discuss the degree of suffering involved.

46. Discuss whether it is cruel to translocate and release displaced mammals captured in a house or city.

47. What moral obligation do we have to protect animals we have domesticated from predation?

48. Discuss the assertion that virtually no agricultural crop, reforestation or home landscaping could survive economically or esthetically if all native mammals were protected and allowed free access to these plants.

49. Do animal damage control practices ever improve the welfare of some animal populations? If so, how?

50. If you oppose the control of any animal or population no matter how much of a pest it or they may be, what do you recommend be done when one has rats and mice in their house, pocket gophers or moles in their lawn or ants in their kitchen?

*Chapter 4. Hunting and Trapping*

51. Since natural predators usually enable their prey to exist at or near their carrying capacity, why shouldn't man help nature

and become a predator where natural predation can no longer exist?

52. Give examples where various harvesting methods can keep populations of wildlife in disturbed environments in a healthier condition than can nature.

53. By using examples, compare the suffering of animals that are shot, trapped or poisoned with the suffering involved in dying of starvation, disease or other vicissitudes of living brought on by competition between members of the same species.

54. Discuss why some people oppose hunting. Is it based on personal or religious reasons rather than biological grounds?

55. Why does the public insist that livestock operators maintain healthy flocks and herds, yet object to a similar management of wildlife populations also living in modified environments?

56. With reference to animal rights, do you believe that we should encourage wolves to reoccupy all of their former range throughout the United States and reintroduce grizzly bears into the Central Valley of California? How much of their former range should such species be permitted to occupy?

57. When species' population densities are declining in an environment people have altered, is it better to try to manage the species or let nature take its course, even if the latter will clearly be at the expense of the population's quality of life?

58. What liberties will you grant to the management and control of competing or predatory species of animals if such action is needed to save an endangered species or to share game with hunters?

59. To what degree does the economic value of being a game animal help save that species' habitat?

60. Why should hunters and trappers have to provide most of the money needed to hire game wardens and biologists to help game animals and also be the major contributor of funds necessary for preserving their habitats?

61. If an overpopulation of deer was caused by our modification of an environment, would it be better to let practically an entire herd of such deer suffer from starvation and cruel diseases rather than trying to prevent this massive suffering by shooting

the surplus animals? Can you think of other effective ways of reducing such deer populations?

62. Can you think of any biological bases for opposing regulated hunting?

63. Analyze whether you think it is equally wrong to trap a muskrat threatening a dam or a beaver causing flooding as it is to take it for its fur.

64. If interested in lessening pain and suffering, why don't organizations that oppose trapping encourage and support research to find more humane ways of harvesting animals or are they opposed to catching animals by any method, no matter how humanely it is done?

65. As long as a species is not endangered, discuss whether it is better for people to follow nature's way and to wear and use animal fur and skins instead of further exhausting the finite supply of oil to make our clothes.

66. How is the quality of life of furbearers affected when their fur is wanted?

67. Discuss whether the regulated use of feathers, furs, skins and other parts of animals is a natural recycling process.

68. Is the quality of life of penned furbearers assured because only quality fur is wanted?

## Chapter 5. Agriculture and Domestic Animals

69. Why might it be morally wrong to domesticate animals for food, fiber or as pets?

70. Discuss whether domestication denies such animals their critical, basic, behavioral and physical needs that exist in their genetically or behaviorally different wild ancestors.

71. Can we justify protecting farm and research animals and our pets from the types of distress their wild counterparts experience when they run free in the cruel natural world?

72. Analyze whether a domesticated animal misses a freedom it has never experienced any more than primitive people miss our public health and life styles.

73. Are we justified in inflicting temporary pain and distress to break a horse for riding? Give other examples.

74. Discuss whether it is wrong to walk dogs and other pets on a leash or to raise inbred strains of white mice, rats, rabbits, pets, poultry and livestock because they are not allowed to run free.

75. List the domestic animals people commonly see and whether or not they would have been born if they had not been wanted.

76. Defend your view as to whether livestock and surplus animals should be left to die from diseases and starvation rather than being humanely slaughtered.

*Chapter 6: Human Population Explosion and Its Impact on Wildlife Habitat*

77. What will happen to the water supply, good soil, clean air and nonrenewable resources if the human population continues to grow at its present rate?

78. How can the growth of the human population realistically be stopped?

79. What would happen ecologically and demographically if an ample supply of nutritious food was provided today to all people of the world regardless of their ability to pay for it?

80. In what ways have people ignored or gone against nature's life-death ethic?

81. How do the effects of an overpopulation of people differ from what can happen if there is an overpopulation of wildlife and livestock?

82. How has our exploitation of animals in research and as food affected the size of the human population?

83. List as many ways as you can that people have damaged the environment?

*Chapter 7: Animal Welfare versus Animal Rights*

84. Do you think keeping pets is justified? If so, what kinds of pets do you condone? Do you think it is wrong for us to exploit any of our finned, feathered or furred wildlife as a sport, material resource or pet? Should all pets be destroyed?

85. If you claim you are not an abolitionist against all human uses of wildlife, list some uses you will tolerate.

86. If you are a vegetarian, explain why you think it is wrong for man to be a predator of wild birds and mammals taken for food or sport, even when such taking (predation) is needed to maintain healthy populations of these species.
87. If you are an animal rightist, give examples with sound reasoning or biological facts upon which you base your desire to change public attitudes and values about humaneness and animal rights,
88. Why do some people think it is more important to use social issues rather than biological facts or basic economics when making decisions concerning the welfare of animals?
89. How much of a personal sacrifice are you willing to make to benefit wildlife? How will you change your lifestyle?
90. If you are an animal rightist, are your beliefs concerning animal rights based on "religious" views or are you willing to debate the related basic laws of nature and biological principles of the dynamics of wildlife populations? If you are shown that your views are mistaken in regard to the biological principles of nature, do you think you could change your mind?
91. When happiness or a quality life are no longer possible for an animal, is a quick death more humane than lingering suffering, pain and distress? Or do you prefer that an animal's death be prolonged for as long as nature will permit in the existing habitat?
92. If a horse needs to have a leg amputated, would you recommend that it be shot instead? Why?
93. Which do you think is more important: the welfare of individual animals or the health and well-being of their populations that can be achieved at the expense of a few others? Why?
94. Discuss whether you think you demonstrate true compassion towards a misplaced individual mammal when you capture and release it at another location where you know the species is common, even though it has been proven that most such translocates do not survive.
95. If you justify translocating misplaced mammals because it gives them another chance to live, however small, discuss whether

you feel it is still justified even if each transplanted animal may cause others of its kind to suffer, as well as suffer itself while searching for its home or a new vacant habitat and mate.

96. Discuss whether wild animals have the same consciousness, emotions and anticipation of pain as people.

97. If you support the artificial feeding of starving wildlife, would you change your view in those situations if you were shown how such feeding will later result in even more individuals suffering from starvation and disease? Explain.

98. If you think all wild animals have as much right as we do to occupy space on this earth, when, if ever, are we justified in taking over the habitat of wild animals or in removing them because we do not want them present in our house, garden or crop?

99. Do you think you have any more of a moral or ethical right to control rats, mice or ants in your house than a farmer has to control animals damaging his crop? Explain.

100. Discuss whether people are morally obliged to provide protection from predation for animals they have domesticated.

101. Do you think animal suffering is all right when it can be classified as "natural"? Do you consider all human activities involving animals as "unnatural" and thus bad?

102. Do you think it ethical to offer assistance to animals that are suffering "natural," not human-caused brutality?

103. Do you think captive pets and livestock usually live much longer than wild animals that must daily face the adversities of climatic extremes, starvation, disease and danger from predators and other animals? Give examples.

104. Since self-righteousness about the sanctity of animal life can result in great cruelty to animals because entire populations can be "loved to death" by overprotecting them, do you agree that proper management and population control are much better ways of conserving our wildlife heritage?

105. Since death is inevitable for all organisms, how do you want wild and domestic animals to die? Be specific.

106. Should special dogs be bred for research and to train veterinarians rather than utilizing unwanted dogs in shelters and pounds that are destined to be euthanized?

107. What are the pro and con ethics of using animals in research?

108. Cite examples of situations in which animals rather than nonanimal alternatives are needed in research.

109. Some groups claim that most of the billions of animals killed annually for materials, food or research die from massive pain and suffering. If you agree, give examples.

110. Do you agree with some that it was wrong to have awarded 70 percent of nearly 80 Nobel prizes in medicine and physiology to scientists who had based their research on animal tests?

111. How can one agree with some animal rightists who claim that we should be willing to forgo all medical treatment developed or tested on animals, such as blood transfusion, anesthesia, pain killers, antibiotics, insulin, vaccines, chemotherapy, CPR, coronary bypass surgery, reconstructive surgery, orthopedic surgery and others?

112. Before contributing money to organizations, ask yourself a question: Is the statement based on sound biological principles or just distorted half-truths?

113. Vested interests trap most of us. How can we make it easier to delist species when they are no longer endangered since vast sums can't be raised doing it?

114. Do you have such strong vested interests in some anticontrol issues that you, like their leaders, cannot financially afford to have them resolved?

115. If you are a paid activist official, don't you have a vested interest in not winning your issues, since your livelihood depends upon the amount of financial support you can raise from the public? What will you do if your current issues suddenly vanish?

116. Since many claim that the news media provide too much attention to adversary groups, would you object to a government agency or a counter-coalition group being

established to raise pertinent questions that adversary fundraisers should then be pressured to answer publicly to help determine their honesty?

117. Do you think the public has a right to insist that their government expose myths being preached by anti animal control groups? Are you aware of any means whereby anticontrol groups police themselves to ensure that their claims are substantiated with facts?

118. Why are so many anticontrol adversary groups headed by environmental lawyers who specialize in litigation rather than compromises? Are these lawyers better communicators or just more skilled at twisting the truth and making money?

# Index

## A

## B

## D

## E

BVG